WORKING FOR THE JAPANESE

WORKING
FOR
THE JAPANESE

Inside Mazda's American Auto Plant

Joseph J. Fucini

AND

Suzy Fucini

THE FREE PRESS
A Division of Macmillan, Inc.
NEW YORK

Collier Macmillan Publishers
LONDON

The Free Press
A Division of Macmillan, Inc.
866 Third Avenue, New York, N.Y. 10022

Collier Macmillan Canada, Inc.

Printed in the United States of America

printing number

1 2 3 4 5 6 7 8 9 10

Library of Congress Cataloging-in-Publication Data
Fucini, Joseph J.
Working for the Japanese : inside Mazda's American auto plant /
Joseph J. Fucini and Suzy Fucini.
p. cm.
Includes bibliographical references.
ISBN 0-02-910931-0
1. Mazda Motors of America (Central)—Employees. 2. Mazda Motors
of America (Central)—Personnel management. I. Fucini, Suzy.
II. Title.
HD9710.U54M394 1990
331.25—dc20 90-34249
 CIP

Contents

Author's Note

THIS book is the product of two years of research and over 150 interviews with workers and managers at the Mazda–Flat Rock plant, UAW representatives, state and local government officials, and residents of the Downriver area. In the course of our research, we made more than 80 visits to Flat Rock. On 5 of these, we visited the Mazda facility at the invitation of the company. We also visited Solidarity House, the UAW's headquarters in Detroit, as well as the union's Region 1A headquarters in Taylor, Michigan, and we attended union dissident meetings in Flat Rock.

Although Mazda initially agreed to cooperate with us, the company, for reasons of its own, abruptly withdrew this cooperation midway through our research (August 1988). A representative from Mazda's public relations department simply told us at the time that the company would no longer be participating in our project. All subsequent calls we made to the company requesting interviews went unanswered. Admittedly this sometimes made it difficult to assess the reaction of Mazda management to events that unfolded at the plant subsequent to the summer of 1988, leaving us to rely on published sources and on the impressions of Mazda workers, whom we continued to interview outside the plant. We have nevertheless tried to recount these events as accurately as possible in a manner that is fair to both the company and its employees. We leave it to the reader to decide how well we have succeeded.

Since the Mazda employee handbook expressly forbids workers to talk to the press without company approval, and since our book

was unsanctioned by the company, many workers were reluctant to allow us to use their real names. These workers, who often earned twice as much at the Mazda plant as at their previous jobs, worried that their inclusion in this book would provoke reprisals from their supervisors. This fear seemed particularly well founded, since Mazda's flexible team system gives supervisors or "unit leaders" an inordinate degree of unilateral, discretionary power to assign jobs and interpret work rules. In deference to this concern, we agreed to change the names of all hourly workers who appear in this book, with the exception of those who became union dissident leaders, since their opposition to the Mazda team system is now a matter of public record. The names of the following workers are pseudonyms: Peter Barrow, Wayne Dodd, Forrest Green, Jerry Healy, Sam Hill, Janet Jones, Becky Mehaffey, Steve Ross, Nate Watson, Darryl Williams, and Judy Wilson. These workers, however, are real people, not composites. The quotes attributed to them also are real and have not been embellished. The experiences they describe actually occurred.

___ Acknowledgements ___

It would not have been possible to complete this book without the support we received from many quarters. Our agent, Julian Bach, did far more than represent our interests. His wise counsel and unfailing encouragement helped to keep our vision clear and our spirits high throughout what was a long and often difficult project. At the Free Press, Erwin Glikes and Robert Wallace delivered timely advice that changed the focus of this book for the better. Claire Weiner is a gracious woman who deserves our gratitude. In the early phases of our research, we received an excellent education in the automobile industry from Dan Luria of the Industrial Technology Institute in Ann Arbor, Michigan. Craig Farrand of the Mellus Newspaper chain gave generously of his time to familiarize us with Flat Rock and the Downriver area. Leonard Woodcock, the former president of the UAW, and Pat Greathouse, the union's former vice president of international affairs, were also generous with their time, providing us with an invaluable sense of the union's history. Robert Fraser, William Lontz, and Read Ross patiently explained government incentive programs to us. Frank Joyce of the UAW's public relations department was courteous and helpful under what were often trying circumstances. The same can be said of Nancy Hennigar and Anne TerMer of Mazda Motor Manufacturing (USA) Corp. We would also like to express our thanks to Ted Anders, Aaron Gillespie, Charles Palmer, Mike Parker, Asae Shichi, and Vince Wicks. Finally, we would like to express our gratitude to all of the Mazda workers we have met. They have proven that, if nothing else, Mazda has at least succeeded in its goal of hiring a "special work force" for its American plant.

WORKING FOR THE JAPANESE

1

A Worker

STEVE ROSS considered himself lucky. In February 1985 he was just a name on a list of 96,500 names in Mazda Motor Corporation's computerized file of job applicants. Only 3,500 of those names would eventually be left on Mazda's list, chosen for jobs at the stamping and assembly plant the Japanese automaker was building in Flat Rock, Michigan, a small industrial suburb 20 miles south of Detroit. Many of those on the application list were laid-off autoworkers who had spent years building cars at plants owned by America's "Big Three" auto companies, and Ross, a millwright who had never worked in a car factory before, worried that his lack of experience would be held against him.

But he had beaten the odds. A little more than a year after mailing in the Mazda application he had clipped from a Detroit newspaper, Ross became part of the first group of 400 American hourly workers to be hired at the Flat Rock plant. Getting the job had not been easy. Almost from the very day—just after Thanksgiving 1984—that Mazda announced it would be building a plant in Michigan, the company's Japanese and American managers had gone out of their way to warn that they would be extremely selective in choosing employees. Mazda would, they promised, do much more than perform standard background checks on job seekers; it would evaluate applicants in a way that no American automaker had ever thought of evaluating potential hourly employees before, having them participate in psychological role-playing exercises and group problem-solving sessions. As part of his evaluation, for instance, Ross was

asked to work with a group of other applicants to develop a plan for counseling an imaginary Mazda employee who was always getting into arguments with his coworkers.

The purpose of such tests, according to Mazda, was to determine how well an applicant worked within a group. Did the applicant have trouble giving or receiving criticism? Was the applicant too aggressive? Too withdrawn? How clearly did the applicant outline goals and express ideas? No American automaker had ever asked these questions before, but the Big Three had been interested only in hiring workers to build automobiles; Mazda wanted people who could become part of a team.

Workers who were fortunate enough to make it through Mazda's demanding screening process would be working together in teams of six to ten. Ross and some of the other workers in the elite group of four hundred original hirees would be named "team leaders" and given the responsibility of coordinating work schedules and job assignments for their teams. Unlike Big Three workers, Mazda's hourly employees would do much more than hang fenders on cars; they would be active participants in the day-to-day management of the plant, designing their own jobs, acting as their own quality control inspectors, and contributing ideas to improving the production process. This was why Mazda had insisted on screening applicants so carefully. Not only would workers at the company's new plant have to be "good communicators," they would need the intelligence and self-motivation required to handle the decision-making responsibilities that went with being "team members," the term Mazda preferred for its employees. "A special work force for a special plant," is the way Mazda managers had often explained the rationale behind the company's meticulous evaluation of job applicants.

Ross was excited by the idea of becoming part of a Japanese team plant. From everything he had seen on television and read in the newspapers, the Japanese treated their workers with much more respect than the Americans did, giving them a real say in how a plant was run. Ross was not sure how he was going to like participating in the calisthenics that Mazda team members did together every morning, or how he would feel about wearing the same blue-and-khaki Mazda uniform that would be worn by everyone else at the plant, from the newest trainee to the highest-ranking executive. (Both evoked images of his not very happy time in the Air Force.) But he did look forward to going to work at a plant that had no artificial barriers separating workers and managers. Everyone at the Flat Rock

plant would, he had read, be called by their first name: Mazda did not allow "misters." There would be no reserved spots for managers in the plant parking lot, and no executive dining room, as there were at American plants. Managers and workers at Flat Rock would sit elbow to elbow in a common cafeteria that served Japanese and American food on a first-come-first-served basis. This pleased Ross, who had always been annoyed by the high-handed attitude of the American managers he had known. The Americans had, he thought, been too concerned about protecting their own authority to communicate with the workers under them. At the American plants where Ross had worked in the past, managers had regarded every suggestion from workers to improve safety or get a job done faster as a threat to their own position. Instead of being praised or rewarded for their good ideas, workers who made suggestions were regarded as troublemakers.

As happy as he was about going to work at a team plant—and as proud as he felt about being part of the select group of Mazda's four hundred original hirees—Ross had to admit that his first reaction to landing a job at Flat Rock was one of relief. The $12.97 an hour he would be earning as a team leader would allow him to provide his wife and two daughters with a measure of financial security they had rarely known in the 1980s.

A man of medium build whose wide eyes and apple cheeks gave him a still-youthful appearance as he approached middle age, Ross had been employed for 16 years at a Detroit factory that manufactured mining and construction equipment. He had spent most of his life in greater Detroit's Downriver section, a name given to the gray and densely packed industrial suburbs—including Flat Rock—that follow the course of the Detroit River as it flows south from the city into Lake Erie. Ross had gone to work at the equipment factory directly out of high school in 1964, but a few months later, when it became apparent he would be drafted into the Army, he decided to enlist in the Air Force. In the Air Force he acquired firsthand experience in metalworking, being assigned to a detail that repaired hangars.

When he returned to the Detroit factory after the service, Ross enrolled in a millwright apprenticeship program. As a millwright he became a member of the skilled trades, an accomplishment that brought with it new stature on the shop floor. Unlike the unskilled production workers who assemble components and operate production machinery—and whose jobs can usually be learned in a matter of days or even hours—millwrights, electricians, welders, and other

skilled trades workers perform the varied and complex jobs needed to maintain and repair factory equipment. Because of their specialized knowledge, acquired over a period of years, skilled trades workers enjoy extra freedom and privileges on the shop floor; they have the flexibility to set their own work schedules and can move around the plant more or less as they please. A good skilled trades worker is not easy to replace. This was especially true in the late 1960s, when Ross became a millwright. No foreman of that era needed to be reminded that any of the skilled trades workers who worked under him could simply pack their tool chests if they became bored or unhappy and be hired by a plant down the highway at equal or better pay.

Ross had always assumed that being a skilled trades worker guaranteed his job security. Should his job at the equipment company ever disappear, he was certain he would be able to find work as a millwright at another plant. He had, in fact, done this once before, taking a temporary job at a local steel mill when his factory was closed for several months by a strike. At other times, when extra money had been needed to meet family expenses or the cost of moving into a new home, he had found it easy to pick up part-time work at mills and factories. Once, he had even held down a part-time job in addition to his regular job for a year, while also attending evening classes at Henry Ford Community College, an institution from which he earned an associate degree in marketing.

But the confidence that Ross had in the door-opening power of his skilled trades training was badly shaken in the late 1970s, when rising gas prices and an influx of imported Japanese cars crippled Detroit's automotive-based economy, throwing tens of thousands of skilled and unskilled blue-collar workers out of jobs. Unable to compete with Japan's efficient, dependable cars, the Big Three surrendered more and more of the U.S. market to their Japanese rivals: 12.7 percent in 1977, almost 23 percent in 1982.[1] As their share of the market declined, American automakers curtailed their production operations, laying off more workers with each plant closing or shift reduction. The pattern of production cutbacks and layoffs was repeated at the hundreds of smaller supplier firms that fed Detroit's big auto plants steering wheels, tires, windshields, paint, and other components.

The factory that employed Ross did not sell directly to the automobile industry, so it did not feel the first shock waves set off by the industry's collapse. But of course it could not escape the effects of the

general recession that followed. The factory's major customers—mining companies and large construction firms—their own businesses hurt severely by the recession, cut back their new equipment orders. The factory owners were unable to absorb their mounting financial losses. In 1983 they were bought out by an out-of-state competitor, who promptly sold the factory and moved its production equipment to a plant in the South. Some of the managers and skilled trades workers at Ross's factory were offered the opportunity to relocate to the southern plant. Ross was not among them.

Ross began his job search by asking relatives and neighbors who were lucky enough still to be working if they knew of any openings at their plants. They offered plenty of sympathy but no leads. Most were worried about hanging on to their own jobs. Unemployment Downriver had been over 20 percent for most of the 1980s. Some of Ross's friends, skilled trades workers like him, had left Michigan for the Sunbelt in an uncertain pursuit of jobs. Ross and his wife had talked about moving to Arizona themselves but dropped the idea because both of their families were in Michigan.

After three months of five-day-a-week job hunting, Ross finally found work as a "machine repair specialist" at a food-processing plant. But less than a year later, the plant's owners cut back their production—and as one of the last hired, Ross was among the first to be let go. He then got a job as a driver for a Detroit delivery firm at 70 percent of his skilled trades wage. His oldest daughter, who was about to go away to college, had to change her plans and enroll in a local commuter school. When the delivery company cut his work schedule from five to four days a week, Ross tried to make up for the lost wages by selling insurance part-time. But having spent over 16 years in the structured work environment of factories, he felt uncomfortable with the uncertainties of commission selling. He found himself brooding over real or imagined "mistakes" on days when, after spending four or five hours calling on potential customers, he came away empty handed. Such days occurred frequently, since the more pressure Ross put on himself, the less successful he was at selling. A few years later, Ross would remember this period, 1984–85, as the most frightening time of his life. A normally mild-mannered man, he had during that year gotten into frequent fights with his wife and daughters, something he had never done before.

When Ross came across the application form that Mazda ran in Detroit-area newspapers in March 1985, he mailed it in without hesitation. Working for Mazda had to be better than driving a truck

and selling insurance, so what did he have to lose? The fact that Mazda was a Japanese company did not bother him. Once, when a relative had made derogatory comments about working for the Japanese, Ross had snapped, lacing into the man about how the Big Three were importing more cars than anyone—selling them under names like Dodge Colt and Mercury Tracer—and, in the process, taking jobs away from workers at their own American plants. So who owed loyalty to American companies anymore? Besides, the new Mazda plant *would* be "American," creating jobs for people right here in Downriver. And, from everything Ross had heard, Mazda treated workers a hell of a lot better than the Big Three ever did.

Ross was working at his insurance office one spring morning in 1986, when his wife telephoned to tell him that someone from Mazda had just called their home asking for him. He dropped what he was doing and dialed the number left by the caller. A woman with a clipped, no-nonsense voice from Mazda's personnel department said that he had been selected to work at the Flat Rock plant. She added that he had two days to think about the job offer. Think about it? Ross found this rather amusing. He said to the woman, "When do I start?"

2
The Union's Chance

IN March 1984 a small delegation of Mazda executives visited Solidarity House, a functional glass-and-steel building on Detroit's East Side that serves as the headquarters of the International Union of the United Automobile, Aerospace and Agricultural Implement Workers of America, as the UAW is officially called. Separated from the urban decay of Jefferson Avenue by a modestly landscaped courtyard and a wide blacktop parking lot marked off by a wire mesh fence, the building resembles a private hospital, built perhaps by a religious order 30 years earlier, before the neighborhood around it collapsed under the weight of poverty and neglect. Until the visit by these Mazda executives, no Japanese manufacturer had ever walked through its doors.

Honda and Nissan, the two Japanese automakers that had preceded Mazda in building American plants, had not seen fit to come calling at Solidarity House. They had, in fact, diligently avoided all contact with the UAW, which they regarded as the embodiment of everything that was wrong with the American workplace. William Usery, secretary of labor under Gerald Ford, who later became a labor relations consultant for Toyota, was speaking of his client in the early 1980s, but his comments applied equally well to Honda and Nissan: "Commies and drug addicts, gambling, fighting, refusing to work—that was Toyota's idea of a unionized American workforce."[1]

Not surprisingly, Honda and Nissan fought the UAW's attempts to organize workers at their U.S. plants, as did the smaller Japanese parts suppliers that followed them to America. The argument used

against the union was the same at Honda, Nissan, and all the lesser supplier firms: The UAW, with its insistence on elaborate work rules and job classifications, and its antagonistic attitude toward management, was too set in the old ways of militant American unionism to fit into a Japanese team system that emphasized close labor-management cooperation. The majority of Americans at Japanese-owned plants appeared to share this view. UAW organizing drives had been soundly rejected at the two main Japanese assembly plants and at almost all of their supplier firms by the time of Mazda's Solidarity House visit. A 28-year-old production worker at Nissan's Smyrna, Tennessee, facility typified the prevailing attitude at Japanese American plants of the era when he told a reporter, "I think unions were fine in their time. But as long as you have a company working like this one is, you don't need a union. It would just get in the way."[2]

But the Mazda executives who drove into the wide black parking lot of Solidarity House on that early spring day were ready to break ranks with their fellow Japanese automakers. They were prepared to accept the UAW in their American plant, provided the union agreed to adopt a more cooperative attitude and allow Mazda to implement a flexible team system, unencumbered by unnecessary rules and job classifications, at its future facility. The men from Mazda would make it clear to their UAW hosts that the company could not accept an American-style contract at its U.S. plant. Mazda could not have its team members divided into more than one hundred different job classifications, the way workers at Big Three plants were: one worker assigned to hang fenders, another to install doors, and a third to drill in engine mounts, with no one permitted to cross over and do someone else's job. The Mazda representatives would explain that sometimes it was necessary to have a door installer hang fenders, a fender hanger install engine mounts, and an electrician do the work of a welder, if a plant was going to have the flexibility needed to respond to changing production demands. Rather than allow one hundred job classifications at its American plant, Mazda would insist that jobs at the facility be divided into only two categories—production and skilled trades.

Given the choice, the men from Mazda would probably have preferred not to be making this visit to Solidarity House. Given the choice, they probably would have followed the example of Honda and Nissan and avoided all contact with the UAW. But unlike its two larger competitors, Mazda had no choice. It had to accept the union

if it wanted to be assured of selling enough cars to justify its investment in an American plant. To be financially feasible, a major automobile plant must be able to produce a minimum of two hundred thousand vehicles a year. Mazda did not have the marketing strength to sell this many American-built cars on its own, without taking export sales (and local jobs) away from its factories in Japan. The company needed a "customer" who would buy a large share of the cars Mazda produced at its American plant—at least in the short run—while the Japanese automaker gradually built up its share of the U.S. market. Ford was the most logical candidate. The number two American automaker owned a 25 percent interest in Mazda. Besides, the idea of buying cars made by Mazda and reselling them under its own nameplate fitted nicely into Ford's marketing strategy. Having downsized its own production operations in the late 1970s, Ford was having trouble producing enough vehicles to meet the suddenly resurgent demand for its products by 1984. Ford was eager to buy American-made Mazdas, but the company could not risk alienating the UAW and its own unionized work force by purchasing vehicles built by a Japanese automaker in a nonunion American plant.

Ford would later deny that it pressured Mazda to accept the UAW, but Mazda's need for an American customer, and Ford's unwillingness to buy nonunion domestic products, left the Japanese automaker with little alternative but to visit Solidarity House. Mazda executives would always be rather candid about their decision to approach the American union. "Of course, one of the reasons for building our plant near Detroit, and for inviting the participation of the UAW, was to smooth the way for us to sell cars to Ford," said Kenichi Yamamoto, president of Mazda at the time the company began its American venture.[3]

Owen Bieber was waiting to greet the Mazda delegation when it entered Solidarity House. Bieber was 54 at the time of the Mazda visit and had not quite completed his first year as president of the UAW. At six foot-five and 250 pounds, he towered over his Japanese visitors. His hair, which had once been very dark, had turned a fox-like silver blue. Brushed straight back, accentuating its natural waviness, it lent a more dignified appearance to a very large face that had begun to grow fleshy with the years. His mouth was his most expressive feature; set over a still-powerful cleft chin, it was capable of showing a wide range of emotions. When he became angry, his thin lips drew together tightly to form a single slit that turned down to present any adversary with an intimidating war mask.

But Bieber was not given to frequent displays of anger. He was a low-keyed, genial man, if somewhat aloof. Union staff members at Solidarity House referred to him as the Lone Ranger because of his tendency to work alone, absorbing himself in the minute details of an issue—the kind that most other leaders delegated to their aides. Deliberate and hardworking, Bieber was very cautious in charting the union's course, methodically weighing his options and quietly building support for his decisions within the UAW's power structure. He was not by nature a risk taker. Nor was he the type of leader who inspired followers with bold rhetorical calls to keep their rendezvous with destiny. "There's an old saying about Owen: before he jumps into the water, he makes sure the temperature is right," Ted Barrett, director of UAW Region 9A in New England, had said following Bieber's election to the presidency of the union.[4]

For all his cautiousness, Bieber's rise through the ranks of the UAW had been a rapid one. Born in the small town of North Dorr, Michigan, near Grand Rapids, he went to work following his high school graduation in 1948 as a border wire bender with McInerney Spring and Wire Company. "It was a tough job," Bieber would later recall. "I had to take five pieces of heavy gauge wire and fit them into a die the width of a car seat."[5] At McInerney, Bieber joined UAW Local 687, which had been cofounded by his father, Albert. Within one year he became the local's shop steward, and he was elected its president seven years later. A succession of appointed and elected positions followed in UAW Region 1D, which covered rural western and northern Michigan. In 1980 Bieber was brought to Solidarity House by UAW president Douglas Fraser and appointed vice president in charge of the union's General Motors Department, his first national position. Only three years later, Bieber became the surprise choice of the UAW's 26-member executive board to succeed the retiring Fraser as the union's president.

Bieber's election marked a watershed in the history of the UAW. The former wire bender from North Dorr became the first president of the union who had not been personally associated with Walter Reuther, the fiery organizer who led the UAW through its most brutal and bloody battles to win recognition from hostile American automakers in the 1930s and 1940s. Reuther, who headed the UAW from 1946 until his death in a small airplane crash 24 years later, is remembered at Solidarity House with the veneration befitting a saint. Portraits of the late labor leader hang throughout the building, his narrow eyes peering sternly at everyone who enters the plain, uncar-

peted lobby and walks down the corridors leading to the union's executive offices. Official UAW histories devote pages to the Battle of the Overpass, in which Reuther and three other organizers were beaten senseless by a group of thugs hired by Ford's security department in 1937, as they distributed union literature outside the gates of the company's River Rouge plant. The attack, captured in all its savagery by newspaper photographers, won public sympathy for the UAW, ultimately pressuring Ford to drop its opposition to the union.

Owen Bieber was aware of the historical significance of his election. In his inaugural address, delivered at the union's 1983 convention in Dallas, he tried to establish a sense of continuity with the Reuther era. "I was not on the battlefield during the great struggles of the 1930s," he said. "But, by God, I am a product, heart and soul, of what was created in those difficult struggles."

But, of course, Bieber himself was not of the Reuther era. He had come of age at a time when young men joined union locals that had been founded by their fathers, not when they got their heads smashed trying to organize workers at the nation's second largest automaker. Experience had not conditioned him to mistrust management with the same depth and passion as it had an earlier generation of union leaders.

Bieber was also assuming control of a union that was far less powerful than the one that Walter Reuther had headed from 1946 to 1970. Reuther's union had drawn its strength from the auto industry in which it operated. In 1955, at the height of their postwar power, American automakers produced 72 percent of the world's passenger cars. The nation's three largest automakers were very rich. They earned combined after-tax profits of $1.7 billion for the year, an amount of money almost four times greater than the value of Japan's entire (industrial and agricultural) exports.[6] Reuther had shrewdly used the Big Three's affluence to wrest generous wages and lenient work rules from them during contract negotiations. Employing a "whipsawing" strategy, the UAW president would single out only one of the three automakers as a strike target before the start of contract talks. This forced the targeted company to face the possibility not only of having its own factories shut down but of being compelled to stand idly by while its two competitors continued to sell cars, increasing their share of the market at its expense. The dual threat invariably scared the automaker into agreeing to the union's demands. Having won what he wanted from one automaker, Reuther had no trouble getting the same contract concessions from the

two other major American car companies. The costs of wage increases and inefficient protective work rules were immediately passed along to the consumer, who had little alternative to American-made cars in 1955, when imported vehicles accounted for less than 1 percent of the U.S. passenger car market.[7]

The American auto industry had, of course, lost its preeminent position by the time Bieber became president of the UAW in 1983, producing just over one out of every five cars made in the world. With imported cars accounting for 28 percent of the U.S. market, a captive American consumer could no longer be counted on to bear the costs of higher wages and benefits. Besides, the Big Three were in no position to grant their workers generous contracts, having lost a combined total of $5.49 billion in the first two years of the decade. The primary interest of the UAW as Bieber assumed office was not to get more money for its members but to help them hold on to their jobs. More than 260,000 autoworkers were on indefinite layoff at the end of 1982. Membership in the UAW, which had been 1.5 million as recently as 1979, had, by the time of Bieber's inauguration, sunk to 920,000.[8]

Under the leadership of Bieber's predecessor, Douglas Fraser, the UAW had begun to make wage and benefits concessions in the late 1970s, hoping that a reduction in labor costs would increase the competitiveness of the Big Three and avert further layoffs. At the same time, the union and the automakers tried to emulate the more successful Japanese by experimenting with modified versions of the team system at selected Big Three plants, allowing management greater flexibility in assigning jobs and bending traditional work rules.

In January 1982 the UAW agreed to renegotiate its General Motors and Ford contracts, both of which had been scheduled to run until September, in order to provide the beleaguered automakers with quick help in their efforts to close the "productivity gap" that existed between them and their Japanese competitors. Lower wages and more efficient work rules were said to give Japan's automakers an eight-dollar-an-hour cost advantage per worker over GM and Ford.[9] (Chrysler, recently saved from bankruptcy by a federal loan guarantee, had already been given a new, more generous contract by the UAW.)

As vice president of the union's General Motors Department, Bieber oversaw the reopening of the GM negotiations. After four months of on-again, off-again discussions, the UAW and the world's

biggest automaker agreed to a new contract that called on workers to make steep concessions. GM workers had to give up all nine of their "paid personal holidays" and one companywide holiday, raising their annual worker hours by 4 percent.[10] The workers also had to relinquish their scheduled 3 percent automatic annual wage increases for 1982 and 1983 and defer all cost-of-living adjustments (COLAs)— pay raises tied to changes in the consumer price index—for a period of 18 months. In addition to granting GM these economic concessions, Bieber's negotiating team accepted a new, stricter "absenteeism control plan" and promised "to be responsive to innovative job assignments" and work rule changes. The UAW granted GM the right to negotiate flexible local contracts at individual plants that lowered the number of job classifications so workers could be assigned to a greater variety of tasks, increased production quotas so they could be assigned more work, and reduced break time and curtailed transfer rights to ensure that more of their time at the plant would be devoted to work activities.

In exchange for these concessions, GM agreed not to close four of seven plants that it had planned to shut down. The company also offered workers a more generous profit-sharing plan, as well as "guaranteed income" protection that promised to pay a minimum of 50 percent base wages to workers with ten years' seniority or more whose plants were closed. But opposition to the concession pact among rank-and-file workers was intense. The renegotiated GM contract was approved by only 52 percent of the workers, a clear sign of discontent in a union in which 80 and 90 percent approval votes on contracts were not uncommon. The renegotiated Ford pact, identical to the GM contract in its economic concessions, but not going nearly as far in allowing more flexible work rules, was approved by 73 percent of the Ford rank and file.

Bieber appreciated the workers' frustration. His personal enthusiasm for team programs was lukewarm compared to that of some of the other, more "progressive" UAW leaders. Some years later, as he was about to begin his third term as the union's president, Bieber looked back on the concessions of the 1980s: "If you go back, we had a long period of time when we were on an upswing. We had the only automobile business in the world in this country. Bargaining was pretty simple. You put your demands on the table. You got caught in strikes sometimes, but it was always a matter of who could out wait who. You always knew that finally you'd be able to get your goal, or at least close to where you were trying to go. We had some

very lucrative times in this country. . . . Now we're living in a much different world. You have to live with that situation. You have to figure out how to survive and how the people you represent will survive through that kind of era. . . . Would I rather have been president of the international union when everything was on the upswing? Well, of course—only a damn fool would say no to that. . . . [But] that isn't the real world. You have to play with the cards you are dealt."[11]

Becoming president of the UAW when he did, Bieber inherited the task of organizing the plants that Japanese automakers and suppliers had begun building in America in the early 1980s to circumvent the "voluntary quotas" the Japanese government had placed on vehicle exports to the United States. In 1982, less than a year before Bieber took office, Honda became the first Japanese company to build cars in this country, when it began producing vehicles in rural Marysville, Ohio. Other Japanese automakers quickly followed. By the end of the decade, there were expected to be seven wholly or partially Japanese-owned automobile plants in the United States accounting for one out of every four passenger cars built in the country.

The UAW tried hard to organize the American plants of Japanese automakers. Union officials visited Honda and Nissan in Japan, hoping to persuade the two automakers to accept the UAW at their U.S. facilities. Japanese union leaders were enlisted to help the Americans in this effort. The union's organizers went to great lengths to project a cooperative image of the UAW, downplaying its traditional Reutherian militancy and emphasizing the "jointness programs" developed under Fraser and Bieber. By doing this the union hoped to overcome the suspicions of Japanese managers, convincing them that the acceptance of the UAW would not jeopardize their team systems. At the same time the UAW wanted to allay the fears of American workers at Japanese-owned plants, who worried that the arrival of a combative union would cost them their jobs by reducing the competitiveness of their plant, ultimately forcing the Japanese to shift production to other nonunion plants in different states or countries. In a full-page ad, taken in the *Marysville Journal-Tribune* during an early Honda organizing drive, the UAW referred to itself as "a quality union for a quality-minded workforce," a message for both management and workers that the union would not be a disruptive force in the plant.

But the Japanese remained mistrustful of the big American union. With few exceptions, most Japanese automakers and suppliers lo-

cated their U.S. operations in rural areas, primarily in the South, with strong antiunion traditions. Most aggressively resisted UAW organizing drives, successfully keeping the union out of their plants.

At the time of Mazda's visit to Solidarity House, the UAW had made little headway in its efforts to organize Japanese-owned facilities. Toyota had softened its earlier disdain for the union and agreed to accept the UAW into New United Motor Manufacturing Inc. (NUMMI), the Fremont, California, joint venture that the company formed with General Motors in 1983. But NUMMI was, in actuality, an existing GM plant with a work force that was made up of recalled laid-off union workers. For Toyota the joint venture with GM was a test run for a future American plant that would be wholly owned by the Japanese automaker. Admittance into NUMMI did not represent the bold embrace from Japan that the UAW had been seeking. Later, when Toyota opened its own American plant in Georgetown, Kentucky, the company would keep the union out.

The men from Mazda who visited Solidarity House in March 1984 brought with them the first, and probably the best, opportunity the union would have to organize a wholly Japanese-owned automobile assembly plant. Owen Bieber would not let this opportunity slip away. Not only would Mazda's American plant, with its creation of 3,500 new jobs (and new union members) be important in its own right, it would also provide the union with the chance to develop a much closer working relationship with a Japanese automaker than it could ever have hoped to develop at the plant that Toyota co-owned with General Motors. If the UAW won Mazda's trust by proving that it could be a reasonable and cooperative part of the team system, the union could take a giant step toward shedding the militant image that kept it from organizing the plants of other Japanese manufacturers.

Gaining acceptance into the eight Japanese-American plants and their supplier firms was of critical importance to the union's survival. Bieber, having just come through the painful concessions process of the early 1980s, understood that much more was at stake than the organizing of workers at the plants themselves. Being unable to organize foreign-owned plants that accounted for 25 percent of the nation's annual vehicle output would put the UAW in a vulnerable bargaining position with domestic automakers. The Big Three would be able to point to the nonunion Japanese plants, with their lower

pay scales and more flexible work rules, during contract negotiations and demand the same concessions. UAW workers at parts plants owned by the Big Three would be caught in a reverse of Walter Reuther's whipsawing strategy during negotiations, being presented with take-it-or-leave-it contracts, knowing that the company could, if they went on strike, simply buy components from a nonunion Japanese supplier firm.

Owen Bieber, the Lone Ranger union leader who kept his own counsel, was not disposed to bare his anxieties to others. But it would not have been surprising if these issues crossed his mind as he welcomed the Mazda delegation to Solidarity House.

Osamu Nobuto, the Mazda executive who would head the automaker's American manufacturing venture, told Bieber that the company was prepared to accept the UAW at its American plant if the union would go along with the implementation of a team system similar to the one Mazda employed in Japan. Nobuto and the Mazda delegation emphasized that the company would need a great deal of flexibility in running its American plant. The union would have to grant Mazda even more concessions than it had given American automakers in the early 1980s. Mazda managers would have to have the freedom to transfer workers from job to job, to redesign jobs as they saw fit, and to assign overtime work when necessary without being impeded by restrictive work rules. American workers and the UAW would, of course, have input into many of these decisions, the Mazda delegation assured their hosts, through team meetings and joint union-management committees.

Bieber and his staff expressed their concerns about job security. If union workers were going to give up the security of protective work rules and job classifications to make Mazda's American plant more competitive, the UAW wanted the company to reciprocate by promising that it would avoid layoffs under all but the most calamitous economic conditions. The UAW president also wanted Mazda to spell out how the company planned to involve workers and the union in the decision-making process.

The two sides agreed at their Solidarity House meeting to form "study teams," which would meet in the United States and Japan to discuss these issues. Mazda had insisted on the use of the term "study teams" rather than the more traditional "bargaining committee," which the UAW would have preferred, because, the company's representatives explained, the ongoing discussions would be at least as much a learning process as a negotiating process. There were so many

unanswered questions that each side had about the other—questions that would have to be answered before a true understanding could be reached. Richard Shoemaker, Bieber's chief administrative assistant, recalled that there was "a great deal more information of all sorts that flowed freely between the Japanese and us than what we have seen historically in traditional plants. I won't say in every one, but historically over the broad scope."

Shoemaker, who was present at every "study meeting," as the discussions were called, was surprised by Mazda's curiosity about the union. "They were concerned [about] what our views were on most aspects of what they were doing." During the course of the discussions, the company had, he believed, come to trust the UAW. "A great deal of apprehension that they had about our union, about union leaders in the United States, a great deal of these concerns were taken care of as we grew to know each other."[12]

Ultimately, the study meetings produced understandings that reassured both sides. Mazda won a "long-term" commitment from the union "to the principles of flexibility, efficiency, and the implementation of work practices and production systems similar to those used by Mazda in Japan." The UAW received a promise from Mazda, later formalized in its contract, not to lay off employees, "unless compelled to do so by economic conditions and financial circumstances so severe that [the] longterm financial viability [of the company's American plant] is threatened." Mazda also committed itself to providing "meaningful joint employee involvement programs."[13]

Agreeing on the specific details of these general understandings sometimes proved to be difficult for the Mazda-UAW study groups. Mazda wanted the power to rotate employees freely from day to evening shifts as it did in Japan. The union explained that American workers would demand more consistency in their work schedules. Morale at the plant would be destroyed, they argued, if individual workers did not know whether they would be working days or evenings from one week to the next. But sometimes it was necessary to change schedules quickly, Mazda countered, to respond to new production demands. Eventually a compromise was reached: Mazda would be able to rotate any employee to a different shift for up to three months during a calendar year. The rest of the time the employee's shift assignment would remain unchanged, barring special circumstances such as a new vehicle launch.

In Japan, factory managers often work on the line alongside hourly employees, when there is a bottleneck or during peak pro-

duction periods. Mazda wanted to have the same flexibility at its American plant, but the UAW feared that such a plan could be used by the company to replace union workers with salaried personnel. For this reason the union had always fought to keep managers from doing the jobs of hourly workers at Big Three plants. But once again the two sides reached a compromise. Mazda managers from Japan, whom the company called dispatches, as well as local American managers, would be allowed to do the jobs of hourly workers when "production difficulties" were encountered during model change-overs and under other special circumstances. Mazda promised, though, that dispatches and other salaried personnel would not be used to take the place of union members.

Other issues to be resolved were economic. Because the start-up costs associated with building its new American plant would be high—and in consideration of its willingness to break ranks with other Japanese automakers and recognize the UAW—Mazda wanted the union to grant it a temporary "wage discount," allowing the company to pay its workers wages that were substantially below Big Three pay rates. The UAW study team reluctantly accepted the wage discount in principle, and after some negotiation it reached an agreement with Mazda about the size and duration of the temporary discount: Mazda workers would be paid 15 percent less than their opposite numbers at Ford but would achieve wage parity through a series of pay increases spread out over the life of their first three-year contract.

By the early autumn of 1984, the Mazda and UAW study teams had resolved the major issues between them. The two sides formalized their understanding in a letter of intent that committed them to "working together to create an organization promoting harmony, cooperation and understanding" at Mazda's future American plant.

Mazda could not officially recognize the UAW as the sole bargaining representative of the workers at its American plant until those yet-to-be-hired workers voted to accept the union. That approval was ultimately given on September 11, 1987, when 87 percent of the plant's workers voted to recognize the UAW. Neither the company nor the UAW had ever had any doubt about the outcome of this election, since Mazda planned to build its American plant in Michigan, the most heavily unionized state in the country.

Although it had yet to be made public at the time the letter of intent was signed, the specific site for Mazda's new American plant had already been chosen by the company, which had agreed to pay

Ford $14 million for the Michigan Casting Center, an ugly, abandoned foundry in Flat Rock that had been closed by the number two American automaker in 1981.

Responsibility for ensuring that the UAW maintained its harmonious relationship with Mazda once the Flat Rock plant began production was given to Bill Judson, a millwright who had served the union in various capacities at the local level for more than 20 years. In 1985 Judson was appointed president of the newly formed UAW Local 3000, which had been established to represent workers at Mazda's Flat Rock plant and those at the plants of the Japanese supplier firms that were expected to follow the automaker to the area. Judson, whose office would be in the Mazda administration building, would be the highest-ranking union official involved with the plant on a daily basis once it began producing cars in 1987. At first glance he seemed an odd choice to lead the UAW local at a plant the union was counting on to project it into a new, international era of labor-management relations. A plain, broad-faced man who wore his hair in an old-fashioned flattop style, he looked as if he had walked directly out of an earlier, more isolated America. Born in rural Washtenaw County, Michigan, Judson had hoped to spend his life farming, and, indeed, he had worked on a farm for a time after high school before being drafted into the Korean War. Returning from the service, he managed a small farm for a widowed neighbor, but when suburban developers from nearby Ann Arbor and Ypsilanti drove up property values, the widow, like other farmers, sold her land. In 1964 Judson went to work for Hoover Universal, a maker of automotive bearings, where he became active in union affairs and was elected president of the plant's UAW local, a position he continued to hold after NSK Corporation of Japan acquired Hoover in 1975.

Judson's experience dealing with a Japanese manufacturer was considered an advantage by Ernie Lofton, director of UAW Region 1A (which included Local 3000), who appointed him president of the Mazda local. Lofton also liked what he called Judson's "stability"— a soft-spoken, steady demeanor that rarely displayed anger, frustration, or other emotions to the outside world. In Lofton's view, the ex-farmer's even-tempered character made him the ideal person to smooth out any cultural misunderstandings that might arise between American workers and Japanese managers.

In the summer of 1986, Judson was sent to Japan, along with Mazda's four hundred original American hirees, for 30 days of intensive training in the company's team management system. At a traditional Big Three plant, it would have been inconceivable for a union leader to participate in a corporate training program. But because Flat Rock would be a team plant, it required a close degree of cooperation between the company and the union. To achieve this cooperation, the two sides would have to build on the trust that was established during the earlier study meetings by continuing to learn more about one another.

Judson visited Mazda's stamping and assembly plant in Hofu, 56 miles southwest of the company's headquarters in Hiroshima. Completed in 1982, Hofu was regarded as one of the most efficient automaking operations in the world. Every month the plant's eighteen hundred workers produced twenty thousand cars and seven thousand knockdown kits (vehicles to be assembled elsewhere), an output that would have required a work force of almost twice that size at a traditional American factory. As Judson surveyed the plant, he could not help but marvel at its technological efficiency. There were robots everywhere he looked. They were welding car bodies and applying primer paint. They were installing spare tires and transporting parts from the loading docks to work stations on the final assembly line. In the stamping shop, where giant presses turned out doors, hoods, and other large stampings, only about 40 Mazda employees oversaw an operation that was as highly automated as anything in the worldwide automobile industry. But Judson was impressed by more than Hofu's technology. The workers at the plant went about their jobs with a speed and purposefulness that he and the other American visitors had rarely witnessed. The movements of every worker were carefully choreographed to avoid wasted time and motion. The Mazda workers never hesitated when reaching for their tools because every tool was stored in its own specially designated place close to the assembly line. They never waited idly, as American workers often did, for work to come down the line to them. When a production employee completed his primary job at Hofu, he immediately busied himself with other tasks, until the next vehicle arrived at his work station. Once a worker finished installing a gas tank on a Mazda 626 as it passed overhead on the "hanger" assembly line, for example, he would race around the vehicle daubing sound-insulating tar to its underside. He would complete this job just in time to reach for another gas tank, fed to him by a machine, to install on the next car

3
Groundbreaking

MAZDA broke ground on its Flat Rock plant, the plant that was to provide new jobs and new hope for dispirited Downriver workers like Steve Ross and a new opportunity for the UAW to regain its lost position, on May 29, 1985. The Reverend Dr. Alfred Tsuyuki, a Shinto priest from Los Angeles, was flown into Flat Rock to perform the ritualistic ceremony. At 10:30 A.M. this bright but blustery morning, the priest mounted the steps of a three-tiered wooden altar that had been set up on an empty field next to the Michigan Casting Center, the former Ford foundry, which stood sullen and neglected against the pale blue sky like an abandoned outpost of a defeated army. Dressed in a flowing, white ceremonial robe, the Reverend Tsuyuki raised his voice heavenward and asked the universal spirit to bless Mazda's new American venture. Then, taking a delicate white paper duster, he bent forward slightly and gently swept the altar to purify the land upon which the Mazda plant would be built. Another prayer, the sacred *Norito*, was recited to thank the spirit for giving Mazda access to that land, a foresaken four hundred-acre-tract in the northeast corner of Flat Rock. When the Reverend Tsuyuki completed his prayer of thanksgiving, he invited the day's nine honored guests to participate in the offering of *Kensen*, a symbolic pouring of the heart into the success of an impending journey. The nine men walked up to the altar individually, each carrying a branch of hollyhock. When each arrived he bowed, held the hollyhock before his chest, turned it over once, and placed it stemfirst on the altar. He then gave two sharp claps of his hands and bowed again before returning to his seat.

as it arrived at his work station. No one at Hofu ever stood still.

Hofu had served as the model for the plant that Mazda was building in Flat Rock. Only minor modifications would be made to accommodate differences between American and Japanese workers. The overhead assembly line at Flat Rock would be built four inches higher to allow the taller Americans to work without bending. The Flat Rock plant would also include women's restrooms, something not found at Hofu because Mazda, like most other major Japanese manufacturers, had no female production employees in its work force. Japanese law prohibited women from working in factories during the late-night/early-morning hours. Mazda, which often ran its plants around the clock, said it did not want to hire workers who could not be rotated to any shift.

The Hofu plant would also serve as a model for union-management relations at Flat Rock. But again there would be differences. The UAW was an industrywide union, beholden to no single company. It was this independence that Walter Reuther had so skillfully manipulated to wrangle generous wage and benefits concessions from American automakers. The union that Judson observed at Hofu was, like all Japanese autoworker unions, a company union. Its members worked only for Mazda, and thus its fortunes were linked absolutely to those of the automaker. This dependence had led the Mazda union to develop a very different approach than the UAW had toward collective bargaining and the labor-management relationship. Rather than focusing on wages and benefits, as the UAW had historically done, Mazda's union emphasized the importance of keeping the economy strong to protect the job security of union members. The Japanese union believed it had a responsibility to help increase Mazda's productivity, and improve its competitiveness, by participating in joint union-management activities that promoted corporate goals. Under this philosophy the union and management were not adversaries, as they were in America, but partners, each working to create a successful company. As it had with the height of the overhead assembly line, Mazda was willing to make adjustments in this philosophy to accommodate the differences between Americans and Japanese. But like the overhead line, the nature of the management-labor relationship at Flat Rock could only be adjusted slightly from the Japanese model. The underlying spirit of trust and cooperation would have to remain unchanged if the UAW-Mazda partnership was going to work.

Stephen Yokich, the vice president of the UAW's Ford Department, a stand-in for the absent Owen Bieber, was among the honored guests. So too were James Blanchard, the boyish, ebullient governor of Michigan, and Ted Anders, the old and kindly mayor of Flat Rock. The 42-year-old governor, who would later win reelection campaigning under the slogan Jobs, Jobs, Jobs, a reminder to voters of his success in bringing new jobs to the state, had invested a great deal of political capital in the Mazda plant. His administration had put together a $125 million incentive package for Mazda that included a property tax abatement on the new plant, job training funds, and a waiver on all building permit fees.[1] To Blanchard the money was well spent. The incentive package, together with the pressure applied by the Ford Motor Company, had persuaded Mazda to build in Michigan. This would not only result in the creation of 3,500 new jobs at the plant itself but create "up to five times that figure in support jobs" at supplier firms, the governor had predicted.[2]

Ted Anders was not so optimistic. Flat Rock had contributed the major portion of the Mazda incentive package, a 12-year, 100 percent property tax abatement worth roughly $80 million, and the mayor questioned the worthiness of this investment. Anders had grown more and more ambivalent about the entire Mazda project as his involvement in the process of bringing the Japanese automaker to Flat Rock deepened. In March 1984, before Mazda announced its decision to build in Flat Rock, a group of Ford officials met with Anders at his office to discuss an upcoming visit by a Mazda delegation from Japan. A member of the Ford group noticed a bronze replica of the U.S. Marines' flag raising at Iwo Jima that Anders, a World War II Army veteran who had fought against the Japanese in the Philippines, kept behind his desk. The man suggested that Anders remove the statue to avoid offending his Japanese visitors. The mayor, a large, heavyset man, exploded, "Like hell I'll remove it!"

Anders had got along well enough with the Mazda group when he met with them in April. A pleasant, normally easygoing man, he bore no special wartime grudges. He had seen enough atrocities committed by both sides in the Philippines to know that neither had a monopoly on cruelty. Later, as part of the occupation army in Japan, he had come to admire the Japanese people for the strength they had shown under adversity. In 1984, when Anders and his mayor pro tem Thomas Wilkins met with the visiting Mazda delegation, they had offered to give the Japanese a 50 percent property tax abatement on the Flat Rock plant. Under Michigan law this was the largest tax

break allowed on a new plant construction project. The Japanese smiled and nodded when Anders and Wilkins made the abatement offer, and the two Americans left the meeting convinced that Mazda was pleased with the idea of receiving a 50 percent discount on its property taxes. Later they were to learn different. In the summer of 1984, the state commerce department informed Anders that Flat Rock would have to grant the Japanese automaker a complete, 100 percent abatement as part of the Mazda incentive package. Mazda would not have to pay property taxes on its new Flat Rock plant for 12 years. When Anders objected, citing the 50 percent legal ceiling on new-plant abatements, the commerce department produced an opinion written by the Michigan attorney general's office that allowed the Mazda plant to be classified as a rehabilitation project undertaken on an existing structure, rather than a new construction project. Under a Michigan law intended to encourage the revival of rundown industrial cities, a rehabilitation project is entitled to a more generous, 100 percent abatement. Mazda qualified for the full abatement even though it would be building its new Flat Rock plant from the ground up, because, as part of its construction project, the company intended to leave a section of the abandoned Michigan Casting Center standing and convert it into a combination warehouse–employee fitness center. In the opinion of the attorney general's office, this constituted a rehabilitation project, even though the "rehabilitated" casting center was not actually a part of, nor physically connected to, the new plant.

Despite the attorney general's opinion, Anders continued to oppose the idea of giving Mazda a "free ride on taxes." A skilled trades worker who had spent more than 25 years working in Detroit factories before a back injury had forced his retirement, Anders knew firsthand what kind of a burden a large industrial plant could put on a small community. Fewer than 7,000 people lived in Flat Rock. The new Mazda plant would, in essence, be increasing the city's population by more than 50 percent. The 3,500 workers and hundreds of outside engineers, vendors, and other visitors who came to the plant every day would place an added strain on the city's resources; so too would the large, belching tractor-trailer rigs that rumbled through town to deliver parts and supplies to Mazda. The city's police and fire services would have to be expanded; its surface streets would have to be widened to accommodate the added traffic; road maintenance and sanitation services would have to be increased. Flat Rock needed more tax revenues, its mayor argued, to defray these added

expenses. Anders and his allies on the city council said they would reject Mazda's abatement request. (The council's approval was required before an abatement could be granted.) Then the state began a carrot-and-stick campaign to pressure the abatement opponents to reverse their position. The carrot was a promise by the state to provide Flat Rock with financial assistance to help it meet several specified expenses associated with the Mazda plant. The stick was more subtle. In late 1985 the state mounted an intensive public relations campaign to generate grassroots support for the 100 percent abatement. Officials from the commerce department and other state agencies crisscrossed the Downriver area speaking at chamber of commerce meetings and business group lunches to promote the abatement plan. At every stop their message was the same: Downriver can get a major new plant, one that will provide up to twenty thousand direct and indirect jobs, but the whole project is being jeopardized because the mayor and city council over in Flat Rock are refusing to go along with this abatement. One luncheon speaker, in a moment of oratory passion, predicted that Detroit's industrial suburbs would be "set back 20 to 30 years if this [abatement] goes down the tubes. No big industry would want to locate here if they knew that a project like this could be put together and then fall apart later on. I'm not crying wolf, but there is a definite possibility that this is what could happen."[3]

The public relations campaign isolated the mayor and his council from the rest of the Downriver community. Anders and his allies started getting phone calls from the civic leaders of other Downriver cities, and from local business owners, accusing them of jeopardizing the Mazda project and the jobs of twenty thousand workers because of their own greed to grab more tax dollars. The pressure took its toll. The council members gradually lined up behind the 100 percent abatement, leaving only the mayor and mayor pro tem in opposition to the plan. But they, too, eventually relented, and on February 19, 1985, the Flat Rock city council—including Anders and Wilkins—gave its unanimous approval to the 100 percent Mazda abatement. Anders, though, was not happy. He continued to harbor resentment toward the governor and other state officials for their pressure tactics. "They waited until the last minute and then pushed us into a corner on the abatement thing," he would later recall. "If we didn't vote for the abatement, we became the bad guys for the entire state. Everybody would blame us for losing Mazda."

Anders's excitement at participating in the groundbreaking cere-

mony was thus mingled with a bitterness that lingered from the abatement battle. The events of the past year continued to play themselves over in his mind. With each replay, he searched for an overlooked strategy that might have been followed to get the city a better deal. As he surveyed the ceremony going on around him, the mayor wondered whether the new plant that would be built on these consecrated grounds would ever be worth the $80 million in lost tax revenues.

Osamu Nobuto also had much to think about as he approached the altar bearing his hollyhock branch. Responsibility for the success of the future Mazda plant rested squarely on his shoulders. A thin, carefully groomed man who wore his graying hair in the blow-dried style of a television news anchorman, Nobuto had, only three weeks earlier, been appointed president of Mazda Motor Manufacturing (USA) Corporation (MMUC), a subsidiary set up by Mazda to operate its future American plant. Trained as a mechanical engineer, Nobuto had joined the company's chassis design department in 1959. Over the years, he acquired the reputation as an innovative manager, adept at tackling new and uncertain projects. By the standards of Japanese businessmen, Nobuto could be relaxed and informal with foreigners. At times, he displayed a disarming sense of humor. Early in 1985 a group of Downriver journalists had dinner with Nobuto at a Hiroshima restaurant. Seaweed baskets with nuts were brought to the table. The Americans ate the nuts but balked at eating the baskets. Noticing that most of his guests were bald, Nobuto remarked offhandedly that scientists in Japan had long known that seaweed induced hair growth, which was why—as he was sure the Americans had already noticed—there were hardly any bald Japanese. The Americans laughed—but they tried the seaweed baskets. Nobuto, meanwhile, had arranged for a plateful of the small baskets to be placed in front of the two baldest Americans.

Nobuto's first prolonged contact with Americans occurred in 1977, when he moved to California to head the Mazda Technical Center in Irvine. Two years later he was back in Japan as manager of Mazda's newly formed Office of International Business Development. From this position he became the leading advocate inside the company of the strategy to build a plant in the United States. Early in 1982 Nobuto was placed in charge of a team formed to study the feasibility of building an American plant. Nobuto's team evaluated potential plant sites in Omaha, Nebraska, and Columbia, South Carolina, before Flat Rock was selected. As the head of Mazda's

American plant project, Nobuto led the company's study team that met with the UAW in the spring and summer of 1984. His team's position during those negotiations was almost as vulnerable as that of the union. Like the UAW, Mazda had fallen on hard times in the 1970s. With the exception of Chrysler, no automaker in the world had been wounded so deeply by the OPEC oil embargo of late 1973, and the subsequent rise in gasoline prices, as Mazda. The company's passenger car sales fell by more than 50 percent in 1974 alone. Sales in the important American market, which stood at 119,004 units a year in 1973, were only 35,350 in 1976. These problems were caused by Mazda's dependence on the gas-guzzling rotary engine. Developed in the 1920s by Felix Wankel, a German inventor, the rotary engine produces power through the orbiting movement of rotors rather than the up-down stroke of pistons. In theory this design makes the Wankel rotary a more efficient power source than the conventional piston engine, but a variety of technical problems had prevented the engine's commercial application. Thirty years after Dr. Wankel's invention, the rotary engine had yet to be installed in a mass-produced vehicle. In 1961, Mazda signed a licensing agreement with NSU Wankel of the Federal Republic of Germany, gaining the rights to manufacture the rotary engine. Although it was a small company with limited resources, Mazda undertook an ambitious campaign to develop a practical version of the Wankel rotary. The company built a special Rotary Engine Development Center in Hiroshima and staffed it with 180 full-time engineers and technicians, headed by Mazda's future president, Kenichi Yamamoto. The rotary team tested prototype engines virtually around the clock. Its researchers recorded their work with television cameras for later viewing and analysis and translated their findings into a digital code so test data could be entered into a newly installed computer. In May 1967, after almost six years of exhaustive research, Mazda introduced the Cosmo 11-S, the first passenger car powered by a rotary engine. Mazda's rotary engine won almost immediate critical and commercial acceptance for its compact size and increased power output. The company's sales rose by more than 113 percent between 1968 and 1972 on the strength of its rotary-powered vehicles. Nowhere was enthusiasm for the new engine greater than in the United States, where nine out of ten Mazdas sold were rotary powered.

If the rotary engine had one flaw, it was its voracious appetite for gasoline. Even under the most ideal highway conditions, a rotary-powered vehicle seldom traveled more than 14 miles on a gallon of

fuel. When OPEC crude oil was selling for \$2.33 a barrel in 1972, this inefficiency was regarded by car buyers as a minor irritant at most, but by 1975, when the price of crude passed \$10.00 a barrel, the rotary's reputation as a gas-guzzler had frightened away most of Mazda's potential customers. The collapse of its rotary market left Mazda unable to pay off the debts it had incurred when gearing up its production facilities to meet the demand for rotary-powered cars in the pre-oil-crisis market. By 1976 the company owed its creditors \$1.6 billion, and no fewer than 62 banks and insurance companies were threatening to cut off its credit. Mazda almost certainly would have gone bankrupt had it not been rescued by the Sumitomo Bank, which agreed to guarantee all of the automaker's outstanding loans. In return for this support, Sumitomo, Japan's most profitable commercial bank, was given a dominant role in directing Mazda's corporate strategy. To raise money for its troubled client and reduce its own financial risks, Sumitomo pushed Mazda into selling a 25 percent share of the company to Ford in 1979. Although the bankers did not realize it at the time, this decision laid the groundwork for the company's move to Michigan six years later.

With help from Sumitomo and Ford, Mazda gradually began to regain its health. New piston-powered vehicles were added to the company's line. A new, more fuel-efficient rotary engine was introduced. The company's assembly operations were redesigned to improve efficiency. Market share and profits steadily increased. But Mazda's comeback was dealt a serious blow on May 1, 1981, when Japan's Ministry of International Trade and Industry (MITI) announced that it would impose "voluntary" limits on automobile exports to the United States. MITI assigned an individual export quota to each of the seven Japanese automakers then selling cars in America. Each company's quota was based on its share of total Japanese car sales in the United States in 1979 and 1980. This penalized Mazda, which had yet to recover from the rotary fiasco, by limiting the company to a share of the American market well below its true manufacturing and marketing potential. Mazda, which had accounted for 27 percent of all Japanese passenger cars sold in the United States in 1973, found itself locked into a 9 percent share of the export market by the MITI decision.

Nobuto and other Americanists at Mazda believed that the export quotas made it imperative to build a plant in the United States. Without such a plant, they argued, Mazda would be essentially locked out of the American market, which had contributed as much

as half of the company's net profits in the pre-embargo era. To support their argument, the American plant advocates pointed to the threat of increased tariffs and other protectionist actions by the U.S. government.

Another faction at Mazda was adamantly opposed to building an American plant. They questioned the necessity of building cars in America, believing that MITI would lift the export quota at the end of its three-year term. This argument quickly lost credibility, though, as Honda, Nissan, and Toyota rushed to expand or begin American production operations in the belief that the export quota would become a permanent part of Japan's trade policy. Yet, opposition to the build-America plans persisted at Mazda. Those who were against the idea of building in the United States worried that because of Mazda's connection to Ford, the company would be forced to accept the UAW into its American plant. Undisciplined, independent, and heterogeneous American workers would be difficult enough to mold into cooperative members of a Japanese team system, they argued, without the radicalizing influence of the militant union. But in the end, economic factors doomed the arguments of the American plant opponents. Mazda could not afford to remain locked into a small share of the American market. It could not sit idly on the sidelines as its larger Japanese competitors built American plants that would allow them to increase their sales in the United States by offering new lines of domestically made vehicles. It could not take the chance that the Americans would not erect new trade barriers. And, as the Japanese yen showed the first signs of what would become a historic ascent, Mazda had to face the fact that Japanese-made automobiles were likely to become less competitively priced in the American market. Despite any uneasiness they may have felt about dealing with the UAW, Mazda's managers could not help but realize by early 1984 that building an American plant was not so much an option as a necessity.

Having decided to build in the United States, Mazda was prepared to wager heavily on the success of its American operation. The company committed $550 million to the construction of its Flat Rock plant, the largest single investment in its 65-year history.* When it was completed, the new plant would cover an area the size of 47 football fields. It would outshine even its Hofu parent in size

* Because of the rising value of the yen, the size of this investment would increase to $800 million by the time construction was completed.

and technological efficiency. The scope of the Flat Rock plant and its importance to Mazda's plans for regaining the company's lost market share had prompted Mazda president Yamamoto to declare: "The future of Mazda depends on the success of this plant." It is doubtful that any of the three hundred people in attendance at the groundbreaking ceremony appreciated the meaning of these words better than Osamu Nobuto, as he turned the hollyhock branch over to give his heart to Mazda's new American venture.

4

A Third-Culture Plant

NOT long before the Mazda groundbreaking ceremony in 1985, Osamu Nobuto settled into a house on Grosse Ile, an island enclave of comfortable homes in the Detroit River about 15 miles south of the city and 5 miles east of Flat Rock, that once served as a summer getaway for the pioneer princes of the automobile industry. Harry Bennett, the thuggish director of Henry Ford's security department and chief orchestrator of the Battle of the Overpass ambush, maintained a boathouse for his yacht on the island. The boathouse was said to have a secret escape tunnel below it and machine gun emplacements built into its upper walls, testaments to Bennet's underworld connections. "Big Bill" Knudsen, the Danish immigrant who, as Ford's chief production engineer, oversaw the construction of the company's early assembly lines and, a man who would later leave Ford to become president of General Motors, purchased a large farm on the island's west side in 1917. The Fisher brothers, famous makers of vehicle chassis for General Motors, also built summer mansions on the island, as did Ransom E. Olds, the Lansing, Michigan, machine shop owner who founded Oldsmobile.

Grosse Ile's legendary automotive estates had long since been abandoned by 1985, turned into country clubs or divided into condominiums and apartments, but most of the island's homes, including Nobuto's, were impressive nevertheless. Nobuto's home was a handsome single-story pale yellow structure set back far off the road behind a large and carefully manicured lawn. Its spacious backyard bordered the Detroit River, affording a pleasant view of the wooded

Canadian shoreline on the other side. In the summer of 1985, Nobuto would host barbecue picnics in the backyard for local high school students and community leaders as a gesture of neighborly goodwill. Ever mindful of the suspicion with which many in Detroit still regarded Japanese automakers, Mazda was eager to prove that the company and its executives could be good neighbors in America's Motor City. As a step toward this end, the company sponsored an exchange program for local high school students to study in Japan. It also presented the city of Flat Rock with two Mazda 626 automobiles (made in Japan) to use as police cars; donated $30,000 to the restoration of a local historical landmark—a building that once served as a stagecoach stop—and promised to donate $100,000 annually to the city's general fund for ten years to make up for some of the revenue that would be lost as a result of the 100 percent tax abatement. "We are very much aware of the diligent effort made by you and the entire Flat Rock City Council in providing an economic package that allowed us to choose Flat Rock as our plant location," Nobuto wrote to Ted Anders when informing the mayor of Mazda's gifts to the city. "We are honored by the faith you have placed in Mazda in taking such a courageous step. We will work hard to maintain your trust."[1]

As the president of a major automaking venture, Nobuto was inevitably drawn into the fraternity of Detroit-area auto executives. This seemed to suit his forthright personal style. He joined many of the same professional associations as the city's other auto executives, participated in the same conferences and seminars, dealt with the same local suppliers, traveled in the same social circles, and negotiated with the same labor union. Yet, despite his successful assimilation, Nobuto would in many ways remain a world apart philosophically from his counterparts at American auto companies. Having come of age in postwar Japan, he had been trained to view the business of building cars from a perspective that differed sharply from that of Detroit's other auto executives. This philosophical difference was so fundamental that it was even evident in the very dissimilar ways in which Nobuto and his typical American counterpart went about evaluating the performance of an automobile plant.

The American manager, having been raised in a bottom-line environment, tended to look primarily or even exclusively at end results when assessing a plant's performance. How many cars was the plant producing a month? What was the defect rate? As long as he received satisfactory answers to these questions, the American manager con-

sidered a plant a success. Little effort was made by the American to evaluate how cars were being built or to look for steps that might be taken to improve a plant's production process and increase productivity. Such an evaluation would have been regarded as tampering with success by the American manager whose plant was meeting its production quota. "If it ain't broke, don't fix it," was an adage that had special meaning for American auto executives of Nobuto's age. Even if an American plant was plagued by a high defect rate, the American manager still preferred to attack the problem on the product rather than on the process level. Was every sixth car coming off the line with a crooked bumper? The American would send them to the redo shop to have the bumpers straightened. This took less time than stopping the assembly line to find the root cause of the problem, and in the short run at least, it allowed the plant to continue meeting its production quota, which made the manager look good to his superiors. The goal of the American manager was to keep cars rolling off the assembly line with no interruptions. Changes, even those that could improve the production process, were regarded as inherently disruptive and therefore undesirable.

Nobuto and other Japanese managers had been taught to evaluate their plants from a more-long-range "process-engineering" perspective. Although they, too, were concerned with end results—the number of cars produced and the rate of defects—their primary focus was on the production process itself. No Japanese manager would consider his plant successful, regardless of how many vehicles it produced a month, if the process by which those cars were made was mistake prone or inefficient. The emphasis of the fluid and mutable process over the static and unchanging product made Japanese managers like Nobuto more adaptable than their American counterparts.

Even if a Japanese plant was succeeding in meeting its production quota, its manager would still continue to study the production process, looking for new ways to weed out inefficiencies, so that the same output could be achieved in less time or with fewer workers. The Japanese called this process of constantly seeking improvement *kaizen*. It was practiced with almost religious fervor at Mazda plants in Japan, where managers and workers seemed always to be holding meetings to discuss plans for "kaizening" (i.e., improving) some part of the production process. Any *kaizen* suggestion that could shave one one hundredth of a minute (0.6 seconds) off the time needed to assemble a car was said to be worthy of consideration. One *kaizen* suggestion would naturally beget others, since an improvement that hastened the work

flow in one area of the plant put pressure on workers in the next area to catch up. If, for example, the workers who welded support pillars to cars devised a *kaizen* plan that allowed them to complete their welding ten seconds faster, the workers down the line who were responsible for grinding the welds smooth would have to come up with a way to take ten seconds off their job cycles to avoid backlogs.

When Nobuto and other Mazda managers spotted a defective vehicle coming off the assembly line, they were less concerned with correcting it—though correct it they did—than with finding the cause of the problem and developing a *kaizen* plan to prevent it from occurring again. They did not believe that quality control could be achieved by final product inspections. Such inspections would only show the results of a problem that had already occurred. As disciples of process engineering, Mazda managers were certain that if they exercised tight-enough control over the production process, the quality of their finished product and the efficiency of their operation would naturally follow.

The products that would be made at the Flat Rock plant managed by Nobuto were the Mazda MX-6 and the Ford Probe.* The latter was slated to be sold through the dealer network of America's number two automaker. Both cars would be built on the well-proved chassis of Mazda's popular 626 automobile, but each would have its own distinctive outer skin and interior cabin features. Both cars would be moderately priced, but the MX-6 would be slightly more expensive. A small but solid two-door coupé, it would have the alert, upright appearance of a German performance car. The Probe, a glassy, low-slung hatchback, would be sleeker and somewhat less serious in its styling. Ford was hoping that the Probe would win over some of the young middle-class consumers who had been buying sporty Japanese imports like the Toyota Celica. More than half the Probe's customers were expected to be women. Because Ford possessed much greater marketing strength than did Mazda in the United States, the two companies had agreed that 60 percent of all vehicles made at Flat Rock would be Probes. Later, after it became apparent that the demand for the Probe was exceeding all expectations, Ford's share of the plant's output would be increased, at times reaching as high as 70 percent.

The process of turning metal, plastic, and rubber into Probes and MX-6s would involve four basic steps. It would begin in Flat Rock's

* In the fall of 1989, the plant would begin making a third model, the Mazda 626.

stamping shop, where large, thunderous presses would stamp out doors, roofs, bumpers, quarter panels, and almost one hundred other parts, cookie-cutter fashion, from coils of sheet steel. The stamped metal panels would then be transported to the body shop, where they would be welded to structural support beams shipped in from outside suppliers to form complete car bodies. More than 4,000 different welds would be performed on each vehicle, 84 percent of them made by gangly long-armed robots sent to Flat Rock from Japan. From the body shop, vehicle bodies would travel by monorail to the paint shop, where they would be dunked like doughnuts into a 350-ton tank of primer and then painted by multiple-axis robots and automated paint machines, each capable of applying 25 different colors of paint as well as sealers and undercoats.

After cars had been painted and dried in ovens, they would be taken by overhead conveyer to the trim and final assembly area. This would be the most labor-intensive shop in the Flat Rock plant, employing about one-third of its work force. Workers in "trim and final" would perform jobs too minute or too delicate to be done economically by robots. They would drill in the engines; bolt on the tires; screw in the mirrors; and install the door handles, radios, ashtrays, and other components that go into making a finished automobile. These parts would be delivered to workers from a materials-handling department and a plastics-molding shop, both of which would border the trim and final area, as well as from several smaller subassembly stations located within trim and final itself. Of all the production areas at Flat Rock, trim and final would most resemble the archetypal image of an auto factory, with workers standing alongside a moving assembly line, performing routinized tasks with mind-numbing repetitiveness.

When Mazda's Flat Rock plant reached its full two-shift production schedule in 1989, about 45 Probes and 25 MX-6s would roll off its assembly line every hour—a rate of almost 1.2 one-ton vehicles a minute, 14 to 17 hours a day.

This output would be achieved with a work force of 3,500, fewer than 3,100 of them involved in actual production, the rest assigned to supervisory and administrative tasks. This would be a remarkable rate of efficiency by American standards. The General Motors Fairfax, Kansas, plant, a facility of roughly the same age and scope as Flat Rock, would require a work force of almost 4,100, roughly 3,800 of them involved in production, to build a little more than 65 Pontiac Grand Prix's an hour.[2] Part of Flat Rock's superior produc-

tivity would be due to the advanced technology employed at the plant; most would be the result of a management system brought to Flat Rock by Nobuto and the four hundred Mazda dispatches sent to Michigan from Japan.

The system was a creation of the Toyota Motor Corporation, which introduced it in the early 1960s and quickly saw it adopted and expanded on by other Japanese manufacturers. Toyota itself had borrowed some ideas from American efficiency experts W. Edward Deming and Joseph M. Juran, but the system was really a natural outgrowth of the Japanese dedication to process engineering. It is a system built on the constant improvement and refinement of the production process; a "kaizening" that strips away layer after layer of redundant manpower, material, and motions until a plant is left with the barest minimum of resources needed to satisfy its production requirements. The system tolerates no waste. It leaves virtually no room for errors.

The system is called *just in time* (JIT), a term that describes its formula for scheduling deliveries of parts and supplies to a plant. A more appropriate name would be "just enough resources," because the system seeks to leave every plant with just enough—and *only* just enough—human and material resources to keep its production process going. A perfect JIT plant (none has ever existed) would be one at which the difference between the amount of resources *available* to meet a production quota and the amount *required* to meet the quota is zero. Such a plant would be perfectly "balanced," according to JIT theory. All backup resources that push a plant over this balanced zero equation are considered waste or, in Japanese, *muda*. Under the JIT system no reserve inventory of parts and supplies is allowed to cover for disruptions in delivery schedules. The materials necessary for building cars are delivered to a JIT plant on what is almost an as-needed basis, usually shipped to the plant from outside suppliers several times a day in quantities large enough to last for three or four hours of production. No backup pool of workers is available to draw on when illness, injury, or vacations remove employees from the JIT work force. Nor is a JIT plant permitted to maintain a work force large enough to meet its labor demands during peak production periods. Under most of these circumstances, temporary employees are brought in to bring the work force up to the required level. A plant with a work force that included permanent employees who were not truly needed 100 percent of the time would be considered wasteful by JIT standards.

Time is another resource that is controlled carefully under the JIT system. No cushion of spare time is built into the production schedule of a JIT plant to account for human error and inefficiencies. Every step of the production process is clearly studied and kaizened to ensure the smoothest flow of work and materials and the most productive use of every worker's time. As Bill Judson, the newly appointed president of Flat Rock's UAW Local 3000, observed when he visited the Hofu JIT plant in 1986, Mazda has eliminated virtually all waiting time and wasted steps from the work routines of its hourly production employees. The workers Judson saw at Hofu were actively engaged in a production activity close to 60 seconds every minute. At the non-JIT American auto plants he was familiar with, workers maintained a 40- to 50-second-a-minute work pace, filling in the rest of their time waiting—waiting for a tool to turn up or for the next car to come down the assembly line. The 10- to 20-second-a-minute difference would not have given Hofu a significant productivity advantage had it applied to only a handful of workers. But when even a 10-second-a-minute differential is applied to a plant with 2,000 workers, the productivity gain will add up to 2,667 extra worker-hours over the course of an 8-hour shift, and 13,335 extra worker-hours over a five-day week. Assuming that every employee at the plant works a 40-hour week, the 10-second-a-minute productivity gain is equivalent to hiring 333 extra workers.

As Judson and other American visitors were to discover, Japanese JIT plants like Hofu (and later Flat Rock) were able to produce more cars per worker because they kept every worker productively employed more of the time.

The efficiencies created by strict control of inventory levels under JIT are often less obvious. The virtual elimination of backup inventories at a JIT plant appears at first to be less logical to many Americans than the Big Three's traditional "just in case" strategy of maintaining a large cushion of spare parts and supplies to protect against unforeseen disruptions in delivery schedules. Deliveries from outside vendors will, after all, sometimes be delayed. The subassembly shops inside a plant that provide parts to the final assembly line (and are not allowed to build up reserve inventories of parts under a JIT system) will be slowed from time to time by absenteeism, injury, or worker error. The assembly line workers themselves, some of whom must fabricate their own parts while waiting for a car to arrive at their work stations (again with no backup parts inventory allowed), will occasionally fall behind in their work because of fatigue,

boredom, or careless mistakes. With no safety net of spare parts to fall back on, the JIT plant is more vulnerable to these interruptions in the flow of work and materials. But the vulnerability that often appears to Americans to be a weakness is in fact one of a JIT plant's greatest strengths. This was true of Hofu, and everyone at Mazda believed it would be true of the Flat Rock JIT plant as well. Because interruptions in the flow of supplies are felt so severely and so suddenly, they cannot be ignored. With their entire production process thrown off balance by the supply problem, JIT managers and workers must move quickly to pinpoint the source of the delay and implement corrective action. (Their task is simplified by JIT's thinly-stretched inventory levels, which leave a problem noplace to hide, making it relatively easy to locate its point of origin.) Because problems occur routinely at a JIT plant, as they do at every plant, the unforgiving bare-bones inventory assures that attention will constantly be focused on the production process.

The removal of spare parts cushions provides a JIT plant with other, more tangible but less important advantages. It reduces the amount of capital that must be tied up in inventory, it reduces the amount of space that must be given over to in-plant warehouse facilities, and it reduces the paperwork and labor costs associated with stocking and maintaining large inventories of parts and materials.

Although individual American plants would make attempts to implement JIT systems in the early and mid-1980s, JIT was not compatible with the traditional product-engineering orientation of most American managers. Focusing as they did on end results, the Americans viewed a large spare parts inventory as essential to meeting their production quotas. Americans valued the security of knowing that simply by reaching into their vast reserves of extra workers and materials, they could overwhelm any glitches in the flow of supplies—at least in the short run—and continue to show the same results (a consistent output) despite inefficiencies in their production process. If the cushion of extra materials and manpower was large enough—and it usually was—the inefficiencies in an American plant could be carried along for years before they became impossible to ignore.

As a JIT plant Flat Rock would have little space given over to warehouse facilities. The absence of backup inventories would make this unnecessary. Where Detroit's other American-owned automobile plants kept enough supplies on hand to cover several days or even weeks of uninterrupted production, Mazda would maintain less than a single shift's worth of inventory for most parts.

The number of workers at Flat Rock would also be kept low in accordance with JIT precepts. Mazda's production work force of 3,100 would be 500 to 1000 workers smaller than the production work forces of comparable American stamping and assembly plants. Mazda would not expand its permanent work force during peak production periods only to lay off excess employees during slow-downs as American plants did. Nor would it carry a cushion of extra employees to cover for worker vacations, absences, or injuries. When extra workers were needed temporarily to fill out the plant's work force, Mazda would be able to summon them from its support member pool (SMP), a group of American workers trained by Mazda, but not on the company's permanent payroll, who were available for short-term assignments.

Like workers at every Japanese-owned auto plant throughout the world, workers at Flat Rock would be organized into teams. Each Mazda team would consist of six to ten workers (or team members) and a team leader, who, like the workers under him or her, would be an hourly employee and a member of the UAW. The media has often presented a glowing image of the Japanese team plant as a place where workers and managers pull together in a spirit of mutual trust and respect as they pursue a common objective. Such shop floor fraternalism is, in fact, a key feature of the Japanese team system, but the organization of hourly employees into teams of cross-trained workers serves another, more practical function, allowing management to maintain a smaller work force by providing it with a readily available means of filling jobs vacated by absent workers without having to hire additional employees.

Mazda, for example, organizes teams around specific work areas: One team will be made up of workers who install different engine components, another of workers who apply different sealants and coatings to the underside of vehicles. The job of each team member is different, yet all jobs within a team share many common features. This makes it simple for Mazda to train team members to perform one another's jobs. With team members cross-trained, Mazda is able to move them freely from job to job within the team (or within similar teams) to fill in for injured, sick, or vacationing workers.

At Detroit's American-owned plants, management was not able to transfer workers freely to different job assignments. The traditional plant's UAW contract did not allow management this flexibility. But the 1984 "letter of intent" between the UAW and Mazda had exempted Flat Rock from traditional job classifications and work

rules. Mazda was not only free to shuffle workers to different assignments within the team, it would have the power to transfer them to entirely different areas of the plant. A worker from trim and final assembly could be moved to the paint shop or body shop if the situation warranted such a move, just as could be done at Hofu.

Nobuto, and every other Mazda executive associated with the company's United States venture, knew that Flat Rock would need a dedicated effort from its American work force if the plant was to become a successful JIT operation. For all their great strengths, all JIT plants have the same Achilles' heel: They are easily derailed by a work force that offers anything less than a 100 percent commitment. Because a JIT plant cannot draw on backup inventories, any worker who does not complete his or her job cycle on time interrupts the flow of parts and supplies, throwing off the entire production process. If the subassembly shop worker making gas tanks slows his work pace or persistently makes careless mistakes, the main production line will soon be held up for a lack of tanks. If a materials handling worker dawdles when loading trim on his or her supply cart, or loads the wrong color of trim, the entire trim and final assembly shop will become logjammed. The fact that the standard work pace in a JIT plant approaches 60 seconds a minute makes it difficult for all but the most committed workers to complete job cycles on time. The relatively small size of a JIT plant's work force also increases its dependence on the dedication of workers. With fewer workers available at a JIT plant, the absence of each employee is felt more sorely. A JIT plant like Flat Rock thus requires employees who have the commitment necessary to show up for work when they have a headache, the flu, or a minor family crisis; employees who are willing to work through minor aches and pains; and employees who will take on added work to cover for absent team members without complaining. Steve Ross, the millwright who was among the first Americans hired by Mazda, recalled that during the question-and-answer segment of his orientation session on health benefits, one of the new hirees asked the Mazda trainer about the number of sick days allowed to Flat Rock workers. The trainer, an American, chuckled in amusement: "You're not supposed to get sick here."*

* Hourly employees at Flat Rock were not given a specified number of "sick days" to take at their own discretion over the course of a year. Workers received 60 percent of their base pay for "excused absences" (that is, absences approved by management), which generally required a doctor's note.

In Japan, with its strong hierarchical tradition and group orientation, assembling a work force with this level of loyalty and dedication had never been a problem for Mazda or any other manufacturer. Japanese culture, with its emphasis on self-sacrifice, respect for authority and social cooperation had, in fact, provided fertile ground for the development of a management system that required workers to commit themselves so completely to job and company. But the United States, with its strong social currents of self-gratification, individualism, and competitiveness, is in many respects the cultural opposite of Japan.

As Nobuto and Mazda's other Japanese dispatches drew up their plans for the company's United States plant, it was widely assumed that the biggest challenge they would face at Flat Rock would be to persuade the company's independent-minded American employees to accept the sacrifices imposed by JIT. The men of Mazda knew that to do this they would have to instill a sense of common purpose in their Flat Rock employees, encouraging the Americans to identify with the company and see themselves as part of a larger Mazda team. If the Americans came to regard the Flat Rock plant as their own, they would have more at stake emotionally in its success. Mazda advisors would explain to the Americans that the only way to ensure the success of the plant—their plant—in a competitive world market would be to implement the more efficient JIT system at Flat Rock.

To encourage workers to identify with Mazda, the company would go out of its way to cultivate an image of itself as a concerned, humanistic employer. In their talks to newly hired workers and in their many interviews with the Detroit media, Nobuto and other Mazda managers made frequent allusions to the company's lifetime employment policy in Japan (job security being presented as a tangible payback for JIT sacrifices). They discussed the company's commitment to providing employees with a safe, comfortable workplace, describing the ergonomic features that would be incorporated into the design of the new Flat Rock plant. They also pointed to the ongoing training programs that would be implemented at Flat Rock, and the Employee Fitness Center that was being built next to the plant, as examples of Mazda's interest in the development of the worker as a "whole person." "People are people before they are assemblers, welders or managers," Mazda's chief executive, Kenichi Yamamoto, said. "Mazda does not take this philosophy lightly."[3]

Mazda hoped to reinforce the sense of unity and common purpose at Flat Rock by exporting egalitarian team symbols from the

company's Japanese plants to Michigan. These symbols were ex-
pected to help break down the barriers that historically had divided
unionized American workers from their managers. The most con-
spicuous symbol was the blue-and-khaki Mazda uniform that would
be worn by everyone at Flat Rock, from Nobuto to the newest hiree.
Everyone at Flat Rock would also do calisthenics together in the
morning and eat lunch together in a common cafeteria at noon. After
work, managers would take workers to Fiorelli's, a local pizza par-
lor, for pizza and beer and some informal shop talk. There would
also be more structured settings for worker-manager dialogue. If the
worker had a problem, an idea, or a complaint, management's door
would always be open at Flat Rock. The accessibility of Mazda
management during the plant's start-up phase would surprise Forrest
Green, a newly hired tool and die maker who had spent 16 years
working at Ford. In the entire period he was at Ford, Green had
rarely talked to a member of management other than his immediate
supervisor. Most of the managers he encountered wore suits and ties
and had an aloof, disdainful attitude toward workers. "The few
times I dealt with a plant manager, it was, 'Yes sir, no sir,' and that
was it," he recalled. "One time, the Deuce [Henry Ford II] came to
the plant for a tour, and they sent us all to the cafeteria for lunch
before he walked in, so nobody would be there to bother him. At
Mazda it was not like that at all—the Japanese were very down to
earth. Nobuto would walk into the cafeteria and plop his butt down
wherever there was a spot. He sat at my table a couple of times. We
[the Americans at the table] were kind of nervous, but he was real
easygoing and nice. We talked about baseball and golf and food. I
got the impression that he was real sincere about not being high-
handed with the workers. You'd hear stories about him, like the time
some Ford people were going to visit the plant and someone told him
he should wear a suit and tie, but he balked and said, 'No, I'm at
work, so I'll wear my uniform.' You wouldn't get that at Ford when
I was there."

The emphasis that Mazda placed on openness and communication
would be reflected in the design of the Flat Rock plant itself. The four
major shops at Flat Rock (stamping, body, paint, and trim and final
assembly) would be located around a central administration area and
computer control room. This "four corner zone" layout, borrowed
from Hofu, placed managers quite literally in the "middle of the ac-
tion," increasing their contact with the shop floor and making them
more accessible to workers. At American plants, by contrast, admin-

istrative offices were located in front of the manufacturing area, separated from the noise and heat of the factory floor by a long and not-too-frequently traversed corridor.

The central administration area at Mazda's Hofu plant was an open office. Desks were stacked head-to-head in the style of a school lunchroom, with no dividers between them. The openness was supposed to encourage an even greater spirit of teamwork among the managers themselves. Mazda wanted to follow this open office design at Flat Rock, but its American managers, accustomed to a different sense of privacy, balked at the idea. The Americans wanted to have enclosed offices, or at the very least, shoulder-high partitions cubbyholing individual desks. As a compromise, Mazda agreed to put small dividers between the desks, which it still insisted on stacking head-to-head. The dividers would be high enough to afford some privacy when a manager was hunched over writing, but low enough to be talked over without craning one's neck. They would not impede open communication.

The modification of Hofu's open office design was only one of the ways in which Mazda would have to adjust its group-oriented management system to accommodate the more individualistic Americans. At Hofu the company maintained a Mazda infirmary for the treatment of workers, a discount supermarket on the factory premises, and worker dormitories. But Mazda could not even consider adding these amenities to the Flat Rock plant, since the Americans, who tended to be suspicious of an employer involving itself too deeply in the personal lives of workers, would have regarded this as paternalism. Even though Mazda would have a high degree of flexibility at Flat Rock by American standards, the company would still have to operate under more, and stricter, work rules than it did in Japan. The UAW, though it had agreed to relinquish most of its protective work rules and job classifications, was still an independent union. Unlike Mazda's company union in Japan, it had some teeth to bare when standing up to the company. Mazda had come to this realization at a couple of points during their negotiations with the American union. The company had wanted to make participation in its morning calisthenics program mandatory, but the union had rejected this, insisting that the exercises be voluntary. "We didn't think it was right to tell workers they had to exercise," said Bill Judson. "The exercises were a good idea, but we felt it was something the workers should decide for themselves."

The distinction between mandatory and voluntary, between in-

structions that were explicit and implicit, was something that Maz-da's Japanese executives would have to learn to appreciate in America. In Japan, with its homogeneous population and close-knit groups, there is no real difference between "should do" and "must do," when a manager makes a request of an employee. Where an American worker would tend to regard the decision to participate in voluntary morning calisthenics, or take on a voluntary job assign-ment, as a matter of choice, the Japanese worker would consider it a matter of duty. Refusing the call to volunteer would be taken as a sign of the worker's disrespect toward management, a gravely serious offense in hierarchical Japan.

Nobuto recognized that Mazda would have to adjust its manage-ment style at Flat Rock, particularly the way in which it communi-cated instructions to workers, if it were to avoid misunderstandings with its American employees. "My understanding is that in America there is a wide range of the way of thinking," he had observed. "Compared to that, for Japanese, the range of thinking is rather narrow. Relatively speaking, in Japan you may find less things to be clearly written, clearly defined in writing, maybe partly because in Japan people work in the same place for many years, perhaps life-long, you know. In Japan there is an expression, *a-un-no-kokyu,* unspoken understanding. Literally, it means even without explana-tions they can understand each other. That, however, is kind of ambiguous [for Americans]. That ambiguity can [cause] a problem [communicating with American workers]. But by clarifying, clearly defining, we can avoid such ambiguity."[4]

Nobuto and Mazda's other dispatches hoped to create what they called a "third culture" at Flat Rock, one that shaped Japanese JIT and team concepts to the American temperament, without signifi-cantly altering the meaning of those management principles. Pouring Japanese clay into an American mold is how their objective could be viewed. The third-culture plant would be American in its external appearance, but its basic substance would always be Japanese.

Mazda's original group of four hundred Japanese dispatches would be responsible for training American hirees in the company's JIT-team system. Every American manager at Flat Rock would have his or her own Japanese advisor, a dispatch who would work side by side with the American to instruct him or her in Mazda's manage-ment methods. Every group of two to four teams (called a unit at Flat Rock) would have a Japanese trainer who would watch over new hirees until they became familiar with the daily factory routine, and

answer questions that were not covered during their earlier ten-week orientation and training session. As the Americans learned their lessons, the Japanese would begin to leave. By September 1988, one year after Flat Rock began to make cars, only a few more than two hundred would be left. The Japanese said that they would eventually be turning over control of Flat Rock to the Americans. This would be the only way to have a true third culture at the plant. It was intimated that Nobuto would be stepping down as president in 1990 to be replaced by an American.

Denny Pawley was the man expected to succeed him. Pawley was the highest-ranking American at Flat Rock, joining Mazda in January 1986, before construction of the plant had been completed, as the vice president of manufacturing. At the time, he was one of a small minority of American plant managers with hands-on experience running a Japanese-style team plant. He had come to Mazda from General Motors, where he was manager of the Pontiac (Michigan) Fiero plant, which made the two-seat Fiero sports car. Opened in 1982, the Fiero plant began operations at a time when GM was groping for new ideas that could reverse the declining market share and quality problems that had plagued the company for almost a decade. The plant was regarded as an experiment by the world's largest automaker, both in terms of its product—a specialty car constructed of fiberglass—and its production process—it was one of the first team plants in America. Borrowing heavily from the ideas of its Japanese competitors, GM organized Fiero workers into teams of ten to twelve. Each team elected its own "coordinator" and each was responsible for meeting its own production schedule and operating budget, performing its own safety inspections and housekeeping functions, and coordinating its own training program. GM also did away with all quality control inspections and time studies at the plant, allowing the workers to be responsible for the quality and productivity of their own operation. Every week, the plant was shut down for 30 minutes to allow workers to hold problem-solving meetings. "Basically, we tried to pass responsibility for running each small piece of the operation down as low in the organization as we could," said Pawley. "It was very close to what you'll find at a Japanese plant. We worked closely with Doctor [W. Edward] Deming for over a year, and I read extensively about Japanese management systems."

Pawley's familiarity with Japanese management methods attracted Mazda to him. It also attracted him to the idea of working for the Japanese automaker. Born in rural Waterford Township, 20 miles

northwest of the city of Pontiac, he had been with GM for 21 years at the time he was contacted by a Mazda headhunter. He had begun his automotive career with some reluctance. His father, a plant lay-out engineer, his uncles, and, it seemed, just about every able-bodied adult male in his family, had spent their entire lives working for the Pontiac division of General Motors. He was determined to avoid a similar fate. After graduating from high school in 1959, he enrolled in Oakland University, becoming a member of the new suburban Detroit school's charter class. Two years later, he dropped out of school to get married, still vowing to stay away from the local car factory. "I told myself, 'I'm not going into that damn plant,' " he later recalled. "So I went to work in the circulation department of the *Oakland Press* [the local newspaper] for three years and almost starved to death. Finally, I bit the bullet and talked to GM about a job." Pawley began at GM as a cost and budget analyst, became a line foreman, and then gradually worked his way up the plant hierarchy—to general foreman, training director, department super-intendent, general superintendent, production manager of the Fiero plant in 1982, and plant manager in 1984. Along the way he com-pleted his college education, attending night classes at Oakland Uni-versity and earning a degree in human resource development in 1982. By the time Pawley was offered the Mazda job, he was ready for a new challenge.

> Looking around me, I could see that if I stayed at GM for another ten or fifteen years, it would be just more of the same. I would move from this plant to that plant, but there would be no chance to do anything really new. Mazda was offering me a small increase in salary, but it wasn't the money that interested me, it was the op-portunity to work with the Japanese. After studying the Japanese system at Fiero, I thought it would be something to really work with the Japanese, and learn from the true experts in the [auto-mobile] business, so when the Mazda offer came, I jumped. . . . The people at GM tried to convince me to stay, telling me what a big mistake I was making and saying I had this great career going for me, but I wanted the experience.[5]

Temperamentally, Pawley seemed ideally suited to a plant that emphasized open communication between management and labor. Stocky and confident, with meat-hook arms and a jaw that still looks square and strong, though the flesh around it has begun to sag with weight and age, he has a blunt, let's-not-stand-on-pretense style that

is appreciated by American blue-collar workers. He did not talk down to workers and never pulled any punches. He said what was on his mind, looking you straight in the eye, and expected his workers to do the same. He was "Denny," not "Dennis," everywhere, not just on the shop floor like some managers who tried to affect a one-of-the-guys image. The basic Mazda work uniform suited him perfectly; a tie looked out of place hanging from his tree-trunk neck. "When you first meet Denny you really like him and think he's a real have-a-beer-with-the-guys type of manager," said Forrest Green, the tool and die maker. "Then after you see him for awhile, you find out that you were right—Denny is very genuine."

During Flat Rock's critical start-up phase, Pawley became almost a father figure for the plant's younger workers, most of whom had never worked in an auto plant before. He encouraged them as they struggled to adapt to the factory routine, trying to take what he called "the fear" out of operating high-powered equipment on a rapidly moving assembly line. He told workers stories from his GM days, like the one about how foremen would walk through a GM plant with shirt pockets stuffed full of grievance slips that had been filed against them by workers. The foremen wore their bulgy pockets like badges of honor to prove that they were not soft, and to show the workers who was boss. It would be different at Flat Rock, Denny told the workers. He was taking almost personal responsibility for that.

"The big thick contracts you've got in your UAW [plants] across the country are there because management proved . . . they couldn't be trusted with general language," he told the *Detroit News*. "If five years from now we have a very traditional type of operating agreement in here, it won't be the UAW's fault, it'd be mine. Because I will have proved that they can't trust me and then they'll say, 'OK, Denny, we tried it and you wouldn't do it, now here's some rules we're gonna live by.' "[6]

Like Nobuto, Pawley believed that the Flat Rock plant would have to develop a third culture that combined elements of Japanese and American thinking. He was certain that the Japanese had developed a better way to build cars, with their emphasis on the production process and their organization of workers into teams. He agreed that Americans should learn to take a longer-range view of the production process, rather than charging head-on to deal with problems only on the results level. But the Americans' take-charge tradition would never allow them to be as patient as the Japanese. Sometimes

direct action *was* the best response to a production problem, in Paw-
ley's view. He was fond of recalling an incident that occurred at
Pontiac in the late 1970s, when a car had slipped off the assembly
line into the work pit below. Pawley, then a line supervisor, had
calculated that the cost of stopping the line to save the car by easing
it out of the pit was greater than the value of the car itself, so he
called for a forklift operator to impale the car and move it out of the
way. The car was demolished, but the line was hardly disrupted.
Some workers at the plant could not believe that their supervisor was
destroying a newly assembled car, but to Pawley there was no logical
alternative.

Pawley had no doubts that American managers and workers
could learn to cooperate with one another in a team system. The
workers especially seemed to be crying out for a system that would
give them some input into the making of plant decisions. But he
doubted that an American team could ever be as serenely harmoni-
ous as Japanese teams, because Americans seemed to be much more
independent. Nor did he believe that American workers, who had
what he called a "hit him square between the eyes" style of commu-
nicating, would ever adjust to the subtle, indirect style of Japanese
managers.

These differences could only be accommodated, believed Pawley,
if Flat Rock became a third-culture plant, one that was headed by an
American, who could communicate with its American work force.
He was convinced that Mazda would turn over control of the plant
to American managers within three or four years. "Every American
here expects that," he told the *Detroit News*. "By then we will have
illustrated our patience to learn the Japanese system and they damn
well better let us implement it. I see no reason why they wouldn't.
That's the reason they came here. They want the American mind as
well as the American effort."[7]

5
A Special Work Force

WAYNE DODD felt uncomfortable. It was an unseason-
ably hot spring day in 1987, and the windowless room in the Mazda
assessment center was stuffy, despite the air conditioning that was
humming faintly in the background. Dodd was sitting at a large
conference table with a group of seven other Mazda job applicants,
working on some made-up problem—the exact nature of which he
has since forgotten—so that the two Mazda assessors who sat silently
at either end of the table scribbling in their notebooks could deter-
mine whether the applicants had the interpersonal skills needed to
work at the Japanese automaker's new team plant.

A quiet and thoughtful man then in his mid-twenties, Dodd was
a little self-conscious about participating in the group exercise, but he
pushed this feeling aside and vowed to himself that he would make
a good impression on the two assessors. He had already got through
a series of paper-and-pencil tests and a personal interview in his quest
for a Mazda job, and he was not about to let a little awkward
embarrassment keep him from getting into the Flat Rock plant. He
plowed into the discussion, offering suggestions for solving the now-
forgotten "problem" in a bright, cheerful voice, listening attentively
when other applicants spoke, and acting like what he hoped was a
cooperative team player. He got the impression that most of the
other people at the table were doing the same thing—trying to over-
come their initial shyness and outguess the assessors. "It was like a
game, but if you didn't play it, you weren't going to get in," he later
recalled. "The assessors were honest; they told us that right up

front—'If you don't participate, you don't get hired.' There were some people who didn't speak up because they were too embarrassed or felt dumb; they probably aren't working at Mazda today."

Dodd had been waiting eight years for a chance to work in a car factory. A tall man whose almost completely hairless head made him appear old for his years and lent a hardness to his otherwise soft and delicate features, he was born in Flint, Michigan. Located about 70 miles north of Flat Rock, Flint was the birthplace of General Motors and the home of the automaker's largest concentration of auto plants. Dodd's grandfather and great-grandfather had spent their work lives laboring at a Buick plant in the city. His father still worked as a skilled trades worker at Flint's Fisher Body plant, the giant GM chassis-building operation started by the Fisher brothers of the Grosse Ile summer estates. Unlike Denny Pawley, Dodd did not wish to escape his family's tradition of carmaking. He hoped to maintain it. The America that his high school class had entered in 1980 was not as hopeful as the one that had awaited Pawley nineteen years earlier. Its graduates were too worried about holding on to the life their parents had known to think about moving beyond it to better things.

There were no new jobs to be had at Flint's car factories in 1980, so Dodd went to work at a local Burger King, an opportunity created by America's service economy. He had become the restaurant's as-sistant manager by 1985, when he came across a Mazda application form in the *Flint Journal*. Dodd did not hesitate to mail in the ap-plication, even though a job at Flat Rock, should he eventually land one, would mean leaving Flint. He could not afford to pass up the extra income that a Mazda job would bring. He and his wife, Rita, had three children and a fourth on the way. The $7.50 an hour he earned at Burger King brought him $18,000.00 a year, not enough to support a family, and there were hardly any benefits.

Dodd was still working at the fast food restaurant two years after mailing in the Mazda application, when he received a letter from the automaker inviting him to come to an abandoned school just north of Flat Rock to take a series of written aptitude tests. The paper-and-pencil tests were the second step in Mazda's five-step screening process, the first being the application that had appeared in the news-paper.

The written tests had proved to be quite easy. Dodd was one of the first to finish the two-hour battery of exams, most of them deal-ing with basic math and reading comprehension, and he used his

spare time to look around the large test room. Few of the other applicants seemed to be having any trouble; most finished the tests well within the allotted time. The one conspicuous exception was a Hispanic woman who spoke limited English; she wanted to return to take the tests on another day but was turned down. Dodd's worst score was on a test that evaluated the ability to detect quality defects, an important attribute, since Mazda had said that its hourly employees would be acting as their own quality control inspectors. Applicants were given a series of illustrations, such as six light bulbs, and were asked to pick the one that had the quality defect—the one with the small crack around its base. The test was simple, but Dodd, who did not wear the glasses he needed, had trouble spotting the smaller flaws.

This problem did not dissuade Mazda from inviting him back to the abandoned school for the third step in its screening process—the personal interview. Again Dodd hopped into his car for the 70-mile drive to the test site. He knew that there would be two and perhaps three more trips, before he completed the Mazda screening process— a total of at least 560 miles of round-trip driving and four or five missed days of work. Even then he might not get the job, but the chance of earning a real income made it worth the risk. The manager of the restaurant knew all about the Mazda application, and he went along with Dodd, arranging schedules so his assistant could drive down to Flat Rock to take the Japanese automaker's tests. Some of the other applicants Dodd met had driven more than seven hours to get to the Mazda test site from Ohio and Kentucky. Some, who were further along in the five-step screening process, had already given up six or seven days of work between the traveling and the testing. They considered themselves lucky to have made it that far.

Dodd's interview lasted 30 minutes. When it was over, he felt certain he would be hired by Mazda. The man and woman who interviewed him seemed impressed with his enthusiasm and his fast food background. "They liked the idea that I was with Burger King, because it has a team concept that is sort of similar to Mazda's," Dodd would recall. "At the restaurant, you had to learn to do everybody else's job, so if someone didn't show up you could cover for them. From what I understood, the Mazda plant was going to be run the same way."

The interviewers wanted to know how Dodd liked working as part of a team at Burger King. He had liked the sense of togetherness it bred. They asked if he would "have a problem" at Flat Rock if his

supervisor asked him to pitch in to help out another team member who was having trouble completing his or her job on time. No, he would be happy to help out a fellow team member by taking on some of his or her jobs in a pinch.

The interviewers were also curious about Dodd's attitude toward unions. Had he ever belonged to a union? No. How did he feel about unions? They were OK. Did he think the UAW and Mazda would be able to cooperate in a team plant? He didn't see why not.

The male interviewer seemed especially pleased with Dodd and his answers. He asked why Dodd wanted to leave Burger King. Dodd did not hesitate: "Not enough money." Flipping hamburgers did not pay as well as building cars. The man smiled and said, "I can understand that." (In 1988, Dodd's first full year at Mazda, he would earn $36,000, double his Burger King income.)

Like every interviewer and assessor Dodd would see throughout the five-step screening process, the man and woman tossing questions at him in the abandoned Southgate school were Americans. (Mazda's Japanese dispatches remained behind the scenes during the interviews and tests.) Both wore the same blue-and-khaki Mazda uniform, and both had introduced themselves by their first names. They were polite, even friendly, but careful to maintain what they no doubt considered was a professional distance. Dodd left the interview thinking that they were lower-level Mazda managers, maybe people he would one day be working under at the plant. Months later, when he would actually begin his job at Flat Rock's trim and final assembly shop, he would recognize the male, a short, solid black man, as Ben Hemingway, one of the plant's six appointed UAW representatives.

But Dodd was unaware of this when he pulled out of the abandoned school's parking lot for the ride back home. His only thoughts at that time were of how well he had done in his interview. He knew he had come off as an "energetic person" and a good potential team member—he could tell by the looks in his interviewers' eyes—but he still had to complete the final two steps in Mazda's screening process. Failing to make the grade at either step would mean no job, despite his successful interview.

A third 70-mile drive from Flint two weeks after the personal interview would give Dodd his first look at the Flat Rock plant itself. Clean and white, the plant shimmered in the early morning sunlight like a giant polar ice cap stretching out over the gray, flat landscape. Mazda had just begun making prototype cars on a "trial build" basis

at the plant in May 1987, when Dodd came to Flat Rock for the "group problem-solving assessment," the fourth step in the company's screening process. Dodd and the other applicants at the Mazda Training and Assessment Center, an institutional building close to the main plant, were organized into teams of varying sizes and put through a six-hour series of problem-solving exercises. The first exercise was supposed to evaluate the applicant's ability to contribute to a consensus decision. This ability would be required in every Mazda team member, Dodd and the other applicants were told, because the company would expect hourly employees to organize their own work schedules and set many of their own quality and production standards. Dodd's team of applicants was asked to create a "rewards program" for the plant that ranked perfect attendance, a flawless safety record, and other achievements in their order of importance and assigned an appropriate reward to each. The group decided to begin by prioritizing the achievements. After considerable debate, they agreed that a perfect safety record should receive the highest reward. As the team worked out its rewards list, a man and woman—both, Dodd guessed, in their late twenties, sat at either end of a long conference table silently studying the job applicants, and periodically jotting down observations in the notebooks that rested on their laps. They were Mazda assessors, and it was their job to decide how well each applicant participated in the discussion. The assessors had made it clear at the start of the exercise that there would be no right or wrong answers: they didn't care whether the group gave a higher rating to perfect attendance or safety. They were interested in *how* the group reached its decisions. How well did its members express their ideas? Did they listen to one another? Dodd had liked the two assessors right away, finding them "very honest."

Dodd joined a new team for his second problem-solving exercise, a test that evaluated the applicant's participation in what Mazda called "*kaizen* projects." The applicants in Dodd's group were issued toy blocks and told to work together as a team to assemble "airboats," while Mazda assessors recorded the time it took them to complete this task. The group was then instructed to use the *kaizen* process of constant improvement to find ways to assemble the boats faster. Could the piles of toy blocks be arranged more efficiently so time was not wasted reaching for materials? Could job assignments be organized better so group members would not get in each other's way and duplicate one another's efforts? Dodd and the members of his team experimented with ideas for squeezing wasted steps out of

their boatbuilding process, while the Mazda assessors jotted down observations in their notebooks. By the end of the exercise, the team had cut the time required to build a boat almost in half.

Another exercise, the one that felt most awkward, and the one Dodd has forgotten, was intended to measure the ability to resolve interpersonal problems. For example, applicants were told that "Pat, a bright, alert and reliable worker, is performing well on the job, but is acting rude and nasty to others. What can the team do to improve Pat's attitude?"

Like Dodd, the other applicants at the center were happy to have made it this far in Mazda's screening process. But as the six-hour series of assessment exercises wore on, he could see that they, like him, were beginning to grow impatient. Many were unemployed. Those who had jobs, usually at or near minimum wage, had already missed three days' wages—money they could scarcely afford to lose—going through Mazda's interviews and tests. In the past, when they had applied for jobs at American plants, they showed up at the personnel office, filled out a short application form, and gave a couple of personal references whom they knew would never be called. Then, if the plant wanted them, they would go to a doctor for a medical to make sure they had no contagious diseases, heart problems, or other ailments that could cause their future employer undue difficulties. But Mazda kept poking, putting its applicants under a microscope, making them go through these assessment exercises, while its assessors scribbled away in their notebooks, to find out if they had the personality to fit into the company's team. Applicants like Dodd, who felt the screening process was excessive for what would, after all, be a job building cars in a factory, were careful not to let their feelings take away from the enthusiasm they put into the assessment exercises.

Dodd passed the group problem-solving assessment and was invited back to Flat Rock in June for the fifth and final series of tests—the simulated work exercise. The purpose of these tests was to see if applicants, who had already proved they possessed the intelligence and interpersonal skills required of Mazda team members, also had the physical coordination and endurance needed to build cars. Dodd was put through a four-hour series of exercises at the training center that simulated factory working conditions. He operated mock production equipment, being asked to maneuver a large and unwieldy drill around an engine without knocking into the engine itself. He assembled a dome light and hopped into a mock car chassis to screw

the light to the roof. He then unscrewed the light, brought it back to a table to disassemble it, then reassembled it, hopped back into the car, and screwed the light to the roof again. Mazda's assessors timed him every step of the way, jotting down observations about his "quality orientation" (for example, was his dome light assembled properly?) in their ever-present notebooks. It was an oppressively hot and humid day and Dodd was sweating profusely under the bump cap and safety glasses Mazda had issued him. He kept asking one of the assessors how he was doing. The man was friendly and encouraged him, telling him he was doing fine. He finished the series of exercises with the second fastest time in his group of six.

Dodd's wife Rita had driven with him from Flint for the final test. She was sleeping in their car in Mazda's lot when he returned from the training center. How had he done? she wanted to know. He told her he was certain that Mazda would hire him.

The idea of working for a Japanese automaker did not strike Dodd as being disloyal to Michigan's American automakers. The Big Three had not, after all, been loyal to America's autoworkers, closing local plants and moving production overseas and even buying foreign-assembled cars and slapping American nameplates on them. To him, a job building Mazdas in Flat Rock was as American as one building Buicks in Flint. No one in his automaking family objected to him applying for work at a Japanese plant, except for Rita's mother. She thought that the Japanese tried to brainwash workers at their so-called team plants. But Dodd had been part of a work team at Burger King, and he had been happy there. He was looking forward to working for Mazda, notwithstanding his regrets about leaving Flint and his slight exasperation with the company's excessive screening process. The money would be good, and the open, supportive environment of a team plant would be much better than the cold and unfriendly plants in which earlier generations of Dodds had worked. Growing up in Flint, he knew firsthand the kind of animosity that existed between American auto companies and their employees. A foreman at GM was as likely to summon a worker by shouting a favorite obscenity as by calling the man's name. The GM worker who made a suggestion for getting the job done faster or better or safer would never be listened to. From everything Dodd had heard and read, he expected Mazda to be more decent.

Mazda's managers at Flat Rock—Japanese and American—went out of their way to explain the reasons for the company's demanding screening process to new hirees like Dodd and to the public at large.

The company had to be very selective in choosing employees, they said, because workers at the Flat Rock team plant would be given much more individual freedom and responsibility than their opposite numbers at Big Three plants. Because Flat Rock team members would be required to participate in joint *kaizen* projects and reach consensus decisions on job scheduling, production goals, and quality standards, Mazda needed to hire people who not only knew how to express their own ideas but could get along with others and resolve their differences constructively. This was hardly an important characteristic to screen for at an American plant, where workers labored in isolation, having no real contact with their fellow plant employees. Mazda's emphasis on cross-training and job rotation created a need for workers who were intelligent enough to learn a variety of jobs and flexible enough to adjust to a work routine that had no rigid job classifications. The constant improvements that would inevitably result from the plant's *kaizen* projects made it necessary to find workers who had the motivation and desire to always do a better job. The success of Flat Rock's team system "starts with the selection process, the type of person you get in," Denny Pawley said. Pawley described the type of person Mazda was looking for: "You need the flexible mind, the person who will sit down with his team and solve methods and layout problems instead of trying to go out and do it all himself."[1]

David Merchant, the vice president of personnel at Flat Rock, would allude to Mazda's hiring policy in the standard welcoming remarks he made to new employees during their orientation. "We like to tell new team members that 'what we really hired is your head. We'd appreciate it if you would bring your body along when you walk through the plant gate in the morning, but what we're really interested in is your head and the contributions that it can make,' " he said. Not only would workers have to be flexible and intelligent to make it through Mazda's screening process, said Merchant, they would also have to possess the desire to "find ways to improve specific tasks as well as everything around them."[2] In other words they would have to be the types of people who could embrace the concept of *kaizen*.

Cool and polished, Merchant did not spring from the factory floor as Denny Pawley had. His background was white collar. Although approaching middle age, his jet black hair and unlined complexion gave him the appearance of a young man not more than five or six years out of law school. He had in fact spent close to 13 years

at Nabisco Brands, becoming vice president of personnel of the Life Savers division, before joining Mazda in June 1985 as the first American hired at Flat Rock. The blue-and-khaki Mazda work uniform looked less natural on his slender frame than it did on the bull-necked Pawley, but during the hiring process it was Merchant who, as vice president of personnel, emerged as the company's chief American spokesperson. Throughout 1986 and 1987 he spoke at local schools and at business seminars and other meetings to explain Mazda's hiring and employee relations philosophy to a curious Downriver community. Mazda would be "a little more innovative" than the Big Three, claimed Merchant, not only in the way it hired workers but in the way it trained and developed them as well. "The average American auto company doesn't spend anything on its workers once it has hired them," he told a group of personnel professionals in March 1986. "Mazda will spend $10,000 a person between now and the spring of 1988 for a three-month training program."[3] This training would not be limited to instructing employees in the operation of factory equipment or the performance of quality control inspections. It would, said Merchant, help employees "focus on things that have meaning, not only at work, but in their social life"— things like stress management, cooperation, and communication skills. Mazda would continue to invest in training its American employees for the entire length of their careers, promised Merchant. This would keep Flat Rock's workers interested in their jobs and save them from falling into the malaise that seemed to afflict many workers at American-owned plants. "The American worker tends to stay on a job until he becomes bored," the Mazda vice president told his audience. "The key for Mazda is job enrichment. The job has its own built-in limitations, but if you give the worker an opportunity to contribute on a daily basis, then it becomes more than just a job." Once hired, workers would not have to worry about the security of their jobs at Flat Rock. Mazda would not lay off workers whenever sales declined as American automakers did, Merchant said, the company was committed to its workers for the long haul. Because of this commitment, and because Mazda would be investing so heavily in developing each employee, it had to be very careful about who it let into Flat Rock. The company viewed the employee-employer relationship as a marriage, not a casual date, and a marriage should never be entered into lightly.

Just as important to Mazda's managers as the qualities they were looking for in prospective Flat Rock employees were the problems

they were determined to avoid. The bright, flexible, and motivated team member sought by Pawley and Merchant had an exact opposite—the sullen, withdrawn, and alienated worker whose name had become legion in the American auto industry in the 1960s. This worker felt cut off from his company and labored in isolation. This worker had no interest in the success of his company and took no responsibility for the quality of the cars it made. If management was lucky, this worker did his job and no more. He never volunteered or made an extra effort to get a job done—and he sometimes vented his frustration by sabotaging production equipment or the cars themselves. Of late this worker had begun, with greater frequency, to relieve the boredom of factory work by drinking and taking drugs on the job. Hiring this worker at a JIT plant, which depended on team members to make an all-out effort to meet tight production schedules and deliver required parts to work stations "just in time," would have been the equivalent of industrial suicide. A JIT plant would provide the disaffected worker with opportunities to sabotage an entire production operation. No one was more aware of this than Mazda's Japanese managers. Although the worker named legion did not represent the majority of American autoworkers, he or she appeared frequently enough to make the Japanese leery of hiring laid-off workers from Big Three plants.

Had the Japanese wanted to justify their apprehension about former American autoworkers, they need only have looked at the previous tenant of the Flat Rock plant site—the Michigan Casting Center (MCC) owned by Ford. Like Mazda's Flat Rock plant, MCC represented the largest single plant investment in its owner's history at the time it was built in 1972. As Mazda would do with its Flat Rock plant, Ford had equipped the casting center with some of the most advanced technology of its era. But unlike Mazda–Flat Rock, MCC did not have a modern management system to go along with its sophisticated production equipment and pollution control devices. In the 1970s MCC, like all Big Three plants of the period, was still being run in accordance with the same "scientific management" principles that American automakers had been following when Wayne Dodd's great-grandfather punched his first GM time clock 50 years earlier. (Although it is no longer openly advocated, scientific management still persists in various forms at plants in the United States.) Created by efficiency expert Frederick Winslow Taylor in the 1890s, and first applied to the mass production of automobiles some 20 years later by Henry Ford, scientific management seeks to increase

productivity by reducing a plant's reliance on skilled human workers, whom it regards as too unreliable and inconsistent to be depended on in an efficient manufacturing operation. To achieve this goal, scientific management calls for as many tasks as possible to be transferred from people to machines. Those tasks that must be performed by people are to be broken down into small segments to allow rigid standardization, which reduces the dependence on skilled labor. For example, if it required 20 different steps to build a given part, training one worker to complete all 20 steps would endow him or her with a valuable skill and, according to scientific management theory, would make the plant too dependent on the performance of this worker. It would also affect the consistency of the parts made at the plant, since if one worker became especially proficient at completing the 20 steps, he or she would turn out parts that were superior to those made by other workers trained in the same job. From a scientific management standpoint, it is more efficient to break down the job of building the part into 20 standardized steps and to train 20 different workers to perform each specific step. This would yield parts that were of consistent quality—though admittedly they would not be as good as the parts made by the best 20-step craftsperson—and it would reduce the plant's dependency on the skills of individual workers.

The effect of scientific management on the morale of workers is the exact opposite of the effect of the team system envisioned by David Merchant. Scientific management reduces the worker's involvement in a plant's production process and erodes his or her sense of pride as a craftsperson by assigning the worker to do a simple repetitive job that bears no visible connection to the finished products made by the plant. It leaves the worker unable to see his or her job as offering any meaning beyond the collection of a paycheck. In the 1920s, before American auto plants were unionized, any worker foolish enough to complain about the dehumanizing effects of scientific management would have been fired on the spot. During the depression of the 1930s, all autoworkers, unionized or not, were too worried about losing their jobs to be concerned about the personal fulfillment those jobs offered. In the 1940s there was a war on. In the 1950s, the workers and their union were primarily interested in making up for wage gains that could not be won during the Depression and war years. But by the 1960s and 1970s, workers had become more secure, more prosperous, and more educated than ever. It was then that the scientific management plants of the United States became breeding grounds of anger and alienation.

At few plants was this discontent more obvious than at the Michigan Casting Center. In its brief history (it was closed by Ford less than a decade after it opened because of a downturn in the demand for its large-engine castings), MCC acquired a reputation in the automobile industry, and in the Downriver area, for its labor problems. "Everything bad you ever heard about an American auto plant was true of the casting center," said Craig Farrand, a Downriver newspaper editor. A former autoworker himself, Farrand had many contacts inside MCC. His contacts told him of widespread drinking and drug taking in the plant (narcotics were dealt openly in some work areas); of violent confrontations between workers; of mutinous employees refusing to follow directions from managers. One MCC foreman who instructed a worker to remove the slag from his oven had a knife pulled on him by the man. Only after the foreman, a large, powerful individual, slammed the worker into a rail and wrested the knife from him did the man relent and clean his oven. "It was like the wild west there," the foreman would later recall of the casting center. "What order there was, was order you established yourself."[4]

Supervision at the large and cavernous casting center was so loose that workers were often able to leave the plant in the middle of their shifts and return later to "punch out" at the end of the day. Most of the truant workers would visit taverns near the plant. A group of skilled trades workers had made the happy discovery that the two-way radios they used to communicate with supervisors when they were repairing equipment in remote corners of the casting center could pick up signals from the plant at a nearby tavern. From that point on, the workers were able to enjoy afternoons at the tavern while still being able to respond promptly to calls from supervisors. Other workers chose to spend their time away from MCC in the parking lots of local shopping centers, drinking beer, harassing female shoppers, and occasionally shoplifting or breaking into cars. "We had a lot of problems out there [at MCC] with crime . . . and a very heavy drug usage situation," recalled Aaron Gillespie, a former Flat Rock city police lieutenant. "I'm not talking only about crime at the plant site, but with employees who were allowed to roam the streets of Flat Rock by the hundreds and cause all sorts of problems." In one of the more bizarre incidents recalled by Gillespie, two men wearing the style of coveralls worn by MCC workers robbed a bank across the street from the plant. Although the robbers were never caught, there was a strong suspicion in the Flat Rock police department that they were MCC employees out on an unauthorized break.

An unspoken but privately acknowledged purpose of Mazda's five-step screening process was to avoid what could be called "the MCC syndrome." The horror stories that came out of the casting center were not unknown to Mazda's Japanese executives. Nor was the case of Vincent Chin, a Chinese American engineering student who was bludgeoned to death with a baseball bat outside a Detroit area McDonald's by two American autoworkers who allegedly mistook him for a Japanese. The 1985 trial of Chin's killers received intensive media coverage in Mazda's hometown of Hiroshima, as did other reports of violence in Detroit. The men from Mazda did not believe that every American autoworker was a violent, destructive brute, but they had seen enough to be afraid. They did not want to let any bad apples into their Flat Rock JIT plant who would spoil the cooperative team spirit that was so essential to its success. They would hire laid-off American autoworkers, but they would be careful. They would ask their friends at the UAW and trusted American consultants to help them weed out potential troublemakers. The lengthy five-step screening process would also serve as an endurance test, wearing down the undisciplined, the unstable, and the uncommitted. Just to be on the safe side, Mazda would make sure that every applicant who passed the five-step screening process took a drug test before he or she was hired.

As a result of the care it exercised in screening potential employees, Mazda wound up with a work force at Flat Rock that is probably more free of troublemakers, malcontents, and drug users than any plant in Detroit. In 1987–88, when Mazda hired the bulk of its Flat Rock work force, a typical group of new hirees gathered at the company's training center could easily have passed for a group of students at a small Midwestern college—young, eager, bright eyed, and earnest. The hirees were invariably proud of themselves for surviving Mazda's five-step screening process. This made them appreciate their new jobs all the more. Later, after they had been working at Flat Rock for one year or more, they would continue to regard the plant's work force as a select group. When asked what they liked most about working for Mazda in 1988–89, many Flat Rock workers would, without hesitation, cite the high caliber of their fellow team members. "We have a bunch of good people at the plant, no druggies, no rowdies. That's one good thing that for sure came out of the screening process," said Peter Barrow, an engine installer from trim and final assembly. Becky Mehaffey, a quiet, attractive young woman who had been laid off from the Ford River Rouge assembly

plant before being hired by Mazda in 1986, compared her experiences with male coworkers at the two plants: "If a woman walked through the plant at Ford it was like a zoo. The guys just went out of their mind; you know, they were screaming, they were whistling. It's not like that at all here. The guys here don't do that. . . . It helps to have a uniform; we all look the same."

Nevertheless, there were others, who, after going through the Mazda screening process, would claim that the company, in its efforts to weed out "druggies" and "rowdies," had—inadvertently perhaps—penalized innocent applicants by unfairly associating them with the MCC syndrome. Some laid-off autoworkers believed that they were not given a fair hearing when they applied for Mazda jobs. This was especially true of those workers who had been active in their union locals. They claimed that they were prejudged as "militant" and uncooperative. One former Big Three worker recalled getting the impression during his Mazda interview that the company "would not have looked favorably on somebody who was a big union man." This worker, who said he was hired by Mazda because of his experience in a skilled trade, hid his earlier union activities from his interviewers. Considering that Mazda's two-person interview teams—such as the one that interviewed Wayne Dodd—often included a UAW representative, the idea of the interview process being biased against a strong union background seems rather odd. But screening applicants for potential rabble-rousers made as much sense for the UAW as it did for Mazda, given the Bieber strategy of creating what for the union would be a new cooperative relationship with management. As the former Big Three worker had pointed out: "If the UAW was not going to act as the same old union, it would be better not to have too many workers around who were indoctrinated with the union's old ways."

The heavy emphasis the screening process placed on verbal skills placed an added obstacle in the paths of older applicants, who were likely to feel less comfortable in the role-playing assessment exercises. The same verbal emphasis also had the effect of giving the process a cultural bias against minority applicants. One of Wayne Dodd's interviewers, Ben Hemingway, was black, but the majority of Mazda's interviewers and assessors were whites from middle-class backgrounds. In judging how an unemployed black autoworker from Detroit participated in a group problem-solving session, they could easily have misinterpreted the applicant's behavior and failed to recognize him or her as a good potential team member.

Blacks would make up 14.1 percent of the Flat Rock plant's work force by the time Mazda had completed its initial round of hiring in 1988. By comparison, 29 percent of the population living within a 26-mile "commuting radius" of the plant was black. Although blacks were clearly underrepresented in Mazda's work force, Flat Rock was significantly better at providing minority employment than were most Japanese-owned auto plants in the United States. Honda's Marysville, Ohio, plant, for example, built in an area where blacks made up 10.5 percent of the population within a 26-mile radius, employed a work force that was only 2.8 percent black. By contrast, at the eight new General Motors plants that were built between 1980 and 1988, 25.4 percent of the work force was black, even though the percentage of blacks within commuting distance was 16.6.[5]

Aside from having a relatively small minority representation, Mazda's Flat Rock work force was very young (average age 31); very inexperienced (more than seven out of ten of the plant's employees had never worked in a factory before, and only one in four had Big Three experience); and predominantly male (women accounted for less than 28 percent of the work force).[6]

Mike Parker, a Detroit electrician and a labor activist and writer, is among those who believe that the relative youth and inexperience of Flat Rock's work force is consistent with the orientation of Mazda's screening process. Parker was one of the 93,000 applicants rejected by Mazda. He applied for a job at Flat Rock in March 1987. At the time he was 47 and employed at a small supplier firm north of Detroit. He made it through the first four steps of the screening process, but was never called in for the final step, the simulated work exercises. Parker, who would later recount his experience applying for a Mazda job in a book about team plants called Choosing Sides, did not fit the common image of an American factory worker. A small, animated man whose round, pleasant face is rimmed by a full-length beard and a generous crop of somewhat unruly dark hair, he holds bachelor's and master's degrees in political science from the University of Chicago. He was on his way to earning a doctorate in the same field at the University of California at Berkeley when he dropped out to become an electrician's apprentice, because, he would later explain, "It offered the fulfillment of working with my hands as well as my mind." Parker has worked as an industrial electrician since completing his apprenticeship program, holding jobs at various

times at Chrysler and Ford plants. Years on the factory floor, however, have not changed an outlook that is essentially cerebral; his guiding lights are rational rather than emotional, ideological rather than personal. He is intensely committed to what he calls "union activism," but a genial personality has kept him free of the ideologue's shrillness.

Before he applied at Mazda, Parker had suspected that his reputation as a union activist would keep him from being hired. But while going through the assessment process, he began to wonder whether the company harbored a built-in bias against former autoworkers in general, regardless of their union politics. Mazda's assessors were all gung ho about the company's team system, convinced that it would herald the beginning of a bright new era of automaking in Detroit. They were equally certain, it seemed to Parker, that Detroit's old system was a miserable and unredeemable failure. Former American autoworkers who were tainted by their past experience would not only have to *learn* Mazda's new system, they would have to *unlearn* all of the bad habits that they had acquired at Big Three plants. One thing Parker was certain of was that the Mazda screening process gave laid-off autoworkers no credit for their greatest asset— car-building experience. "The company placed no weight on the fact that a worker had survived ten or fifteen years at an auto plant and perhaps had picked up some valuable knowledge about building cars along the way," he said. The mere act of "surviving" ten or fifteen years in an auto plant would, Parker realized, seem like an absurdly insignificant accomplishment to anyone who had not actually labored in a plant, but he knew differently. Surviving in an auto plant, with its relentless production pace, intense heat, and ear-shattering noise levels required a person of steady nerves and stoic endurance. Those who lacked either would quickly be eaten alive in a real plant. To think otherwise was naive beyond belief.

Parker was struck by the naïveté of the Mazda applicants in his group during a problem-solving exercise. The assessors presented Parker and the other applicants with four problems and instructed them to develop a plan for dealing with each. One problem involved a worker who was causing discontent among other team members because of his unfriendly attitude. Another involved a team member who had been missing a lot of work lately because of her son's asthma and needed help in improving her attendance. A third was to decide whether the team should play in a plant volleyball or bowling tournament. And a fourth was to find a way to stay comfortable even

though it had become "too hot in our part of the plant of late." Parker's group decided to prioritize the problems so they could work on the most important one first. They put the question of hot plant conditions at the bottom of their list as the problem of least significance. Parker, who had seen workers collapse from heat exhaustion in the summer, when outside temperatures, the heat from machinery, and the sweat of 2,000 men and women turned the factory floor into a steam bath, was stunned. He knew that temperatures inside an auto plant routinely reach past 90 and even 100 degrees in the summer, because no automaker—including Mazda—could afford the expense of air-conditioning a two-and-a-half-million-square-foot factory. Heat exhaustion was one of the most common health concerns of autoworkers everywhere. As he sat and listened to the young Mazda applicants dismiss high temperatures as a minor concern next to the weighty issue of whether to bowl or play volleyball, Parker remained silent. Looking at the group, he could not help thinking how innocent they were.

6
Learning
to Think Japanese

DAVID MERCHANT was right. No automaker in the history of Detroit had ever come close to matching the energy and resources that Mazda committed to training its first two thousand hourly employees in 1986–88.

At an American auto plant, new workers were given a pamphlet that outlined wages and benefits and explained work rules. They were then sent out to the shop floor to watch other workers perform the same narrowly defined jobs that they had been hired to do. They would watch for two or three days or, if the job was especially difficult, perhaps for a week. After that, they were on their own. Further training was considered unnecessary, since workers were expected to remain at the jobs for which they were initially hired, with no variation introduced into their work routines.

Mazda's orientation and training program for new employees would, by contrast, last ten to twelve weeks, depending on where in the plant a worker was assigned. The Japanese automaker would not train its workers in only one narrow job, as American automakers did, but would cross-train them to perform a variety of different tasks, so they could rotate job assignments to keep their work routines from becoming dull. This cross-training took time, but it was not the only reason, or even the main reason, for the greater length of Mazda's program. (The company had already said that most cross-

training would not begin until after the plant had been building cars for awhile, probably in mid-1988.) Much more time in the orientation and training sessions was given over to teaching the Americans how to view their jobs as hourly employees through, what for most of them was, a new and very different perspective—the perspective of the Mazda team system. Even those employees who did not have to un-learn bad habits picked up at Big Three plants would have to change their way of thinking to adjust to Mazda's concept of teamwork.

The clear lines of demarcation that Americans often used to sep-arate the responsibilities of one worker from another would have no place in Mazda's new team plant. Nor would the wide and often impenetrable lines that Americans used to separate managers and workers and distinguish company time from personal time. "That's not my job," or, "I'm on a break," were excuses that did not apply in the one-for-all-and-all-for-one environment of a Japanese team plant, where every worker was expected to feel personally responsi-ble for the overall success of the company, and not merely the com-pletion of his or her narrow job routine.

It had become obvious during Mazda's five-step screening process that this philosophy was alien to most American workers. Mazda interviewers had asked the job applicants: "What would you do if your neighbor was having trouble with a Mazda automobile?" The American applicants had often been taken aback and appeared some-what confused by this question, uncertain about what it had to do with the job they were seeking. But by the time they completed their training, those Americans who had been hired by Mazda would, it was expected, answer this question without hesitation: "I would try to solve the problem, and I would apologize to my neighbor on behalf of Mazda." By then they would understand that standing behind a company and its products was the only correct thing for a worker to do. They would have grown to identify with their com-pany, Mazda, in a way that was less American and more Japanese.

Mazda began its orientation and training program with a three-week common orientation. The first days of orientation were given over to paperwork and administrative details. New workers filled out forms for the plant's labor relations department. They were fitted for safety shoes and measured for the blue-and-khaki Mazda uniforms that would be worn by everyone from the receptionist at the plant's administration building to Nobuto and other top managers. (Female administrative employees had the option of wearing a blue skirt or blue slacks with their khaki work shirts; most chose the latter.) The

hirees were familiarized with Mazda's dress code: Uniforms must be worn at all times in the plant; to avoid scratching vehicles, no watches, rings, or earrings could be worn on the shop floor; no patches, other than those issued by the company, or buttons could be worn on uniforms; long hair and dark glasses also were not permitted. Workers were issued lockers at the plant, and it was recommended that they change out of uniform before going home, since Mazda was afraid that they might be harassed for working at a Japanese plant.

New employees also had their wages and benefits explained to them by a Mazda labor relations representative. Although Mazda was a large corporation by the standards of most industries (its 1986 sales were $9.7 billion), it was dwarfed by its giant competitors in Detroit, Ford and General Motors, the labor representative told the new hirees. "We are a small company and a new company," the representative said of MMUC, the Mazda subsidiary that officially owned the Flat Rock plant. "At first, we must all be willing to sacrifice and tighten our belts so we can get off to a successful start." Belt tightening for Flat Rock's hourly employees meant accepting an initial wage that was 15 percent below the Big Three standard. But, as the labor representative pointed out, Mazda had already publicly committed itself to increasing wages at the plant in steps, until they caught up to Ford wages in 1991.

Like virtually every orientation speaker, the labor relations representative was an American. Only a few of the highest-ranking Japanese managers spoke briefly to the hirees. MMUC president Osamu Nobuto appeared with Denny Pawley and David Merchant during the first day of orientation to welcome new employees to the "Mazda family" and present them with Mazda pins. Nobuto told new employees that he looked forward to the day when they would regard Mazda as their own company, and he expressed his hope that their lives would be enriched—and not just in monetary terms—from their association with Mazda.

Pawley and Merchant spoke at greater length, both reiterating the same basic message. It may have been OK to just follow orders where you worked before, they would tell hirees, but at Mazda things would be different. Here, everyone will be expected to take the initiative and participate in the management of the plant. This participation will take many forms: not only will workers be contributing ideas to the design and constant improvement of their own jobs, they will be expected to help maintain quality control standards throughout the

shop floor. There were yellow and red cords running alongside the entire production line, the new employees were told. If you see a defective part coming down the line, pull the yellow cord, and your team leader or unit leader will come running over. If the problem persists, pull the red cord, and the entire line will come to a halt. Workers at General Motors, where Pawley had come from, were not given that kind of "stop-line" power; neither were workers at Ford or Chrysler. But this was not going to be like the American plants. The old walls that had divided workers and managers were not going to apply here.

Not only would workers be invited to contribute ideas on the shop floor, they would also be given a voice in making higher-level decisions. This message was repeated by a procession of orientation speakers and reinforced by Mazda's training literature. For example, the "interpersonal problem solving" workbook that was given to hirees—a book that expanded on the themes of the group problem-solving assessment from the screening process—included exercises that required new workers to resolve a conflict over maintenance budget classifications and to determine an appropriate means of recognizing an employee's outstanding effort to push a department "over the top" in its United Way campaign.[1] Determining budget classifications and deciding how to reward achievements are matters that fall entirely under the domain of management at a traditional American plant, where hourly workers are not consulted on even the most trivial questions. The idea of sharing in management's authority was heady stuff for Mazda's hirees; their excitement was heightened when they were issued business cards, which, they were told, were of the exact same design and quality as the cards carried by the plant's top managers.

David Merchant told new employees that they were a special work force, not so much *hired* by Mazda but *chosen* by the company to help bring about a new era of carmaking in Detroit. Mazda hirees were reminded that they, and they alone, had been selected from a group of 96,500 people who had wanted jobs at Flat Rock. They had been selected not only because the screening process had shown that they were more intelligent and in possession of greater interpersonal skills than the others, but because they had what Mazda training literature described as "the will to participate." They should be proud of themselves for their achievement and excited about the opportunity to become a part of a plant of such historic significance.

Mazda's new American workers were also reminded that they

were now part of the Mazda family. This message was driven home by one orientation speaker after another. Mazda cares about you, not just as a worker but as a whole person. Your safety was our number one priority when we designed this plant; we chose the safest tools and equipment we could find, and we tilted the overhead assembly line, so you could work under the bottoms of cars without craning your neck the way the workers at GM and Ford do. We built this giant fitness center, where you can play sports or exercise. It even has a driving range. At American companies only executives get perks like this, but here we're all part of the same team. We're going to offer you classes in Japanese language and culture and other nonwork subjects to broaden your horizons. We're going to cross-train you in advanced skills like robotics, so you can rotate jobs and have a more varied and rewarding work life. If you're having problems at home—your kids are sick or having trouble at school—tell us, and we'll do what we can to help arrange your work schedule around the problem. The emphasis here is on pulling together like a family.

Judy Wilson was eager to join the Mazda family. The 37-year-old mother of a teenage son and daughter, she had lost her husband only six weeks before the start of her Mazda orientation to a long and ugly battle with cancer. Her late husband Jim had mailed in a Mazda application form for himself and one for her when the company had run its help-wanted ads in Detroit newspapers back in February 1985. A little over two years later, Judy was invited to the abandoned school outside Flat Rock to take Mazda's written tests. Jim's application was never answered, but by then he was already terminally ill. Judy was reluctant to apply for the Mazda job, but her husband urged her to go ahead. He had only a small life insurance policy, and the money she earned clerking at a Downriver convenience store would not go far supporting her and the children. Judy, a small and animated brunette, had never worked in a factory before. She was frightened, but she did well enough in the tests and interviews to make it through Mazda's screening process, completing the fifth and final step in April 1987. She purchased an answering machine, so she would not miss Mazda's call should a job offer come. After a few weeks passed and she had not heard from Mazda, she panicked and called the Flat Rock plant, even though the company's assessors had been adamant about job applicants not calling the plant. The woman she spoke to at Mazda had been understanding, though, agreeing to

look for Judy's name on the "hired" list—"Yes, Judy, you're in. You'll be starting in September. You should be getting a letter soon."

When Judy attended her first Mazda orientation session, she was swept up in the good feelings. "Everyone from Mazda seemed so nice, and they kept stressing that they were family oriented and understood our problems," she later recalled. "I sat there thinking, 'Wow, this is the place for me. I'm going through a bad situation right now, and these are a bunch of very supportive people.' I remember one of the women from Mazda telling me that one of the nice things about working here was that because we get off at three-thirty, we could get home in plenty of time to have dinner with our kids."

Judy felt even better about Mazda after going through the company's one-week series of interpersonal relations exercises. The exercises, which emphasized the importance of building empathy and trust between team members, reaffirmed her belief that she was about to go to work for a sympathetic employer. Like the group problem solving assessments in the screening process, Mazda's interpersonal training relied heavily on role-playing exercises. In one training exercise on "communicating problem situations," Judy had to tell a man who worked next to her every day that he needed to shower more often. The interpersonal problem-solving workbook that Mazda had given her, the videotapes of "correct" and "incorrect" problem-solving interactions that she had been shown, and the discussions that her group already had with their trainer, gave her a good idea of how to approach the odorous team member. She knew the cardinal rules of Mazda's problem-solving technique: Be specific and direct (she did not drop subtle hints or make vague references to the importance of good personal hygiene, but told the man in clear language that he needed to shower with greater frequency); be nonpunishing by criticizing the problem (not showering) rather than the person (she was careful not to accuse him of being sloppy), and by avoiding both anger and sarcasm ("he will only hear your hostility and not your suggestion," her trainer had advised), mix criticism with praise (she said something nice about the man's personality and work habits before criticizing him for not showering), and explain the consequences of the problem (she pointed out that not showering was interfering with his relationship with other team members). After Judy completed her exercise, other members of the group evaluated her performance. "The whole idea was to be able to criticize without hurting anybody's feelings," said Judy.

Other exercises that Judy's group participated in showed the new

Mazda employees how to "recognize and reinforce" positive actions, how to diffuse another person's anger, how to be a good listener, how to avoid ambiguity when "communicating situations." These how-to exercises were preceded by icebreaking sessions intended to loosen up the hirees and get them used to talking to one another. "Is anyone having problems at home that they'd like some help in dealing with?" the group's trainer had begun one such session. One hiree said she was having trouble keeping her daughter from tying up the telephone. Everyone laughed. Then came a suggestion: Install a separate phone for her, but have her pay for it with the money she makes baby-sitting. A lively discussion ensued on the pros and cons of this suggestion. Another hiree complained that he was having trouble convincing his wife's brother to help care for their aged and infirm mother. The group offered their emotional support. Judy told of her ordeal with Jim's illness and the problems of raising two children on her own. By the end of the session, the hirees felt an emotional bond with one another. Their trainer said they were going from being "just a group" to being a team.

During their training the new team members were taught how to work together to arrive at consensus decisions. Every decision made at this plant is made by consensus, the hirees were informed. At American plants a supervisor could just issue orders in the autocratic style of a dictator, neither seeking nor accepting outside counsel, but no one at Mazda, even Nobuto himself, made decisions unilaterally, according to the orientation speakers. Nor would any decisions at Mazda be put to a vote if this could at all be avoided. Voting was a sacred American institution, and it was fine for electing presidents, but it had no place in a team plant that depended on close cooperation among its members. Voting sometimes polarized people by presenting them with a stark take-it-or-leave-it choice—"either you're with me or against me." This had the potential to promote divisiveness when people had to work in close contact with one another every day, especially when a small majority—say, 50.1 percent—was able to impose its will on a large minority of 49.9 percent. A consensus decision does not represent the triumph of one point of view but a collection of many different views, the new Mazda workers were told. Ideally it bears the imprint of every team member, and because of this it is much more conducive to a harmonious team relationship. "In a [team plant] voting is not a good process, and if we've got groups that have to resort to voting, what we do at that point is move in and give them more training in prob-

lem solving and decision making," David Merchant would later re-
mark. "I won't say it never comes down to a vote, I'll just say it's not
a good process; just like in the more traditional system, it's not a
good idea for me as a boss to call shots all the time. If I'm doing that,
I need more management training."[2]

Merchant described Mazda's idea of consensus as "working to-
gether . . . being willing to bend, being willing to argue your point,
but being willing to be convinced." Everyone was expected to con-
tribute to the consensus process, and everyone was expected to go
along with the final decision. Concepts like "silent majority" or "loy-
al opposition" had no place in the consensus process. The consensus
decision itself did not necessarily represent a compromise between
opposing positions. Mazda's consensus process only committed man-
agers to *listen* to the views of employees; it did not obligate them to
act on what they heard. The company's training literature was ex-
plicit on this point, stating in its section on consensus: "It goes with-
out saying that the person responsible for business accomplishments
also has the responsibility to make the final decision." Denny Pawley
would later elaborate on this distinction when describing how con-
sensus worked at Flat Rock: "My definition of consensus—it's prob-
ably different from what you may have heard before—but the way I
see it work . . . if you have an issue you're talking about, the manager
calls the appropriate people together who have a stake in the issue.
The highest-ranking man in the room . . . would try to draw out all
the opinions of everyone in the room. The objective there is to be sure
you've drawn out and gotten all the input of all the players. Then if
the group doesn't come to a clear consensus on a joint unified action
everyone agrees upon, consensus means that the top-ranking man-
ager will make the decision—but only after he has made sure he has
drawn out everybody's opinions. It doesn't mean you sit there until
everybody reaches [the manager's] opinion. Probably half the time
they don't, and someone has to make a decision."[3]

New Mazda workers practiced reaching consensus decisions in
group problem-solving exercises and in team production projects.
Hirees worked together to build paper airplanes. After charting the
flight of their planes for distance, the hiree teams were instructed to
redesign the planes to see if they could increase the length of flight. As
the teams sat at their tables debating the size and shape of wings and
the position of tails, a Mazda trainer watched. Instead of silently
taking notes as the screening-process assessors had done, the trainers
actively coached their teams. Their advice and suggestions did not

have anything to do with building planes, but with how group members went about reaching their consensus decisions. "Take more time to explain why you are making your suggestion." . . . "Be more patient when you defend your idea from criticism." . . . "Don't sandwich your specific suggestion in vague generalities."

As David Merchant had predicted, Mazda's training in interpersonal problem solving and consensus-building had an impact on the personal lives of new employees. By the end of their training period, Flat Rock workers were "communicating problem situations" to spouses, children, and friends in the "direct, nonpunishing" language they had learned at the training center. ("Just look at this pigsty! How can you be such a slob?" was replaced by: "Johnny, you're a wonderful son, but you must clean up your room so you'll be able to find things easier when you need them.")

"The training we got about dealing with other people was great," said Forrest Green, the former Ford tool and die maker. "Mazda brought this guy in from California, and he was brilliant. We had a week of him. He showed us how to get your point across in a nice way, how to have an argument with someone—or let's say someone's really mad at you and is screaming at you—how to calm that person down and find out what's really bothering them. I've used that training so often at home with my wife and kids."

After their sessions on interpersonal problem solving and consensus decision making, new Mazda employees turned their attention to what the company considered to be the most important subject in its training program—*kaizen*. Few hirees had even heard of *kaizen*, the process of constant improvement, when they applied for jobs at Flat Rock, but by the time they left the Mazda training center, *kaizen* would come up naturally—and often—in their conversations: "We're going to kaizen this operation (make it more efficient). "She kaizened the cost of that" (got it done for less money). "They kaizened out a team member" (got the same job done using one less worker).

Kaizen is not a corporate policy directive at Mazda, at least not in the rigid and impersonal American sense of the term, as much as it is a mind-set on the part of individual Mazda workers. Constant improvement cannot occur at a plant unless its workers are committed to the idea of constantly striving to do their individual jobs faster and more efficiently. If workers do not share management's conviction that "nothing is ever good enough," they will not be motivated to seek ways in which mufflers can be clipped onto cars a second faster, or side molding strips installed using less sealant.

Mazda tried to instill this sense of commitment in its new employees by explaining to them why *kaizen* was essential to the company's survival in the competitive world automobile market. The company introduced *kaizen* with the slogan, Everlasting Effort for Everlasting Competition. The message, repeated throughout the training program, was clear: Mazda cannot compete against the likes of General Motors and Toyota unless you help us lower costs—and increase profits—by squeezing waste and inefficiency out of the production process through *kaizen* activities. New employees were shown a graph comparing Mazda's annual vehicle output per employee to those of Nissan and Toyota since 1976. Mazda trailed its two larger rivals badly in the early years displayed on the graph, when the company was still reeling from the Wankel engine disaster, producing less than half as many vehicles per worker as Nissan, and only about 38 percent as many as Toyota. Mazda has caught up in recent years, equaling and then passing Nissan and coming to within striking distance of Toyota. If Mazda is to continue gaining ground on its largest Japanese competitor and beat back challenges by Honda, Nissan, and the resurgent Americans and Europeans, every worker must always be searching for ways to increase his or her own efficiency. "We feel the most important thing is not to be satisfied with present conditions, and thus to always challenge a higher (quality, production or safety) target," a Mazda manual declares.[4]

The worker's payback for expending this everlasting effort is primarily financial. Waste and inefficiency are "irrevocably linked to higher costs and will be reflected in your future pay," Flat Rock hirees were cautioned.[5] They will also be reflected in reduced job security, since a company that is burdened by excessive costs will be less competitive and will be forced to curtail its operations, laying off workers. Mazda's new workers were told that through the *kaizen* process, they had an opportunity to control the future success of their plant as well as their own financial destinies. This opportunity was not available to workers at Big Three plants, whose rigidly defined job classifications and relative isolation made it all but impossible for them to change things on the shop floor. As David Merchant said of the Flat Rock plant, "[Workers] control their destiny here more than anyplace else."

The chief target of any *kaizen* program is *muda*, the Japanese word for waste, one of the "Three Evil Ms" that every plant must strive to eliminate. (The two lesser evils are *mura*, the irregular or inconsistent use of a person or a machine; and *muri*, the placing of

excessive demands on workers or production equipment.) *Muda* comes in many forms, Mazda warned its hirees. One of the most common types of *muda*, and the one that had most bled American automobile plants, was idling *muda*, the wasted time that occurred when an employee stood around waiting for work to come to his or her work station. "If you are simply standing in front of a machine doing nothing, you yourself are not gaining respect as a human being," Mazda told workers. "And moreover, because this results in higher costs of a car, the customer will not buy the car."[6] Another form of *muda* hirees were warned about was motional *muda* (wasted motions that occur when workers search for misplaced tools or components).

During the course of their training, Mazda hirees learned how to find and eliminate *muda* in all its forms. This was not only supposed to make them better workers but happier and more productive in their personal lives. The hirees' education began with instruction in the plan-do-check-action (PDCA) problem-solving system that had become popular in Japan in the 1960s and 1970s. Adapted from the quality control "Deming wheel" introduced to Japan by W. Edward Deming, PDCA was used by Japanese manufacturers to evaluate broad corporate policy decisions as well as to solve localized problems on the shop floor. As taught to Mazda hirees, PDCA is made up of four problem-solving steps. The first, "plan step," is to identify the problem, determine its cause, define its solution, and develop a plan for achieving that solution. The planned solution is put through a trial run in the second, "do step," and the results of this trial are evaluated—and any necessary revisions in the plan are made—in the third, "check step." Once all the bugs have been worked out, the plan is ready to be implemented in the fourth, "action step."

Denny Pawley, who years earlier had made the quick decision to impale a Pontiac to keep his GM assembly line moving, wondered whether American workers would have the patience to adjust to Mazda's methodical Japanese approach to problem solving. But the hirees at the training center took quickly to ideas like *kaizen* and PDCA. "Some people have tried the kaizen around the house," one hiree told a Downriver newspaper in 1987, adding that by following the Mazda philosophy, a worker could become "just a better person in general."[7] Other new workers told of how they saved time by organizing personal errands to avoid *muda*. One hiree who had "just stood in line" at the bank now used the time to work on her grocery list; another realized she could cut time from her regular Saturday

errands by filling her car with gas on the way to pick up her daughter from dancing school on Fridays.

Mazda trainers explained to hirees that the company had eliminated "inventory *muda*" at its plants by implementing a JIT system. But the more important purpose of JIT, new employees were told, is that it accelerates the *kaizen* process by exposing problems quickly. The hirees were shown two illustrations of a boat steaming down a river. In the first illustration, the river's water level (supply of parts) was high, and the boat was undisturbed by the jagged rocks (production process problems) at the river's bottom. But when the water level (parts supply) declined in the second illustration, the rocks (problems) protruded above the surface and blocked the boat's progress. As long as the rocks are covered by a high water level, there is no incentive to remove them, Mazda's trainers explained, but Mazda purposely keeps its water levels low so problems cannot be ignored.

New Mazda workers got to apply the principles learned in their *kaizen* sessions by participating in three days of flashlight-assembly exercises. The hirees were divided into teams of five. Each team was given bins of ten different flashlight parts, along with a detailed description of what the finished product should look like. They were also given cardboard and tape to build "fixtures" to help them in their assembly process. Then they were left to their own devices. The mood in the training center when these exercises began was always high-spirited. The hirees dubbed the flashlight drill "insanity training." None of them seemed to have any idea of what they were doing. Invariably a box of lenses would splatter across the floor or an "assembled" flashlight would come apart in somebody's hands, and the whole team, along with the trainer, would burst out laughing. Gradually though, the mood would become more serious, as the teams, with some gentle prodding from their trainers, caught on to "applied *kaizen*." The number of flashlights the teams assembled in their three-minute exercise intervals steadily increased—15, 20, 25. Then, just when they seemed to be peaking, their trainers asked them to equal the same output with one member less. "Most of us thought, no way that this can be done," recalled Judy Wilson, "but we all did it. My team went from five to four and got the same efficiency, just by combining jobs and getting rid of wasted motion. It was pretty impressive what you could do with *kaizen*."

Mazda videotaped the flashlight-assembly exercises to allow the hiree teams to study themselves to find wasted motions. The new

workers were taught to do this by performing "motion studies," breaking down each step in the flashlight-assembly process into the smallest possible segments so it could be analyzed to find redundant or inefficient motions.

The workers also learned how to perform time studies on themselves. A time study measures the amount of time it takes a worker to complete each "work element" of a job, and compares it to a "time standard" that has already been established for that element. The hirees practiced doing time studies on one another as they assembled flashlights. They also participated in "paper cup exercises," timing themselves as they shuffled cups of water between circular spots on a table. Their trainers went to great lengths to explain why time studies would be necessary at Flat Rock to help adjust time standards at the new plant and detect *muda* so productivity could be increased. When an American automaker conducts a time study, the workers at its plant almost always object, often deliberately slowing their work pace to sabotage the study, which they regard as a form of spying used by management to pressure them into moving faster. But like a lot of things, time studies would be different at Mazda, the trainers assured their charges. Mazda would not cloak its time studies in secrecy as American automakers attempted to do, usually without success. Instead, time studies would be performed in the open at Flat Rock by team leaders, unit leaders, and company engineers with the full knowledge of workers. Mazda also promised not to use time studies to push workers into a mindless acceleration of their work pace. Mazda time studies would, when combined with motion studies, help to increase work speed by pinpointing unnecessary motions and other inefficiencies that could be kaizened out of the job cycle, allowing the job to be completed in less time, not by forcing the worker to move faster but by simplifying his or her work steps. As Denny Pawley would later remark about the kaizened job routine of Mazda workers: "When you look at [the] situation, they're doing more elements [of work] per worker, but they're doing it with much less effort."

This argument persuaded Mazda hirees with Big Three experience to view time studies in a new, more favorable light. Becky Mehaffey, the former Ford worker who recalled the rowdy behavior of her male coworkers at Ford's River Rouge plant, described the different reactions to time studies at Ford and Mazda. "At Ford, there was one man who did time studies. He hid behind boxes. Word passed around when he came to the plant. Everybody knew he was

there, so we slowed down our pace on purpose. Here it's different. . . . In orientation we were made to understand why we need time studies, so there's a lot of cooperation."

Having learned how to break work down into minute time and motion elements, Mazda's new hirees were taught how this information is recorded and communicated on "programmed worksheets." At first glance a Mazda programmed worksheet looks like something torn out of a child's coloring book—a single sheet of paper with crude, almost stick-figure panel drawings of a car and a character, described by Judy Wilson as "a funny-looking little man." But in reality, the programmed worksheet is, as David Merchant observed, "one of the most critical documents in the . . . plant." Using illustrations of the man and car, and brief written commands, a programmed worksheet describes every step required to perform a job in sequential order, listing the exact amount of time—down to the second—needed to complete each step. For example, the programmed worksheet for the one-minute-and-four-second job of applying exterior sealant to the driver's side of a two-door car lists 14 illustrated steps, beginning with the 25-second step of applying sealant with a spatula to seven designated spots under the hood, and concluding with the 17-second step of finishing the sealant with a brush at two spots over the door. Every job at Flat Rock would have its own programmed worksheet, hirees were told, except for the skilled trades maintenance and repair jobs, which were too unpredictable. Flat Rock workers would have input into the design of their own programmed worksheets by working with their fellow team members, team leaders, and unit leaders, the Mazda trainers promised, but once a programmed worksheet had been written, it had to be followed to the letter without variation, every time a job was performed—no exceptions. Any *kaizen* ideas for improving the way a job could be done would be written into its programmed worksheet, but only after it had been discussed and analyzed at a team meeting. The programmed worksheets must be followed for the Flat Rock plant to remain competitive, the trainers cautioned. At American plants there were no programmed worksheets, so workers performed their jobs inconsistently. This created waste and kept the Americans from matching the productivity of the Japanese.

For Steve Ross and the four hundred other original hirees, the Americans tapped to be future team and unit leaders at Flat Rock, Mazda's training program included a 30-day trip to Japan. The Americans were sent to Japan in groups of 40 to 50 between July

1986 and February 1987. Ross was in the first group to go. He and
a group of 15 other skilled trades leaders and about twice that many
production leaders took an early morning flight out of Detroit Met-
ropolitan Airport and, after changing planes in Los Angeles, arrived
in Osaka 18 hours later. From there they took a flight down to
Hiroshima for two days of handshaking, speech making, and public
relations appearances at Mazda's corporate headquarters. The Jap-
anese were naturally curious about this first group of Americans
from Detroit, a city about which they had heard so many terrible
things. They were relieved that the Americans seemed like such a
pleasant, cooperative bunch. The Americans nodded and smiled ner-
vously when they toured Mazda's Hiroshima facilities, bending for-
ward slightly when they were asked questions to better hear their
shorter hosts and giving their answers in slow, deliberate voices,
mouthing every word carefully to be sure they were understood.

From Hiroshima the Americans took a train to Hofu, a city 56
miles to the southwest, where their real training would begin. There
they visited the Hofu plant, the facility that had served as the model
for Mazda's Flat Rock operation. They donned Mazda uniforms and
worked on the Hofu line alongside Japanese team members. They sat
in on team meetings and "quality circles" (meetings at which *kaizen*
plans were put through PDCA analysis), the proceedings translated
for them by Japanese interpreters. They also attended classes in *kai-
zen*, JIT, "total quality control," and consensus building at the six-
story training center located next to the plant. The Japanese originally
scheduled full-day (eight-hour) classes for their new American em-
ployees, but the Americans, who found the class routine tedious,
prevailed on Mazda to cut the classes to half-day sessions and give
them more time on the shop floor. The experience the Americans
gained in the plant and the lessons learned about the Mazda man-
agement system in the classroom, would, predicted Osamu Nobuto,
"deepen their confidence in being able to put the system into practice
in their future at Flat Rock."[8]

The first thing that struck the Americans, particularly those from
industrial backgrounds, about the Hofu plant was the absolute clean-
liness of the shop floor itself. The American plants that they were
familiar with were Dickensian dungeons compared to the bright and
spotless Mazda plant that greeted them at Hofu. There were no
burned-out lightbulbs at Hofu as there were at so many American
plants, where every other light seemed to be out; no discarded equip-
ment tossed into a corner away from the line to collect dust; no tools

strewn about the work areas like a child's toys; no metal scraps and shavings speckling the floor; no rivers of oil running down the sides of machinery gathering into greasy puddles. Craig Farrand, the newspaper editor and former autoworker who had visited Hofu a year earlier, soon after Mazda announced its decision to come to Flat Rock, exclaimed when he first saw the plant: "You people can't be making cars here—toy cars maybe, but not real ones. It's too clean."

Farrand, familiar as he was with the Michigan Casting Center syndrome, also could not help but marvel at the high level of morale at Hofu. Every worker seemed so happy and enthused, Farrand began to wonder if at least some of the team spirit was not being put on to impress a visiting American journalist with how great it was to work for Mazda. Later, when he was able to speak to some of the Japanese workers alone, Farrand brought this up with them. "Don't you guys ever get mad or upset with the boss?" he asked. Of course, they acknowledged, and yes, they were putting on their best face for their visitor from the hometown of Mazda's future American plant, but the harmony and the enthusiasm were no act. They were happy at Mazda. It was like one big family.

Jerry Healy, a skilled trades worker who was part of the original group of American Mazda hirees that visited Hofu, was also struck by the team spirit of the plant's Japanese workers, and the way in which they seemed to get behind consensus decisions quickly with no discord. But Healy, who had come to Mazda after being employed as a skilled trades worker at a food-processing plant in Grand Rapids, Michigan, wondered whether American workers could ever subjugate their strong individual opinions to the will of a group so effortlessly as did the more hierarchical Japanese. "There's a lot of differences between American and Japanese workers; I know from when I was in Japan," he would later recall. "In Japan, they can all wear the same shirts, but they know who's got the authority. They got a lot more respect for position over there—it's part of their culture."

As a skilled trades maintenance worker, Steve Ross was most impressed by what he termed "the *kaizen* for maintenance" displayed by workers at Hofu. Throughout the plant, maintenance people seemed to be anticipating problems before they occurred, replacing parts on machinery not because they were broken but because they were aging and might break soon. Whenever a piece of equipment malfunctioned, the maintenancce people did not simply repair it, they held a meeting to find out what had gone wrong and

developed a *kaizen* plan to prevent it from happening again. This dedication to preventative maintenance would have been unheard of at the American plants Ross had worked at, where it was often an effort just to get a supervisor to approve of a basic grease and oil job on a machine that was still running. Apparently management had a different attitude at Hofu. When Ross toured the plant with a Japanese skilled trades maintenance team, its leader would point to a machine and say, "What can we do to ensure this machine's operation? What will we need to lubricate; what will we not need to lubricate?" Ross recalled his Hofu team changing air cylinders in equipment before the cylinders broke down. "They'd say, 'This air cylinder has been on the machine a year now, and its life expectancy is a little over a year, so we're going to change it now, on a weekend when we're not running production,' " said Ross. "It was a way of thinking that we [American] skilled tradesmen were glad to hear. We felt that way when we worked at the other plants we came from, [but when] we wanted to do those things . . . they'd say, 'Oh, no, wait till it breaks. . . . We're not going to pay you overtime to work on machinery that's got nothing wrong with it.' We would tell them, 'It's going to break, and then you're going to have unnecessary downtime—which is better: Pay me eighteen dollars an hour to come in on Saturday or pay me to fix it when it breaks, plus pay an operator or two who are standing there waiting to get their machine back?' "

The Japanese made sure their guests from Detroit had plenty of leisure time for shopping, sightseeing, and socializing during the Americans' four-week stay in Hofu. Mazda arranged weekend bus tours of historic sights, telling its new American employees that their presence on the bus was not mandatory, but would be "deeply appreciated." Mazda went about the business of being a tour guide with the same kind of methodical thoroughness it applied to kaizening its production process, lining up ancient shrine after imperial garden after natural wonder, in precise order. But, like the full-day training classes, the company's crowded tour itinerary made the impatient Americans restless. "They showed us sights and explained what we were looking at," Ross recalled of the Mazda tours. "There's a large cave over there like Mammoth Cave in Kentucky, and they took us to that. They took us to shrines and gardens. It got to be like going down to Florida and seeing all the gardens—if you've seen one, you've seen them all. So we would express that—'Hey, really, another garden; give us a break!' We'd say, 'How about if we got a

cooler, everyone pitched in a couple of bucks, and we got some pop or beer and had a picnic?' Our trainers would say, 'Hey, that sounds all right,' so that's what we did. . . . The Japanese worked their butts off trying to keep us happy."

Like the other Americans who visited Hofu, Bob Ramp, a veteran UAW official appointed to the bargaining committee at the new Flat Rock plant, also came away with good memories of Japanese hospitality. Ramp and Bill Judson, the UAW Local 3000 president, accompanied the first group of hirees to Hofu in 1986. On their second night in the city, a group of Japanese trainers came to Ramp and Judson's hotel to invite them to a local *karaoke* bar where patrons take turns going up on a small stage to sing songs selected from a large playbook of Japanese and American standards (the lyrics are flashed on a small on-stage video screen), with musical accompaniment provided by a compact disc. For awhile several of the Mazda trainers took turns on stage, most singing *enka* songs, melancholy compositions about lost loves and faraway homes, others rendering familiar Elvis Presley and Beatles hits. Then a couple of the Japanese started tugging on Ramp's sleeve, "You get up there . . . you get up there." Ramp, a small, round, and very likable man, was delighted. "Oh, man, I'm telling you, I'm a ham anyway. I get up there and do some country stuff, and I was having a good time," he later recalled. "They were having the fifteenth anniversary of the place, and they had a *karaoke* singing contest coming up, and they asked me if I'd be willing to sing at eleven in the morning and I said sure. So they sent a car the next morning to pick me up at the hotel. I went down there and sang [an audition], and they invited me to come back in the evening and sing again in the contest, so I did. Anyway, after I finish my song I turn around to leave and there was this lady in a traditional Japanese kimono, and she had this big bouquet of flowers. Then the manager of the body shop had a nice blue Mazda blazer for me, and he said there were only six of them in all of Mazda. All these people in traditional Japanese garb, but speaking pretty fluent English, were around me saying, 'Very good—love country music very much. Maybe *karaoke* contest next year we have country music.' "

Despite his warm feelings toward his hosts, Ramp felt occasional tugs of uncertainty about how American workers back home in Flat Rock would adjust to a management system that was so grounded in the culture of Japan. An early riser, he was up every morning at five in Hofu and showered and ready to go by six. Half a world away from home, he would then enjoy a few moments of solitude looking

out the window of his hotel room. Not long after six every morning, he would see young children arriving at a local school yard, more than two hours before school started, to practice baseball. The children seemed intensely dedicated and purposeful, committed in a way that most American children were not. This is the way the Japanese are raised, Ramp thought. It was not the way Americans were raised. He could not help but wonder what implications this difference would have for everyone at Flat Rock.

The same issue was raised for Ramp when he toured the Hofu shop floor. "They were so dedicated there," he said. "I saw a young man there putting trunk lids on cars, and every move this young man made was calculated. He didn't waste a motion. In fact, they admitted he was so good that if he were to be off, it would take two people to replace him." As he watched, Ramp wondered how Americans would adjust to the work pace set by factory olympians like the young trunk installer before him.

American workers who did not go to Japan, a group that included all of those hired after the initial group of four hundred, were introduced to Japanese culture and customs through an orientation class on the subject. The class was taught by salaried American employees of Mazda who had spent years living and studying in Japan. One of the teachers explained the purpose of the class as being "to create a climate of understanding in the plant and to show workers that the American way is not the only way." To impress this point on their pupil-workers, the teachers showed them a video of different people from around the world enjoying dinner—some ate with chopsticks, some with forks, others used their fingers, some sat at tables, some sat on the floor, some squatted in huts, others stood at fast food counters. "Everyone is not like Americans," the teachers reiterated after showing the video. They then proceeded to explain just how the Japanese differed from Americans. Japan is a small country geographically, the teachers informed their students; its 3,900 islands equal a landmass that is only about one-twentieth the size of the United States—about the same size as Montana. Yet Japan's population is over 119 million, about half the size of America's. The crowding of so many people into so small a space has created a society in which teamwork and cooperation are highly valued. Japan's isolation as an island nation, along with the cultural and ethnic uniformity of its people, has strengthened this sense of group con-

sciousness. The Japanese dispatches you will be working with will be polite and eager to be your friends, American hirees were told, but many things about American culture will be unfamiliar to them, and though most of them have taken English in school, they will not always be fluent in conversational English, so be patient when explaining things to them. The teachers said that the dispatches shared many leisure interests in common with American workers: They liked sports, especially baseball and golf; they enjoyed the outdoors; they were fond of American movies and television shows, both of which were popular in Japan. There were, however, differences that the Americans should appreciate. The Japanese diet is quite unlike ours, with fish and rice as its main staples. The Japanese often eat fish raw, either in thin slices called sashimi or as slices over small blocks of rice called sushi. Other sea products eaten by the Japanese are *nori,* a dried seaweed pressed into flat sheets, and *kamaboko,* a hard gelatin of ground fish flesh. The idea of eating raw fish and seaweed might strike the American workers as odd, but the teachers assured the class they had a surprisingly delicate flavor. (Later, when the Flat Rock plant was up and running, traditional Japanese dishes would be served in the cafeteria side by side with American standards like hamburgers and roast beef. The American workers wound up eating Japanese lunches with greater frequency than their Japanese trainers and advisors ate American.)

Most of the American hirees "found it exciting to be exposed to Japanese culture," recalled Forrest Green, the tool and die maker. They continued to study Japanese language and culture after their original orientation session ended, taking classes taught by the wives of Mazda dispatches in the plant's administration building. They questioned their Japanese advisors incessantly about everyday life in Japan—"Do you have horoscopes?" "Do you celebrate Christmas?" Intimate exposure to an exotic culture, especially one that had attracted so much attention in the white-collar world beyond Downriver, was one of the things that made working for Mazda special.

Not all the Americans were happy with Mazda's extensive orientation program, however. Some of the older hirees, particularly those from the skilled trades who had come from Big Three backgrounds, grew impatient with the lectures on Japanese culture and *kaizen* and teamwork. They were tired of playing the same role-playing games they had been forced to endure during the five-step screening process; tired of putting a stopwatch to themselves as they moved paper cups around on a table; tired of building paper air-

planes and flashlights like schoolkids in a freshman shop class. They had been hired to build cars, and build cars is what they wanted to do. At the conclusion of a lecture on "line balancing" held during the third week of orientation, the speaker, a young outside efficiency expert hired by Mazda, asked if there were any questions. One of the older hirees in the room, a man who had spent years working at a Big Three plant, raised his hand: "Yeah, when the hell do we get to work?"

Phil Keeling, a 32-year-old electrician, laughed to himself when he heard the older worker's question. The same question had crossed his mind during the line-balancing lecture, but he was careful to hold his tongue. He had already mouthed off once during this endless orientation, and one of Mazda's young cheerleaders had read him the riot act. He was not about to draw attention to himself again and lose this job before he even set foot in the plant. Keeling's confrontation had occurred a few days earlier, after his orientation group had seen a videotape of workers at Mazda's Hofu paint shop applying sealant. The job of applying sealant is rather tedious, involving a lot of bending and walking and the constant juggling of spatulas, brushes, and sealant guns, but the Japanese workers in the video, following the carefully choreographed steps in their programmed worksheets, were moving at an unbelievable pace, sprinting around cars and switching tools with the sleight-of-hand speed of a magician. When they finished with one car, they raced to the next, not pausing to wipe the sweat from their brows. When the video was over, Keeling found himself saying to no one in particular: "If I thought I had to go in the plant and do that, I'd be heading south on I-75," referring to the interstate that runs next to the Mazda plant. His voice, a rich baritone that seems to draw its strength from deep within his muscular six-foot-four-inch frame, filled the entire room. The Mazda engineer who was conducting the class was taken aback but quickly regained his composure; looking squarely at Keeling, he said: "I hope we can get that kind of productivity here." During a break a short time later, a young woman in a Mazda uniform who had been sitting in front of the classroom marched up to Keeling until she was almost standing on his toes: "Just why are you here, anyway?" she demanded, before delivering a shape-up-or-ship-out ultimatum. She was, said Keeling, "one of the whiz kids Mazda hired right out of college to help us workers by figuring out how we could work faster and harder. Of course, none of them had ever worked in a factory before, and they weren't going to work in one now, but

they knew best. They were going to kaizen out this and kaizen out that, so we could be more productive. The more they talked, the more it sounded like this whole team thing was just a way to squeeze more work out of every worker, with a good dose of old-fashioned paternalism thrown in to keep everybody happy."

With his big frame, sandy hair, and close-cropped beard, Keeling evokes the image of an ancient Viking warrior. This image is intensified by his clear blue-green eyes; large, prominent brow, and sturdy jaw. When he becomes angry or excited, the eyes and brow narrow into a powerful stare and the jaw juts out defiantly. When he is amused, his mouth curls into a short, wry smile and the brow becomes softer, but the eyes continue to burn intensely, as if they do not wish to let any detail escape their attention. Born in the small hamlet of Scott Depot, West Virginia—the high school he graduated from in the nearby town of Winfield had fewer than three hundred students—he followed in his father's footsteps and became a building trades electrician. Keeling was working as an electrician in the spring of 1987, when he saw a Mazda ad in the Charleston paper seeking electricians with "good communications skills and at least eight years journeyman's experience" for the company's new Michigan plant.

Mazda advertised for skilled trades workers in newspapers throughout the South and Appalachia because the company was having trouble finding enough skilled trades workers in Michigan. By 1987 the state's economy had begun to improve, and although untrained workers were still desperate for good-paying jobs, skilled trades workers could often find something better than a job at Mazda, with its 15-percent-below-Big-Three-wages. But many of the Michigan skilled trades workers who did seek Mazda jobs were, like Mike Parker, the electrician from Detroit, weeded out by the five-step screening process, their attitudes or communication skills apparently being judged unsuitable for a team plant. Neither Mazda nor the Michigan governor's office was eager to call attention to the out-of-state employee search while local skilled trades workers were being rejected by the company, since the $125 million Mazda incentive package, which was funded largely by state and local tax dollars, had been justified as a means of creating new jobs for Michigan residents.

Keeling, who had just come out of a divorce, was looking to start a new life. He was also eager to get out of the building trades, which required a lot of traveling, something he felt had contributed to his failed marriage. Besides, building trades electrical work had become routine, requiring him to run simple conduits and do the other fa-

miliar grunt work day after day with no chance to broaden his skills as a tradesperson. Mazda was promising to cross-train its skilled tradespeople in all of the new high-tech skills involving robotics and computer controllers. From all Keeling had heard and read, the Japanese team system also gave workers more input into plant decisions and made it easier to get promoted into supervisory positions. He thought that if things worked out, he might even get into management at the Flat Rock plant.

Keeling reported to a building in downtown Charleston to take Mazda's paper-and-pencil tests. The tests were administered by an older man with a crew cut wearing a Mazda uniform, who, Keeling would discover, was Bill Judson, the president of UAW Local 3000. After passing the written test and a personal interview in Charleston, Keeling was asked to travel to Michigan at his own expense to complete steps four and five of Mazda's screening process, the group problem-solving assessment and the simulated work exercise. He passed, and in May 1987 he rented a small apartment in Flat Rock, less than a mile from the plant. He was ready to begin his new life. At the end of his first week of orientation, a young woman from Mazda's labor relations department spoke to Keeling's group. "She was just so excited, she was standing in the front of the room on her tippy-toes telling us how much we were going to love to wake up every morning and come to work at a place where we could be so involved and so appreciated, so much a part of a family," Keeling recalled, the sarcasm very evident in his baritone. "The younger people ate it all up. They were ready to walk through the wall for Mazda. But some of us who'd been around the block took it all with a shovelful of salt." Although he had come to have serious doubts about his new employer, doubts so strong they would almost lead him to quit Mazda before he started, Keeling decided to stick it out at Flat Rock. He did not believe the company's talk about team spirit and family and involving workers in management decisions, but he did think that Mazda would be providing him with valuable cross-training, and he expected that the company's *kaizen* projects would give him a chance to get involved in some creative problem-solving work. Eventually, Mazda was going to start building cars there, and before they did this they were going to have to stop playing games and teach their workers some real skills. Then all the whiz kids would be gone. Things would get a lot better, he told himself, once they got down to business inside the plant.

7
Working Together

AFTER completing their three-week orientation, Mazda hirees were sent inside the plant for what David Merchant described as "job-specific training." Since most of the new workers were young and inexperienced in the ways of an auto factory, the early part of this in-plant training was given over to basics: how to operate an air gun, when to use a spot welder, what to do when a welding gun pulls to the left or right. Aside from a brief walk-through tour of the production area taken during orientation, this was the first time that most of the workers had ever set foot inside a big industrial plant, and many were clearly awed by what they saw. "Nothing that they can say or do in orientation can get you prepared for what it's like out there," Judy Wilson, the recently widowed mother of two, said of the plant. "The noise, and all the activity, you can't understand until you get out there."

In September 1987, during Wilson's first week in the plant, she witnessed a knock-down, drag-out argument between two team leaders, both men in their early twenties. She never learned what the argument was about, but the shouting and finger pointing stayed with her. "It was like, welcome to the real world," she later recalled. "We had just heard all this talk about family and problem solving, and here are these two guys ready to kill each other." The new employees in Wilson's team "looked at each other like we couldn't believe it."

Denny Pawley was a well-seasoned factory hand. He knew that Mazda's young, inexperienced workers would go through a period of

"culture shock" before they adjusted to the realities of the factory routine, and he worked hard to keep their spirits up. He was a frequent visitor to the shop floor, walking up and down the line exhorting workers to stick with it: "Don't get discouraged, in a couple of weeks running that machine will be child's play for you." "Body shop work is rough, but it'll get easier once your arms are built up." Pawley would sit with young team members in the common cafeteria. His insider's tales of the automobile industry, told in the earthy language of the shop floor, encouraged a sense of bravado in them, as if they believed that by absorbing his experience they could become old hands themselves. In 1987 he described how Mazda would be bringing along its young work force: "A lot of people come in here who have never worked in a plant before, and they look at one of those big weld guns, and they say, 'Oh my God, I'll never be able to run one of those.' Well, we try to make that weld gun friendly to the person. Instead of throwing them on the end of that thing the first day they walk in the door, they gradually learn it. They learn all the names of the pieces on it. . . . They learn that this is a weld tip and what it does, and this is a water hose, and you try to take the fear out of the tooling and the automation before a person has to go out there and get thrown in the middle of it."[1]

For most of the new workers, the training described by Pawley took place in "training cribs," classroom areas located to the side of the shop floor that, in addition to blackboards and chairs, contained samples of the equipment found in the plant itself. Trainees would be assigned to the cribs to practice on sample equipment from the department in which they would eventually be working, and to familiarize themselves with its safety and maintenance features. When their Japanese and American trainers felt they had mastered the equipment sufficiently, the new workers were sent out to the shop floor as part of work teams for several weeks of on-the-job training.

The amount of classroom training production workers received varied considerably, depending on where in the plant they were assigned. Workers in the body shop, for example, spent close to 80 hours in training cribs, learning 4 different types of welding and becoming familiar with the operation of sanding and polishing machines. But in the trim and final assembly area, where Wayne Dodd, the former fast food employee from Flint, was assigned, classroom training totaled less than 10 hours. Dodd started working at Flat Rock in September 1987, just as the plant had begun to make automobiles full time. (Before September, Mazda had conducted four

months of trial builds, producing a limited number of cars to work out start-up bugs in the plant's production system.) Dodd began working on the line after only two hours of classroom training. "Every morning we had a class in tools or safety, and then we were sent out on the line for the rest of the day to work," he recalled. "My first job was installing struts—this was on my first day in the plant. They showed me how to do it, and then they had someone work alongside me until I got the hang of it. That didn't take long, because it was a simple job, and we were only getting one car coming down the line every three minutes back then [compared to over one car per minute in 1989], so we had plenty of time. . . . After a while we went to another job and did the same thing. That was the extent of my training—we didn't spend much time in the classroom."

Skilled trades workers received more extensive training at Flat Rock. Mazda divided the skilled trades into three divisions, or "section occupation groups" (SOGs)—tool and die, mechanical, and electrical. American automakers, by contrast, had as many as 25 narrowly defined skilled trades categories at their stamping and assembly plants. The numerous classifications made the American plants less efficient. At times their entire production process would be halted while workers waited for the properly designated skilled trades "specialist" to arrrive to push the restart button on a machine or replace a broken tip on a welding tool. Mazda's managers said that the company would be avoiding this problem at Flat Rock by training skilled trades workers to perform a broad range of jobs, so instead of having, for example, ten millwrights, ten pipefitters and ten welders, it would have thirty workers skilled not only in these three trades but in a variety of others as well.

When tool and die maker Forrest Green joined Mazda in 1987, new skilled trades workers were receiving six weeks of cross-training. "They spent a lot of hours and dollars training us," said Green. "We were trained and certified in arc welding, the use of torches, and crane operating—we did all our own crane work with electronic cranes."

As a tool and die maker at Ford, Green had been accustomed to having the special status of his trade scrupulously respected. Tool and die makers build the dies that are used to stamp out metal panels like doors, hoods, and fenders. No one at a traditional Big Three plant would even consider asking them to do anything else. The importance of their work and the high degree of individual artistry it requires have given them a special status on the shop floor. Other,

less skilled, workers were called in at a Big Three plant to do minor welding on a die, burn off its excess metal, or operate the crane that transfers it to the stamping press. Asking a tool and die maker to perform these mundane tasks, as Mazda was doing at Flat Rock, was akin to having a world-class chef wash the dishes.

Despite the priority that Mazda placed on finding "flexible" workers in its screening process, and despite all the orientation talks about the need for cross-training, the company's new tool and die makers were often insulted by the requirement that they learn lesser jobs. "I personally [feel] that running a crane [is] beneath me," said Green. "We could hire somebody and pay them three dollars an hour less to run the crane. We talked about that with the Japanese—a lot of the other die makers felt the same way. We spent a lot of years being trained as die makers. It took a day and a half to learn how to run the crane. We talked about that—'If you're going to treat me with dignity and respect like you said you were, then why am I running a crane?' They went through the rhetoric of explaining that because we were trained as die makers, we should worry about our tools and dies. It was an extension of our job . . . because we knew the intricacies of a die, we would be more careful in handling it. This was ridiculous."

The need to learn arc welding made more sense to the tool and die makers, given the difference between the Japanese and American approaches to die making. The Japanese employ a die making method that Mazda's American tool and die makers describe as "chunk-and-chew." Making a die out of inexpensive, soft steel, the Japanese grind the edges of the die and then weld a strip of more costly hard steel around it for mastering. When the hard metal strip begins to grow loose, the die is sent back to the shop and a new strip is put on, and the mastering process is repeated. American tool and die makers build their dies out of expensive hard steel that does not require frequent welding and remastering. "Both methods make sense for what the different countries want," said Green. "The Japanese like to run small lots because of their just-in-time system. At Mazda they may run a thousand doors and then pull all the dies out, so why waste money on an expensive die that's going to last and last? When I was at Ford, they'd leave the same die in the press for weeks on end and make thousands and thousands of doors, so you needed a die of greater strength. . . . The thing is that under the Japanese system, the better you could weld, the less grinding you had to do. This was the Americans' downfall. We didn't have fifteen years' welding experience. We got [the welding] done, but it wasn't very good. The Jap-

anese used to kid us about our welding, but eventually we got as good as them."

Although they conceded that Mazda's chunk-and-chew method was better suited to the needs of a JIT plant, with its frequent die changes and small press runs, many of Flat Rock's tool and die makers complained that the company's use of "disposable dies" did not allow them to utilize all their professional skills. Because of their experience building durable hard steel dies, the Americans were familiar with a wider variety of diemaking tools than their Japanese trainers, and they were often more skilled than the Japanese at die repairing. "The Japanese allocated tools for the die shop, and when the Americans got there we said, 'Hey, we need more than this. [We need] different sized grinding wheels and different textured wheels to do different jobs.' " said Green. The Japanese gave the Americans the tools, but they were skeptical about the supposedly "specialized" skills of their new employees. The Americans got a chance to prove themselves in late 1987, when an electronic eye on one of the stamping shop's automatic transfer presses malfunctioned, causing the press to break an important die in half. "The Japanese said that it would take three weeks to get a new bottom half of the die from Japan," recalled Green. "We told them we'd have the press running in 19 to 24 hours. They said we were nuts. We used American technology and a lot of Ford steel, and we fixed that thing in 22 hours. . . . We basically took the broken part, put it back together, built a framework around it to hold it, welded it, and got it back in the press. . . . The Japanese were amazed."

Unlike tool and die makers, the other skilled trades workers at Flat Rock did not regard cross-training as an affront to their professional pride. Their most frequent complaint was that the cross-training provided by Mazda was not extensive enough; that it taught skilled trades workers only enough to allow them to perform basic maintenance and repair jobs on specific equipment in the plant and did not provide them with a comprehensive background in new trades. "It was strictly 'plant-specific' training," said Phil Keeling, the electrician from West Virginia. "You were cross-trained just enough to know how to push a button or change a filter on Mazda's equipment, and that was all. It was like if I took you out and had you watch me clean my carburetor and said, 'Okay, now you're an auto mechanic.' Then I took you and made you watch me put a new washer on my faucet and said, 'Okay, now you're a plumber.' If you went into that plant as a welder, you wouldn't have learned enough

[about electricial work] to help your neighbor wire his garage. A lot of guys said, 'Thank God I already knew a trade before I came here,' because this cross-training is chicken shit—it wouldn't be worth anything outside the Mazda plant, because it's all so basic."

During the plant's startup phase, when equipment snafus were common, Mazda farmed out most major skilled maintenance jobs, with the exception of tool and die work, to outside contractors and the service departments of its equipment vendors. This further alienated skilled trades workers, who felt they were being deprived of a valuable cross-training opportunity every time the company called in an outsider to perform a complex job. "Mazda wanted to minimize the importance of skilled trades, so any job that was too involved got sent outside," claimed Keeling. "This let the company get away with hiring [fewer] skilled trades people than anyone thought they would hire." By the end of its first year of production (September 1988), Mazda employed fewer than two hundred skilled trades workers at Flat Rock out of a work force of three thousand, about half the number of skilled trades workers employed at similar Big Three plants.[2] Keeling believes that by keeping down the number of skilled trades workers, Mazda not only hoped to save money but to assure itself of having a more compliant work force, since skilled trades workers were regarded as more independent than production workers. (Every UAW president, and many of its most militant spokespersons, have come from the skilled trades.)

Not every skilled trades worker felt this way. Jerry Healy, the skilled trades worker from the Grand Rapids food-processing plant and one of Mazda's original four hundred hirees, believes that the company provided its skilled trades workers with plenty of opportunities for cross-training. The catch, in Healy's view, was that the workers had to seek out these opportunities on their own initiative. "A lot of (skilled trades) people expected hand-fed training when they got to Mazda," he would later recall. "This created some problems. Mazda had the best [training] literature and documentation on equipment of any place I worked. . . . [Skilled trades] workers could have pulled a book out, but they wanted people to tell them what to do; they didn't put their own initiative into training. . . . In the initial [plant] start-up, we had a lot of vendor-type training, but that's a once-in-a-lifetime deal. A lot of people expected that the vendors would keep coming in to hold classes, but this isn't practical. But guys viewed it like, 'Hey, they said they were going to train me, so I should be in a classroom eight hours a day.' "

Yet Healy acknowledged that the small size of Flat Rock's skilled trades work force made it difficult for workers to find the time to train themselves: "There were too few people in the plant . . . so people got demotivated. The plant was running extremely lean, and everyone was always busy. If they had hired a few more people, it would have given everybody more time to train themselves and look at books."

Training provided most of Mazda's American employees with their first prolonged contact with the Japanese. More than four hundred Japanese dispatches were sent to Flat Rock from Mazda's facilities in Hiroshima and Hofu in 1986–87, when the bulk of the American plant's work force was hired. Every unit at Flat Rock (consisting of two to four teams) had at least one Japanese trainer during the plant's start-up phase. A trainer followed his team's performance on the line, coaching members in the Mazda system and helping them solve problems that came up. If a trainer's English was very limited, he was assigned an American or Japanese interpreter. One of the first things that impressed Mazda's new American workers about their trainers was the willingness of the Japanese to let workers figure things out for themselves. Most of the Americans had come from jobs where a manager had simply laid down the law about the way work should be done or a problem solved. But a Japanese trainer always wanted to know what his American workers thought. The Japanese trainer may have been welding roof pillars for twenty years, but when a problem came up, he would turn to a couple of hirees who had been on the job all of two weeks to see if they had any ideas. The hirees would suggest something, and the trainer would tell them to try their idea. When they came back an hour later to report that their idea had not worked, he would ask how they wanted to modify it. Then, after their revised plan had failed, he would show them the "right answer," which, of course, he had known all along. At first the Americans were confused by the behavior of their Japanese trainers. Why let us waste time making all these mistakes? they wondered. Then, after a week or two of training, it began to make more sense—by forcing team members to figure things out for themselves, the Japanese, in the spirit of process engineering, were ensuring that the Americans would not only learn the right answer but—and this was more important—the problem-solving process that was used to arrive at that answer. Or, as Forrest Green explained it: "The Japanese will let you make all the mistakes you want. . . . They will let you fail, so you will win in the end."

Early in the Flat Rock plant's start-up, some of the Japanese, especially those who spoke limited English, tended to keep to themselves. But the Americans went out of their way to make their Japanese trainers welcome, inviting them to share lunch and join in card games. "They used to have more trouble with English than they do now," Steve Ross said of the Japanese in the summer of 1988. Two years earlier, when Ross had become one of the first Americans hired by Mazda, the company gave its American and Japanese employees lists of different types of restaurants with basic menu items printed in English and Japanese. It was always a sign that a Japanese dispatch had begun to feel comfortable with his English, and his American dinner companions, when he ordered a meal without struggling through his list.

Friendships between Japanese and Americans developed throughout the plant. Even those workers like Phil Keeling, who were critical of Mazda's management system, became friendly with the company's Japanese dispatches. "As far as people go, I love the guys," said Keeling. "Every time I've gone out with them, I've had a blast. . . . To me, the complaints I've had have been a management-labor thing, not a Japanese-American thing."

Keeling, who was assigned to work in Flat Rock's paint shop, developed close relationships with several Japanese trainers in his department. A photo album he keeps in his Flat Rock apartment includes pictures of him, another American worker, and a group of Japanese dispatches, taken while they were on a rafting trip through the rapids of his native West Virginia. Keeling loves to get back to West Virginia, a state that, despite large pockets of poverty, is blessed with uncommon natural beauty. Its mountains, though not as awe inspiring as the Rockies, are kinder and more soothing, covered by lush foliage and separated by fertile valleys. Keeling likes to show off his home state to the friends he makes in Flat Rock. It is an unwritten law: If you become friends with Phil, sooner or later you'll see West Virginia. The Japanese in the photos obviously enjoyed his friendship. They are looking directly into the camera, chins up, chests out, broad smiles on their faces. They are wearing brightly colored life jackets that shimmer in the sunlight. They appear tired from their journey down the rapids but pleased with the camaraderie and the adventure they have just shared. The expedition was one of those rarest of greatly anticipated outings—it lived up to everyone's expectations.

Keeling did not try to hide his reservations about Mazda's man-

agement system from his Japanese friends. Why did Mazda insist on downgrading the importance of the skilled trades? he would ask. Why didn't they hire more people at the plant? How could Mazda's Japanese union be so cozy with management and still represent the interests of workers? For their part, the Japanese did not understand why Americans like Keeling were so concerned about petty work rules and rigid job descriptions. The Americans talked about being democratic, but didn't they realize that their elaborate rules and regulations allowed some workers, especially those with seniority, to get by doing soft, easy jobs, while others had to work harder to pick up the slack? "The Japanese didn't appreciate our ideas about seniority," said Keeling. "They didn't see anything wrong with filling jobs based on who was the best person available for that position, instead of who's been at the plant the longest. They didn't see why they shouldn't be able to take the youngest, strongest, most athletic worker and use him to set the work [pace] standards for everybody else. You know, if a forty-year-old can't keep up with this guy—too bad."

A Japanese-owned plant building automobiles in America's "Motor City" had the potential to arouse powerful nationalistic resentments. Mazda's Japanese managers were aware of this, and they worked hard to diffuse local hostility. They pointedly referred to the plant as "MMUC," the name of the company's American manufacturing subsidiary, rather than "Mazda"; they relied on American executives to make public appearances on behalf of the company whenever possible; and they repeatedly told the press that the company planned to produce cars with more than 50 percent "local content" at Flat Rock by 1990. (More than half of the value of each vehicle made at the plant would come from American parts and labor.) In 1987 Kenichi Yamamoto, then the president of Mazda Motor Corporation, had gone out of his way to assure the Detroit media: "Please understand, we have no intention to transfer our Japanese culture to the United States. We want to combine the Japanese and the United States in a new culture which has a potential to prosper in the future, a new blend that has not been done before."[3]

But Mazda's executives at Flat Rock, both Japanese and American, also inadvertently offended many Detroiters with their frequent criticisms of the local auto industry. It sometimes seemed as if Mazda managers could not make it through a newspaper or television interview without disparaging the way other local automakers did things. In describing Mazda's virtues, they invariably criticized—

either explicitly or by implication—the flaws of the Big Three. Not only was Mazda a caring and concerned employer, the American companies were callous and indifferent. Not only did Mazda's team system bring out the best in workers, the American system brought out the worst. Not only was Mazda quality conscious, American automakers were sloppy. In describing the concept of *kaizen* to a group of engineers in Ann Arbor, Michigan, MMUC president Nobuto remarked: "While I observe that many Americans and American companies are very concerned about quality, they do not always have this dedication to constant improvement which is essential to insuring quality. It often seems that if something is 90 percent right, there is a tendency to believe that further improvement is either unnecessary or not worth the extra effort. . . ." Commenting on the growth of Japanese-owned plants in the United States, Nobuto told his audience: "For American manufacturers, both the automakers and the component suppliers, you are now facing, perhaps for the first time in your history, real competition. . . ."[4] Nobuto's comments, though not made in a spirit of arrogance or malice, left many Americans feeling patronized. It was as if Henry Ford, Walter Chrysler, Alfred Sloan, and all the other Americans who had been building cars before the Japanese came to these shores with their *kaizen* and JIT, had somehow not been capable enough to provide one another with "real competition."

Local resentment toward Mazda was fueled by the failure of the Flat Rock plant to meet the unrealistic claims that were made for it as a creator of "spin-off jobs" by state politicians eager to sell the $125 million incentive package to voters. The flood of Japanese supplier firms that was supposed to follow Mazda to Michigan never materialized. Instead of creating up to twenty thousand jobs, as the governor had predicted it would, the plant had created about half that amount by 1989.[5] Few people thought this figure would ever get much higher. "Flat Rock gave up everything and all we wanted was a shot at some jobs," the mayor, Ted Anders, would later say of the 100 percent tax abatement. "But we didn't even get that."

Yet resentment against Mazda would have existed regardless of what its executives said, or how many jobs its plant created, simply because the company was Japanese. Japan-bashing had become much less common in Detroit by the mid-1980s, especially among younger, working-age people. Japanese cars were spotted much more frequently on the city's streets, even in blue-collar neighborhoods. For the most part, local government and business leaders had toned down

their anti-Japanese rhetoric since 1982, when John Dingell, Down-river's longtime congressman, referred to the Japanese as "the little yellow people."[6] The level of tolerance had reached such heights that in 1988, when Isaiah Thomas, the captain of the Detroit Pistons basketball team, signed a contract to do television commercials for Toyota—an act that would have created a public outcry five years earlier—his popularity in the community did not suffer at all. But hostility toward the Japanese was still very much in evidence. As recently as May 1989, a Detroit city council member used the term *Japs* during a press conference he called to attack Chrysler for hiring a Japanese firm to do design work at the company's new Jefferson Avenue assembly plant in the city.[7] Criticism of the Japanese usually centered around that country's allegedly unfair trade practices. At times it was laced with vague references to World War II atrocities. Often it included strong but unspoken undercurrents of racism. No one associated with the plant, least of all the Japanese dispatches, discussed the issue of racism publicly, but privately they could not help but wonder if many of the white Detroiters who appeared so eager to complain about Mazda's actions at Flat Rock would have been so critical had the plant been built by a German or French automaker.

Mazda's Japanese dispatches were harassed by American bigots. This harassment began in 1985–86 during the construction of the Flat Rock plant. Some members of the American construction crew hired by Mazda's Japanese contractor, Kajima, wore T-shirts with an illustration of an atomic mushroom cloud over the caption: "Made in the USA, tested in Japan." The T-shirts had to have been especially offensive to Mazda dispatches, who visited the unfinished plant to check on the installation of equipment and familiarize American hirees with its layout. Many of the dispatches had come from Hiroshima and had lost family members in the 1945 atomic attack. (Mazda, then called Toyo Kogyo, had almost half its factory destroyed by the bomb. The plant would have suffered even greater damage had it not been separated from the rest of the city by a small hill.) Yet the dispatches showed no emotional response to the T-shirts. Neither did they respond to the occasional obscenities shouted at them when they walked through the construction site. Nor did they react to the racist graffiti that were scrawled on the walls of the site's portable bathrooms. Some of the construction workers were clearly spoiling for a fight, but the Japanese carefully avoided all confrontations and quietly went about their business. Later they

would voice their objections to their American managers, who would complain to building union representatives at the site, who would promise to talk to the workers—but the harassment continued. "It really was rough when they were building the plant," recalled Steve Ross. "We would go over there with Japanese trainers, and the construction workers really took offense to the Japanese. Not all of the construction workers—but a number of them—were rather rude and boisterous about Japan and the atomic bomb. . . . [They] would also make comments like 'Go home, Japs' . . . [and they would write] 'Today's slap a Jap day' in the portajohns."

The majority of people Downriver, however, were eager to welcome the Japanese to their community. In Monroe, Michigan, an industrial city south of Flat Rock where many Japanese settled, the local chamber of commerce established a "host family program" to help dispatches from Mazda and the company's seat supplier, Delta Kogyo (which built a plant in Monroe), adjust to daily life in America, by matching them with local families. Generally, dispatches arrived in the United States about one month before their families to allow themselves to settle into their jobs without the distraction of having to establish a household routine in a strange, new country. For their first one to two weeks in this country, the dispatches who participated in the Monroe program lived with an American family, sharing meals, watching television, and going to baseball games and movies. Later, when the dispatch's family arrived, the host family would help them get settled. David Bagnall, the chamber of commerce president who started the program, wondered at first if enough local people would be willing to participate in it. The response he received was overwhelming, providing many more volunteer host families than there were Japanese dispatches in Monroe. Host families and their Japanese guests often developed friendships that outlasted the dispatch's two- or three-year assignment in the United States. "A lot of people have become real friendly with their Japanese families," said one woman who participated in the host program. "You won't find Japanese people who don't have a dinner to go to on Thanksgiving and Christmas—there's plenty of invitations."

But the problems with the construction workers at the plant site were not an isolated example of harassment directed against the Japanese. For every 50 friendly shoppers who would help Japanese wives, showing them which box of detergent was for laundry and which was for dishwashing, there would be one huffy American who would push her cart away muttering something about how people

should go back where they belonged. For every 50 Americans who patiently gave a Japanese family directions to a school or shopping mall, there was one who made an obscene gesture out of his car window. Mazda's American employees also found themselves harassed. Peter Barrow, the engine installer, once went to cash his paycheck at a Flat Rock bank. Not having an account at the bank, Barrow expected to pay a small service fee. The bank teller, looking down at the check and then back at Barrow, told him that although she ordinarily waived the service fee for people employed by local firms, she was going to charge it to him because he worked for Mazda. Barrow was angry but not surprised. As a Mazda employee, he had encountered that kind of hostility before in the area around the plant. In 1987, when Barrow was in training at Mazda, he and a group of other American employees would stop off at a tavern near the plant after work. Without fail, some of the bar's patrons would start needling the Mazda workers soon after they walked through the door about being "Jap lovers" and "lackeys," until the bartender, wishing to preserve the peace, came over and quieted them. A short time later, Barrow took his Japanese trainer on a fishing trip to northern Michigan. When they stopped at a restaurant in a rural area, a group of men in the parking lot began yelling out references to Pearl Harbor.

For the most part, Mazda's American employees were as restrained as their Japanese trainers when confronted with this verbal harassment. "I wore my uniform to bars, and quite a few people would make derogatory comments about the Japanese," recalled Forrest Green. "They'd say, 'The Japanese are taking American jobs.'" Green never argued with his tormentors, even though he believed that the Japanese at Mazda were creating jobs for Americans. These people already have their minds made up, he would tell himself, and arguing will only alienate them further.

Being a part of the first Japanese auto plant in America's industrial heartland brought with it a certain amount of pressure for Japanese dispatches and American employees. Both groups were very aware of the plant's unique position and of its importance, given the complicated nature of their two countries' relationship. Good-natured teasing and practical jokes often were used to diffuse tensions in the plant and break through the awkwardness that sometimes developed between Japanese and Americans. The Japanese took pleasure in panicking American workers—hiding an important tool right before a shift started and "losing" a worker's car keys when it was

time to go home; insisting that an American try an exotic Japanese dish and then watching his expression when they told him it's made-up, and extremely vile, list of ingredients; switching an American's full beer can with an empty one and laughing uncontrollably when he picked up the suddenly lighter can. "The Japanese were great kidders," said Green. "You really had to be careful with those guys, they were such practical jokers. They liked it when you played jokes on them too. . . . We had this high-pressure wash system that we used to wash out every die when they brought it out of the press. When the first Japanese trainer was going home to Japan, someone trapped him, and we put him in the wash and hosed him down. The Japanese all thought this was hysterical. When the next guy was supposed to go back to Japan, his friends would come over and say, 'So-and-so is going home, can you give him a wash too?' It got to be that whenever someone went back to Japan, he got washed down."

Green and most of the other Americans in his department grew very close to their Japanese advisors. Every Friday the two groups met at a popular local bar, where the owner reserved a large "Mazda table" for them. They also went golfing and bowling together, and on several occasions, the Americans did what many Detroit businessmen do when entertaining out-of-town clients—they took the Japanese to the striptease clubs across the river in Windsor, Ontario. The Americans were amazed by the stamina the Japanese displayed when pursuing a good time. "They're party animals," Green said of his Japanese trainers. "No American can keep up with them. . . . They didn't want to quit. At two A.M. they'd stay out, still going strong. Then they'd be right there at work at seven the next morning."

As the Americans grew closer to their trainers, they learned more about the fears and anxieties of the Japanese. The dispatches were very homesick for the familiar insulated world of the Hiroshima-Hofu corridor. They were not worldly men. Like the Americans they trained, they were the products of an industrial backwater, located far from the nation's cultural center. They were less sophisticated than the workers of Honda, Nissan, and Toyota, who came from the more cosmopolitan Tokyo area. Most of them had been recruited by Mazda directly out of high school or after graduating from the local college—Hiroshima University. They often found it difficult to understand the unfamiliar, and occasionally hostile, world around them in Michigan. They lived in fear of crime and were dismayed by the abandoned and decaying buildings they saw in Detroit. Is this not still the richest country in the world? they would ask their American

friends when they drove by the buildings. Those too young to re-
member the wartime destruction of Japan had never seen buildings
like that. Nor had they ever seen stores with bars on the windows to
keep out criminals. At first they had refused to go into the city of
Detroit out of fear. When they had to drive from Flat Rock, which is
south of the city, to a Japanese food market in the northern suburb
of Southfield, they would map out a route that circumvented Detroit
even though it lengthened their journey considerably. Mazda's Amer-
ican workers gradually helped them overcome this fear, taking them
to baseball games at Tiger Stadium in the city, and to Greektown, a
downtown area of ethnic shops and restaurants.

The Japanese were also worried about their wives, who felt lonely
in America, cut off from their families and friends back in Japan.
Some of the wives kept busy teaching Japanese classes at the plant,
attending classes at Henry Ford Community College, and involving
themselves in local PTA activities. But the many wives with a limited
knowledge of English found very little to occupy their day. None of
them could get even part-time jobs, because they had not been issued
work visas.

The Japanese wives worried a great deal about their children, and
by extension, their husbands worried too. They worried about their
children being harassed in their new American schools, though the
friendships between Japanese and American children developed so
quickly that this concern soon became moot. But a deeper anxiety
remained. The Mazda families worried that after spending two or
three years in American schools, their children would fall far behind
their classmates in Japan, particularly in mathematics and the sci-
ences. (In contrast to the United States, where students are given
more work in college than in the lower grades, in Japan students
follow a more demanding curriculum through high school and relax
more in college.) The children of dispatches attended a Saturday
school in Bloomfield Hills, Michigan, sponsored by the Japanese
Society of Detroit, where they studied math and science as well as
Japanese culture. But their parents knew that the once-a-week classes
would never make up for the real Japanese education their children
were missing. The classes also could not compensate for the missing
exposure to Japanese cultural values. Nor would they eradicate the
bad "habits" that the children were picking up from American
schoolmates—habits that included a greater self-assertiveness and a
more casual attitude toward homework. Mazda mothers worried
that their children would never be fully assimilated back into the

tight-knit, homogeneous society of Japan after their American experience; that they would, instead, be forever branded *uchi no gaijin* (insider-outsider), a term used to describe someone who, though accepted as an ethnic Japanese, is regarded as tainted by his or her exposure to foreignness.

Although the move to Flat Rock caused them and their families considerable stress, Mazda's dispatches never considered turning down their American assignments, which lasted anywhere from several months to three years for ordinary workers, and longer for top executives like Nobuto. Refusing or even resisting the company's request to go to Michigan would have been unthinkable to Mazda's Japanese employees. When a curious American asked a dispatch why he had "volunteered" for the Flat Rock assignment, the man laughed at the naïveté of the question, then explained that in Japan this kind of volunteering was simply something one had to do out of loyalty to the company.

Japanese and Americans had very different ideas about the degree of loyalty and obedience a company should expect from its employees. Despite the warm feelings that developed between Japanese and Americans at the plant, this difference sometimes caused friction and misunderstandings between the two groups. The conflicts had started even during the plant's trial-build phase in the spring of 1987. Mazda issued its American employees company baseball caps, with the understanding that the caps were a voluntary accessory to the mandatory blue-pants-khaki-shirt Mazda uniform. Taking the term *voluntary* to mean that they had a choice whether or not to wear the caps, many Americans elected to come to work bareheaded. This upset the Japanese, who regarded not wearing caps as a sign of disrespect toward the company. When the Japanese pressed the issue, the Americans countered that cap wearing was voluntary. True, the Japanese acknowledged, but if you really cared about the company you should *want* to wear your caps. The Americans, who could accept being told what they *had* to do by an employer, took offense at being told what they should "want" to do. As far as they were concerned, Mazda had overstepped its boundaries by trying to force them to do something that was supposed to be voluntary. *Mandatory-voluntary* was the term they began to use to describe the company's cap directives. The harder the Japanese pushed them to wear caps, the more stubbornly they resisted. In the end the issue proved to matter more to the Americans than the Japanese. After several months of bickering, the company agreed to make cap wear-

ing voluntary in the American sense of the word. In the years that followed, most Americans would continue to go to work capless.

Similar confrontations erupted during the plant's start-up phase. The Japanese consistently expected the Americans to give up unpaid "personal time" for work-related activities, and the Americans consistently refused. When the plant began building cars in 1987, Japanese trainers would instruct American workers to clean up their work stations after the quitting bell had rung at three-thirty. Are we getting paid overtime to do this? the Americans would ask. No, the Japanese would say, but cleaning up after yourself is part of your job. If it's part of our job, the Americans countered, then we should get paid for it. The argument went back and forth, with the Japanese demanding that the Americans clean their work stations and the Americans refusing. Eventually the Japanese relented and allowed the Americans to clean up before the end of a shift.

In the beginning Japanese trainers would try to get the Americans to talk about *kaizen* projects or review safety procedures during their twice-a-day 15-minute breaks. The Americans, already fatigued from maintaining a rigorous JIT work pace, were in no mood to talk about these subjects. They preferred to read a newspaper or play a quick card game. Some of the Japanese prohibited workers from pulling out newspapers or cards in their break area and attempted to plow ahead with work discussions. The discussions usually got nowhere, as workers sat at the break table in stony silence. Again the Japanese backed off, and workers were left to pursue their own activities on breaks.

Although they gave in to the Americans on specific issues like the wearing of caps and the reading of newspapers during breaks, the Japanese generally refused to accept the sharp distinctions that the Americans drew between personal and work time and between individual and company interests. To the Japanese one did not work for a company as much as one *belonged* to it, in much the same way that one belonged to a family. A worker's responsibility toward his company did not end when the quitting bell rang, any more than his responsibility to his family ended when he left home in the morning. The dispatches may have griped about their jobs and their American assignments, but they gave Mazda this familial loyalty without question. They drew their identities from Mazda and expected the Americans at Flat Rock to do the same. When the Americans, who tended to have more complicated and diverse loyalties, refused to share in this commitment, the dispatches felt hurt—it was as if the Americans were rejecting their family.

Peter Barrow felt this division between Japanese and Americans soon after he arrived at the plant in 1986. "The biggest difference between us and the Japanese is that we work to live and [they] live to work. The Japanese are all the same. You can take ten Japanese and say 'work together,' and they will. They've all been brought up the same. But Americans are from all walks of life. We don't think alike. You can bring [Americans] together, but you can't tell them to like each other; it's not going to happen. . . . The Japanese try hard to understand us, and we try hard to understand them, but we have this difference. Japanese guys will go into the plant without getting paid for it—show me an American who will do this. If Mazdas don't sell in Japan, [the workers] there feel responsible . . . you don't see that in this country."

Sometimes it seemed that the Americans and the Japanese at Flat Rock viewed the worker-company relationship from completely opposite perspectives. The Americans, though usually sincere about wanting to give their employer a "fair day's work for a fair day's pay," were first and foremost interested in what their company owed them. The Japanese, though eager to advance their own individual careers, were primarily concerned with their obligation to their company. This difference led to serious misunderstandings over Mazda's orientation promises to involve American workers in *kaizen* activities and provide them with cross-training. Americans walked into the Flat Rock plant assuming that they would be spending a good share of every work day discussing *kaizen* projects at meetings that were very much like the problem-solving exercises to which they had devoted so much time during their three-week orientation. They also assumed that Mazda would be committing part of each day to training them in computers, hydraulics, and other technologies. To them, *kaizen* activities and training classes were "perks" that went with a Mazda job. But to the Japanese, *kaizen* and training were responsibilities to be assumed by workers on their own time. Mazda did offer its Flat Rock workers limited opportunities to participate in *kaizen* projects and to attend a very small number of advanced-training classes during normal work hours, but the company scheduled most *kaizen* and training sessions as voluntary, nonpaid activities after work. Many Americans saw this as a sign that Mazda was going back on its orientation commitments, refusing to make good on its promise to provide workers with off-line activities. To the Japanese, the Americans' reluctance to devote thirty minutes or an hour to something that could make them better, more productive workers

was an indication that they were shortsighted and not fully committed to the success of their company.

Despite their complaints Americans often participated in after-hours *kaizen* meetings. Not only were the Americans eager for the opportunity that *kaizen* seemed to offer them to use their creative and intellectual facilities, they also believed that by contributing to improvements in their work stations they would be making their own jobs easier. As one American Mazda worker told the trade paper *Automotive News* in February 1988: "I think we are going to have to get used to . . . doing things for the company on your own time, not expecting to get paid all the time for it. It may take a half hour, but it may be the only time you have to do it. And it's basically your comfort as against that little bit of pay you might get."[8]

The Japanese, with their emphasis on process over end results, were unwavering in their adherence to protocol and standard operating procedures. If safety procedures required all workers to wear helmets, glasses, and gloves, then all workers wore them, even if those workers were not assigned to the factory floor but to a specialty shop, where the safety gear was an unnecessary inconvenience. Forrest Green and other tool and die makers objected to Mazda's strict adherence to the safety-gear rule. "I never worked anyplace where I had to wear a helmet as a die maker," said Green. "There's nothing overhead where we work that could hurt you—it's not like the assembly line. . . . From a safety standpoint [the helmets] hurt more than they helped, because they obstructed our vision. They were always falling off, because we did a lot of bending. The Japanese had straps to keep helmets on, but these were uncomfortable. . . . [The Japanese] also wanted us to wear gloves, which made no sense. It's hard to be a die maker with your hands covered."

Tool and die makers showed their displeasure with the safety-gear requirement during the "point-and-call" drill that was held at the start of every shift. Pre-work safety inspections, point-and-call drills group workers on a team into pairs so they can check one another's safety gear. As the team leader or Japanese trainer reads off a list of required safety gear, every worker points to the designated item on his or her partner and calls out: "Helmet okay," "Glasses okay," "Gloves okay." As a protest, some tool and die makers started to give their point-and-call responses in Polish, Russian, or in imitations of what to them sounded like a foreign language.

The Japanese were unmoved. The rule about wearing safety gear remained in place. Some tool and die makers complained about the

rule at a "diagonal slice meeting" conducted by Denny Pawley. Diagonal slice meetings were held frequently at the plant during its start-up phase. They brought together fifteen to twenty randomly selected team members and leaders from a given department to meet with upper-level managers to talk about problems on the shop floor. Only Americans attended. The workers were happy when the popular Pawley chaired a meeting. He seemed to listen more carefully than the other managers, and he always took notes so he could follow up better on worker complaints. Unlike many of the other managers, he was not afraid to admit when the company was wrong: "No, you're right, your job requires good safety gloves, and if the gloves in your team's bin are torn, your unit leader has got to replace them. . . ." Then he would write something in his notebook—and the next day there would be new gloves in the bin. Pawley told the tool and die makers that if they wanted to dispense with the helmet requirement, they should conduct a study to show the safety and health department that the rule's removal would be in the plant's best interest. Document your case, then if safety thinks you have a logical point, they will pursue the matter further, he advised. The tool and die makers found the prospect of documenting a study rather daunting, so they decided that they would learn to live with the helmets.

Many American workers resented what they considered to be the patronizing attitude of some of the Japanese trainers. The workers respected the ability of Mazda's dispatches, but the pride and confidence of the Japanese sometimes inflated into arrogance on the shop floor. It was then that the Americans felt they were being talked down to, treated by their trainers like members of a backward nation who could never be as smart or as skilled as the Japanese. When a problem developed in the plant, the dispatches on the scene often would only go through the motions of listening to suggestions from workers, as if they assumed that Americans could not contribute an idea that had not already been apparent to them.

On one occasion, Jerry Healy's maintenance team was called to repair a filter on the paint line. When the team got there, a group of Japanese engineers was already working on the problem. Healy, the team's leader, protested, telling the engineers that the maintenance job fell under his team's jurisdiction, but the Japanese dismissed him, as if the problem was too critical to wait for Americans to try to solve. The Japanese made it clear that they did not need the Americans' help. The members of Healy's team were angry, feeling that their pride as craftspersons had been insulted, but Healy, who had

experienced this sort of treatment before from the Japanese, calmed them down. "I told . . . my guys, forget it," he recalled. "We're not going to waste our time. If they want to do it, we'll let them do it."

Hiroshi Ueno, the Flat Rock plant's chief production engineer, reflected the attitude of many dispatches when he questioned the abilities of American workers during a discussion with visitors to the plant in the spring of 1988.[9] Ueno told his visitors that he hoped Mazda's designers in Japan would de-emphasize the mig weld that connects the roof to the rear quarter of vehicles on future Mazda models built in the United States. When asked why, Ueno explained matter-of-factly that mig welding, an exacting job that requires a very high metal finish, was not "matched" to the skill levels of American workers. "A highly trained person only can do this," he said. "We sent people [Americans] to Hofu for one month of special training . . . but this is something I want to avoid in the next model design." The Mazda public relations representative, an American who was with Ueno, promptly interrupted him, explaining to his visitors that the Japanese engineer was having trouble expressing himself in English and did not really mean to disparage the quality of American workmanship. But Ueno, a sincere and cordial man who apparently saw nothing patronizing in his remarks, politely brushed off his would-be defender and insisted that he meant exactly what he had said. He told his visitors that it was "not normal to find this highly skilled worker in the U.S. market."

Mazda's dispatches were under intense pressure to get the $550 million Flat Rock plant up and running and at full production as quickly as possible. This, together with their homesickness for Japan and their repressed anger at being the object of racial insults, caused some dispatches to snap and take their frustrations out on American workers. "Some of the Japanese would just lose it from time to time," recalled an American team member. Americans who failed to catch onto a trainer's instructions quickly, or who made a mistake that disrupted production, sometimes came under a barrage of insults from the Japanese. When production equipment malfunctioned, some of the Japanese would forceably shove Americans to the side to get at the problem themselves. "The Japanese can get really angry," said Peter Barrow. "They jump and yell, and make people feel really embarrassed. . . . [They] also had this bad habit of calling us stupid." Barrow recalled several incidents early in the plant's history when Japanese trainers would tap workers on the helmets with long pointers. "The Japanese had these pointers that they used to show you things on the line. Sometimes, if they wanted to get your attention,

they'd tap you with their pointers. It was a custom for them to do this in Japan, but the Americans got pretty upset by it. I remember a few people got mad and just grabbed the pointers and broke them, and that put a stop to the Japanese tapping people."

American maintenance workers often got into confrontations with Japanese trainers over what the Americans believed was the willingness of trainers to compromise the safety of maintenance crews for the sake of meeting production schedules. The production-driven Japanese did not like to see the line stop for equipment repairs. They thought nothing of risking their personal safety by jumping on top of a moving conveyor to free a jammed gear or climbing into a giant piece of equipment to inspect a circuit board while the machine was in operation. The important thing was to keep the line going, since even a slight disruption in the flow of work and materials can upset the delicate balance of a JIT plant. The Japanese expected the Americans to take the same risks. Trouble arose when the Americans refused. American maintenance workers would turn off a piece of equipment and climb inside to work on it, only to have a Japanese dispatch come by and restart it while they were still in the machine. When the Americans could not turn off equipment because some power was needed to check its circuitry, they would hang danger tags called "sky cards" on the machine. The sky cards warned production workers that the machine was not to be used. (The cards were also placed on malfunctioning machines that maintenance considered unsafe to operate.) Some Japanese advisors made a habit of walking through their departments and plucking sky cards from equipment.

The dispatches' disregard for safety prompted an angry reaction from the Americans. "We've been real lucky that no one's been hurt. We've had so many close calls with the Japanese, where our guys have had their hands in a press or a machine, and the Japanese [have gone] up and started it up on them," Phil Keeling said in November 1988. "There's almost been fights because of this. My [Japanese] friend was up on top of a lifter with me, and we had this car stuck up there on the overhead [paint] line. We figured out how to get the car down by rigging up this brake and big lever. But we had to be careful when we released that brake, because there were people crawling all over the place below us—and once we let go [of the lever] that car was going down. I had my team leader on the radio, and I said to him, 'Ok, tell me when it's safe to release this thing.' But [the Japanese dispatch] couldn't wait. We kept saying, 'No, wait,' and he kept trying to release the brake. I had to grab his hands—I almost hit him."

Bob Ramp, the UAW representative who had gazed out his hotel window in Hofu two years earlier and wondered how Americans would adjust to a Japanese-inspired team system, now found himself confronted with the type of cultural clash that had then been a vague fear. Complaints were coming across Ramp's desk about Japanese trainers pushing, shoving, and verbally abusing workers in the body shop, the area of the plant he represented. The complaints were not coming in giant waves, but they were frequent enough to alert Ramp that this was more than a case of a few workers not getting along with their boss. Ramp had already acquired a reputation in the plant as a "worker's rep." He was a little more aggressive than most of the other UAW officials at Flat Rock in following up on worker complaints, even if it sometimes meant upsetting the harmony of Mazda's team system. He investigated the reports of abusive trainers, talking to American workers and Japanese dispatches. In most cases, he found that the incidents were the result of either production schedule pressures or the language barrier that separated the two groups. A talk with the workers and trainers involved in an incident usually cleared up misunderstandings quickly. "Sometimes the Japanese are prone to become a little acrimonious, and I haven't taken too kindly to that," Ramp said in 1988. "But I think it's just because of the pressures on them. . . . They want us to be as good as we can be; I think that's where the frustration lies. They are so dedicated, they want to make sure this plant is a great success. . . . There's also a problem with a lot of the trainers speaking limited English, so they might come out and say something like, 'Team member—team leader no good.' I don't think they really mean that you're no good, but their limited English sheds a bad light on it." In a handful of cases, however, Ramp believed that Japanese trainers had known exactly what they were saying—they were trying to intimidate workers with statements like, "Team member no good; take money back." When this happened, Ramp would have to confront the trainers: "Look, maybe this is the way it's done in Japan, but you're in the U.S. now—and when in Rome you do as the Romans do."[10]

Eventually, after the Flat Rock plant completed its first year of building cars, and the early glitches in its production system were ironed out, tensions between Japanese and Americans abated. The Japanese no longer screamed and shoved and tapped with pokers. They no longer expected Americans to conform fully to the Japanese ideal of the worker-company relationship. Although disagreements still existed with Americans over safety, the emotional conflicts be-

tween American maintenance crews and Japanese dispatches became less frequent. As Peter Barrow would observe of the Japanese during the plant's second year of production: "They've loosened up a lot." By then the number of Japanese at the plant had fallen significantly— from 400 in September 1987, when production began, to a little more than half that amount one year later. Much of the day-to-day authority on the shop floor itself had been transferred to Americans, though major decision-making power still rested firmly in the hands of Japanese upper-level managers. Most American workers sincerely missed the trainers who had returned to Japan. The camaraderie and good times at ballgames and bars had left a more lasting impression than the confrontations on the shop floor. The Americans were, for the most part, understanding about those confrontations. The majority of incidents that had occurred were really no one's fault, they would say, but simply a matter of start-up pressures and cultural differences getting in the way of open communication.

The 560 American women who worked at Flat Rock in 1987–88 tended to be less understanding than their male co-workers.[11] Unlike the plant's male workers, women team members did not have memories of good times shared with the Japanese dispatches, all of whom were men. The Japanese were less chummy with female workers on breaks and at lunch, and they seldom included American women in their after-work outings.

On the contrary, the Japanese tended to treat female employees much more shabbily than they treated males at Flat Rock. Women workers were pushed around more often and more forcibly, and screamed at more harshly by trainers. It appeared to many female workers that the Japanese believed that women were inherently weaker and less capable than men and thus had to be watched more closely. "If a machine broke down and there was a woman around, the Japanese just naturally assumed it was her fault," recalled one female team member.

Other Japanese seemed to have the impression that a woman working in a factory had to be sexually loose. The Flat Rock plant had "some problems with Japanese patting women on the derriere," according to Peter Barrow. But, as Barrow and other American workers emphasized, upper Japanese management quickly brought this form of harassment to a halt.

Japanese dispatches were unsure of how to react to female American workers during the early phase of the plant's history. Because of Mazda's prohibition against female production employees in Japan,

the dispatches, virtually all of whom had been with the company their entire careers, had no experience working with women. Mazda knew it would have to accept women into its production work force at Flat Rock, and the company tried to prepare its trainers to deal with female workers, but many of the Japanese were surprised by what they considered the "assertiveness" of American women. This became evident when the original group of four hundred American hirees visited Hofu for 30 days. Mazda offered the Americans the chance to take Japanese cultural classes in addition to their job-related training. Trainees were given the option of attending classes in Japanese flower arranging (*ikebana*), the Japanese ceremonial tea ritual (*chanoyu*), or the more aggressive samurai sword drills. To the astonishment of the Japanese, about half of those who participated in the samurai drills were women. More amazing still, many of the male trainees attended the flower and tea classes. Takashi Itakura, the deputy general manager of Mazda's human development division, ranked this "sense of equalness" between the sexes as the most conspicuous difference between American trainees and Japanese trainers at Hofu. "I believe women are very gentle and beautiful, and man is strong and not so beautiful," he observed. "So man should go out into the mountains and battle with a bear or something, not do quiet flower arranging." But Itakura allowed that because of cultural differences, an American man might find "importance" or "value" in flower arranging and concluded: "It's nothing I should say anything bad about."[12]

Mazda dispatches brought their perception of women as the "weaker sex" with them to Flat Rock. This made it difficult for female hirees to receive equal treatment during in-plant training sessions. At first many Japanese trainers simply ignored the women in their classes, showing only the male hirees how to operate a drill press or read an andon board.* After class, the American men would explain the lesson to the women. The women complained about this unfair treatment to upper management, and the trainers were forced to begin addressing the women directly. Since they could no longer ignore the women, some trainers decided to intimidate them by acting exasperated if they asked questions or failed to catch on to a lesson right away, and by addressing them in very sarcastic tones. "The Japanese weren't so pleased about having to train women, and they let us know it by acting all impatient and huffy in a way that they would never do with the guys," said one female worker.

* Lighted displays positioned over each work station, andon boards show the production goals and current rate of production for each station.

Just as they had modified their attitudes about many other things, however, so too did the Japanese grow more accepting of female workers as they became accustomed to the American workplace. The harassment and intimidation stopped, and the Japanese became more evenhanded in their treatment of male and female team members. But despite this progress, women often had to prove themselves to each new dispatch from Japan. In 1988 a Japanese who had just arrived at Flat Rock saw a woman spraying cars in the paint shop. Spraying is one of the most difficult jobs in the paint shop, and the new dispatch could not believe that anyone at Mazda would assign it to a woman. He marched over to the woman, reprimanded her for doing a job without authorization, pushed her aside, and began doing the spraying himself.

Female workers at Flat Rock also had to contend with a special set of off-plant problems in 1987–88 as a result of Mazda's unpredictable work schedule and intense overtime demands. Normal quitting time for the day shift is three-thirty, but Mazda often informed workers near the end of a shift that the company was adding one or two hours of mandatory overtime to the day's production schedule. Consequently, when they left for work in the morning, workers could never be sure when they would be returning home from the plant. This uncertainty made it difficult for women workers, many of them single mothers, to schedule child care services, family doctor visits, and other domestic errands. (Despite requests from its female employees, Mazda refused to provide a day-care center at the plant.) In 1988, when the Flat Rock plant was struggling to keep up with the demand for the popular Ford Probe, the length of the Mazda workweek—which often stretched for over 50 and even 60 hours—made it especially difficult for female team members to balance the responsibilities of job and family.

Judy Wilson, who had been so positive about Mazda's "family values" when she joined the company in September 1987, was dismayed one year later by the effect that her job at Flat Rock was having on her family life. "I get up at four-thirty in the morning and almost never get home before six," she said. "By nine or ten I'm in bed. My whole first year at the plant I worked only two forty-hour weeks—most weeks I work six or seven days. I wish I had more time for my kids, but I can't get off, and I can't quit because we need the money. This isn't the way they said it would be in training. . . . They never talked about sixty-hour weeks." The demands of her job made it difficult for Wilson to provide her two children with the support

and supervision they needed in the wake of their father's death. She was losing influence with her teenage son and daughter. They were becoming sullen and uncommunicative, and their grades, which had always been at least average, had begun to fall. A teacher suggested that Wilson come to school for a talk about a problem one of her children was having. Wilson asked her unit leader (an American) for permission to take an afternoon off so she could meet with the teacher. The leader refused her request, telling her that she should "take care of personal business on personal time," and threatening to issue her a written reprimand if she missed work. (Mazda employees who receive five reprimands, with less than one year elapsing between the last two reprimands, can be fired at the company's discretion.) Wilson went to the school anyway, and true to his threat, her unit leader officially reprimanded her. When she received her reprimand, Wilson looked back sardonically on the early orientation speeches that had welcomed her to the Mazda family. "It would have been better if they didn't stress the things they did in orientation, and we just thought we were going into a regular plant. They talked a lot about family, but this is no different than any other plant. . . . They push you all the time to meet the production schedule, and they don't care about anything else. . . . I know women who've had kids sick at home, and they couldn't get permission to use the phone for five minutes to call them, because it would throw off the production schedule."

Japanese dispatches found it difficult to empathize with the problems of American workers, male or female, who had to juggle the sometimes-conflicting demands of job and family. In Japan men assume virtually no direct role in managing day-to-day family affairs. These matters are left in the hands of Japanese women, who, denied access to outside careers, assume the responsibility of running the home. It is the women who must deal with school problems, doctors' appointments, and other domestic matters in Japan. The Japanese factory worker, knowing how sorely his presence would be missed at a thin-stretched JIT plant, is reluctant to take even the full number of vacation days allotted to him every year. The idea of placing anything short of a life-threatening family crisis over his obligation to the company would strike the Japanese worker as completely disloyal and selfish. This point was driven home to Phil Keeling soon after he began working at Mazda, when the wife of one of his Japanese trainers was involved in a serious car accident back in Hofu. The trainer was visibly upset after he learned about the accident. The Americans in his group went over to the man to express their sym-

pathy, but he kept muttering, almost complaining, thought Keeling, about having to go back to Japan before his job at Flat Rock was completed. Keeling could not help thinking, "This guy's wife just got messed up in an accident, and he's sitting here bitching that he's not going to be able to finish his job."

Black workers at Flat Rock were often ambivalent about their new employer. The success that Mazda and other Japanese automakers have enjoyed since the 1970s has helped to deflate the myth of white supremacy that had long been used to victimize blacks and other minorities. This was certainly good, but at the same time, the Japanese seemed to be second to none in their prejudice against blacks. Former prime minister Nakasone's remarks in 1986, blaming blacks and other minorities for the decline in U.S. academic performance, were well known to black workers at Flat Rock. So too were other examples of Japanese insensitivity toward the feelings of American blacks, including the widely publicized popularity of Sambo dolls in Japan, and the comments made by a leading Japanese politician, Michio Watanabe of the Liberal Democratic Party, accusing blacks of having a nonchalant attitude toward bankruptcy.

Japanese prejudice against blacks prompted a group of civil rights organizations, including the NAACP, to sponsor a boycott of Japanese products during the 1988 Christmas season. Especially disturbing to civil rights leaders was the tendency of Japanese automakers and parts suppliers to build their American plants in rural areas, often in the South, with small black populations. Toyota in Georgetown, Kentucky, Nissan in Smyrna, Tennessee, Honda in Marysville, Ohio, Mitsubishi in downstate Illinois, and Fuji-Isuzu in Lafayette, Indiana, had all located their new plants in largely white areas. By choosing a plant site in an industrial suburb of Detroit, Mazda became the sole exception to this rule. The Japanese have consistently denied that their choice of sites was racially motivated, citing instead the relatively cheap cost of land, the offer of attractive tax incentives, and the availability of good transportation facilities as the pivotal factors in their decisions. But to civil rights leaders, these denials have a hollow ring. This is especially true in the case of Honda, which required that all job applicants live within a 30-mile radius of its Marysville plant when it began hiring workers in 1982. The hiring radius—the only one established by a Japanese automaker in the United States—effectively excluded residents of Columbus, 35 miles

away, the only nearby black population center, from consideration for Honda jobs. Not surprisingly, Honda has wound up with an American work force that is 2.8 percent black, compared to the 17.2 percent Big Three plant average.[13] (Honda has paid $6.5 million to settle various Equal Employment Opportunity Commission complaints since opening its American plant.) With Japanese-owned auto plants expected to account for 25 percent of all passenger cars made in the United States by the early 1990s, civil rights leaders have worried about the commitment of Japanese automakers to providing equal employment opportunities. Being locked out of such a large share of the auto industry is especially troublesome for black Americans, since the industry has historically provided the black community with one of its most solid economic underpinnings. The first automaker to hire blacks in significant numbers was the Ford Motor Company, which employed more than 10,000 black workers—one-tenth of its total workforce—by 1926. For the next 40 years, a job at an auto plant was one of the only routes to a middle-class income open to black blue-collar workers. In the mid-1960s, when most good-paying industrial jobs were closed to blacks, roughly one out of four production jobs in American auto plants was held by a black worker. In 1980 one of the key factors that persuaded a reluctant President Carter to support the Chrysler loan guarantee package was that the number three automaker by itself provided 1 percent of black America's total income.[14]

The publicity surrounding Japanese-black problems made many black Mazda workers unsure about the company. True, Mazda had broken ranks with its fellow Japanese automakers and built its plant in an area with a large black population, but everyone knew it had done so under pressure from Ford. It was also true that blacks made up between 14 and 15 percent of the plant's work force, which was a lot better than Honda but not impressive when one considered that blacks accounted for 29 percent of the local population. Besides, as every black in the plant knew, the percentage of blacks steadily declined as one went up the management ladder from team leader to unit leader to area leader (a manager in charge of several units). To make matters worse, it appeared to some black workers at the plant that their numbers were shrinking in 1989. "Every time we turn around, it seems like there's fewer of us," said one black worker. "It seems like almost every time there's a black that leaves the plant for whatever reason, there'll be a white that comes to take his place. We have a joke about that—every time we see a new white, we'll say to each other, 'There's fewer.' "

Still, blacks have rarely encountered blatant racial discrimination at the plant. When they have, it has more often come from white Americans than from Japanese. Most blacks say they get along with the Japanese, but they will usually describe their relationship in terms of the problems that have been avoided rather than the good times that have been shared. It is: "They don't bother me, and I don't bother them . . . ," or, "They treat me the same as everyone else. . . ." It is not: "When we were at the baseball game . . . ," or, "When we went bowling. . . ." Blacks, it seems, have not shared as many good times as white workers have with their Japanese trainers. "The Japanese are either afraid of black people, or they just don't like us," said Nate Watson, a black worker in the materials handling department. "Whatever the reason, they want less to do with us than they do with whites." On one occasion, Watson and a group of other black workers invited some Japanese trainers and their families to a Sunday picnic at a suburban Detroit park. The Japanese indicated that they would try to attend, but on the appointed day none of them showed up. Sometime later, when he attended a barbecue organized by a group of black and white workers, Watson ran into the Japanese trainers. To him the incident typified a Japanese double standard: "The Japanese didn't feel safe going around a group that was all black, but it was okay if there were whites involved too."

Other blacks at Flat Rock, however, have a different view of the Japanese, finding them friendly and accepting. Janet Jones, a black unit leader, has experienced less discrimination at Flat Rock than she had at her previous jobs with American manufacturers. "I was surprised I was so accepted by the Japanese," she said. "The Japanese tend to accept [you] based on your ideas and performance," and not, she indicated, because of the color of your skin. Jones spoke extensively of her respect and admiration for her Japanese trainer, and noted that she and her husband had been out to dinner with the man and his wife on several occasions. "My trainer is a super person; working with him has been a real joy for me. . . . He accepts me as me, not as a 'black woman.' "

When Mazda workers, black or white, went to their UAW representatives with complaints about Japanese trainers, the plant's excessive overtime demands, or other problems, their grievances rarely prompted decisive action. Bob Ramp's confrontation with abusive Japanese trainers in the body shop notwithstanding, the six UAW

representatives at Flat Rock, including union local president Bill Judson, maintained a low profile. Modeling itself on the cooperative company union that Judson had seen at Hofu, the Flat Rock UAW local worked hard to preserve what the union called a "nonadversarial relationship" with Mazda. In the past, when a worker at a Big Three plant went to a union representative with a complaint, the rep never hesitated to carry the battle directly to management. But, as Flat Rock's union representatives were quick to point out, that kind of confrontationalism had only got the UAW and the American automakers into trouble. It had also given the union a reputation for militancy that was keeping it out of the new Japanese plants in America. At Flat Rock, confrontation would be replaced by quiet diplomacy—the union would work together with Mazda to settle differences calmly, without relying on strikes, shrill arguments, or the filling of formal grievances. As Judson had observed: "It's a lot easier for everyone to come to work in the morning if they know they're not going to get into four or five arguments with management . . . and the end result is that you get things resolved a lot more quickly."[15]

In the spirit of working together, UAW representatives shared an office with American and Japanese members of the plant's labor relations department. Members of management, the labor relations staffers represent the company in contract negotiations and in worker grievance procedures. This role puts them inherently at odds with a plant's union representatives, whose job is to represent workers in the same negotiations and grievance filings. The relationship between the two is, in many ways, similar to that of a prosecutor and defense attorney. At a traditional auto plant, having representatives of the union and labor relations department share an office would be as inconceivable as putting the public defender and district attorney together in the same quarters. But the UAW and Mazda reasoned that by closely coordinating the activities of union and labor relations representatives, they could respond faster to problems on the shop floor and maintain a more harmonious environment in the plant. The UAW representatives and company labor relations staffers made rounds of the plant together, checking on potential problems and talking to workers as a de facto "labor team." Early in Flat Rock's start-up phase, many of the younger workers, who had never been employed in an industrial plant before, made no distinction between the plant's UAW representatives and its labor relations people. As far as they were concerned, both wore Mazda uniforms, and both were always walking through the plant together to deal with

"labor issues." Some of the older, more experienced workers were disturbed by this closeness. "It was very hard to get a UAW guy by himself," Forrest Green recalled of the plant's first year. "They would always come around in twos—the union rep and the labor rep. This made the UAW guy very careful and inhibited about what he said." Desiring to maintain harmony in the plant above all else, UAW representatives always counseled workers against filing formal grievances. Not surprisingly, this advice was enthusiastically supported by the labor relations representative, who usually was present during the discussion. This kept the grievance rate at the plant close to zero—but it led to a loss of face for the union. "Whenever someone complained to a [union] rep about anything, we got the same answer—'That's a matter of management discretion, but don't worry, we'll talk to the company and take care of it,' " recalled Wayne Dodd, the former Burger King worker from Flint. "Then nothing would get done about it at all. Pretty soon we started saying, 'If everything here is management discretion and the union can't do anything about it, what do we need a union for?' "

More and more during the plant's first year, workers came to dismiss the union as an ineffectual relic, something carried over from the past as window dressing to appease the local politicians and Mazda's partners at Ford, both of whom still had to worry about maintaining peace with the UAW. The workers signed their union cards and voted for the UAW to be their exclusive bargaining representative in September 1987, because they knew that this was expected of them. (Prior to that time, the UAW, though not formally endorsed by the workers, had staffed the plant with a full contingent of representatives on an unofficial basis.) Mazda itself had shown its approval of the UAW by signing the letter of intent with the union before the plant was even built and the first worker hired. But as far as daily work life in the plant was concerned, the UAW was, in the view of many workers, merely a spectator. The contract the UAW signed with Mazda gave the union very little power, and although Mazda talked about forming joint committees with the union to deal with training, safety, and other issues, most of the committees never got off the ground. Those that were formed basically did nothing. It would be, as Judy Wilson later observed, "like we don't have a union at this plant."

Not surprisingly, workers at Flat Rock were more prone to air their grievances at team meetings and diagonal slice meetings than at the Sunday union meetings. To most workers the union meetings seemed like a waste of time. The UAW representatives there were often

more interested in repeating management's message about the need for teamwork and cooperation than they were in hearing what the workers had to say. It was almost as if they were a junior branch of management, thought Phil Keeling. At Keeling's first union meeting, local president Judson gave the workers a speech about the need to reduce absenteeism at the plant. What kind of union is this, wondered Keeling, where the top man gets up and talks about attendance? We aren't paying union dues so we can hear someone repeat the same speeches that management gives us. They got it backwards—the union is supposed to be representing our interests, not management's.

With few exceptions, Flat Rock workers did not identify with the plant's UAW representatives. Plant manager Denny Pawley, not Local 3000 president Judson, was the person most workers would rather have gone to with a problem. Judson's quiet personality was in keeping with the low profile the union maintained at Flat Rock. In 1987 Judson was 53, an age when some men, like Pawley, still maintain an attitude and appearance that makes it easy for them to cross generational lines and establish a rapport with those 20 or 30 years younger. But Judson, with his close-cropped white hair, seemed grounded in a different era. He had a difficult time relating to the young communicators that Mazda had hired. He did not mingle easily with workers in the common cafeteria. He did not go around telling entertaining stories like Pawley. On most days he ate his lunch quietly with a few associates from the labor relations department.

Judson and the plant's other UAW representatives had been appointed to their positions by the union's regional office. The workers were told that they would be given a chance to elect their own union local president and representatives at an unspecified date in 1989. Few seemed to care. The election would, they believed, be a mere formality, with Judson and the other incumbents, backed by Solidarity House, running against token opposition put up by one or two gadflies. Besides, most workers did not think it was important who ran the local union; whoever it was, he or she would not have much influence on the way things were done at Flat Rock.

8
Exit Interviews

MAZDA workers heard a startling announcement at their morning team meetings on Wednesday, February 17, 1988—Denny Pawley, the highest-ranking American at Flat Rock, was leaving. Pawley, the crusty veteran whose can-do spirit had given courage to young workers during the production start-up the previous fall, was resigning, the workers were told, to take a job with United Technologies' Otis Elevator division in Farmington, Connecticut. The unit leaders who broke the news to workers made a point of saying that Pawley had not been job hunting. He had simply received an offer from Otis that was too good to turn down. He was not, the leaders emphasized, bailing out because he was unhappy with the Mazda team system.

Despite the assurances of their leaders, the workers were apprehensive. Like passengers on an airplane told by a voice on the intercom to fasten their seat belts because the flight might get a little bumpy when they go through a storm front that's a few miles ahead, the workers could not help feeling suddenly vulnerable, even as they were told everything was all right. How could Denny, the Denny of the orientation sessions, the Denny who gave those wonderful speeches about how this was going to be the best job they ever had, the Denny who had told them how they were going to look forward to coming to work every morning, be leaving Mazda? What could be so attractive about a job building elevators for an old East Coast company that would make it preferable to staying here and implementing Mazda's team system at a brand new auto plant? True, there

had been some problems during the plant's trial-build and start-up phases—that was no secret. But Denny, more than anyone else, had always counseled patience—there may be some rough edges now, but things will get better once the bugs are worked out, he would say. He had even made the learning process seem like a giant adventure. "The next two or three years around here are going to be wild," he had told *Automotive News* only a few weeks earlier.[1] Now Denny was leaving, and the workers wondered if he knew something about Mazda that they did not. Was his departure really a career move, as the unit leaders insisted, or was it a sign that the Mazda system had problems that went beyond a few start-up glitches?

The workers in Peter Barrow's engine unit debated this question among themselves. "Our main concern was why he left—was it money or something else," recalled Barrow. Most of the workers decided that it had to be the money. There were rumors going around the plant that Pawley had increased his income threefold by going to Otis.

In the paint shop Phil Keeling took a more cynical view of Pawley's departure. Pawley was only one of several high-ranking American managers to have left the company suddenly. Several area leaders and administrators had preceded Pawley out of the plant. To Keeling these Americans were using Mazda as a springboard to advance their careers—a place where they could stop off and learn the "secrets" of Japanese management and then go on to sell their newly acquired expertise to an American company for a handsome price.

But Pawley did not quit for money. He left Mazda because he had become frustrated with the constraints that the company's Japanese management had placed on him. After two years and one month with Mazda, it had become obvious to the burly, high-spirited car man, who had once impaled a Pontiac to keep his line moving, that because he was an American he would never be given real authority at Flat Rock.[2] He had, he believed, worked patiently with the Japanese to learn their system, in the belief that one day he would be combining this knowledge with the experience he brought with him from General Motors to create the "third-culture plant" that Mazda's executives had so often talked about. But, as he would later observe, "It started looking more and more to me [like] the real decision making would always come out of Hiroshima, and [this] just didn't offer me the opportunity to use my broad-based management experience."

Pawley was certain that his power at Flat Rock would always be limited to implementing specific directives, making sure that orders from the Japanese were carried out. Like every American manager,

Pawley had a Japanese advisor, whose duties at the plant overlapped his own. Not to be confused with the Japanese trainers, who were sent to Flat Rock for relatively short periods to instruct workers in the operation of equipment and other specific job skills, advisors remained at the plant longer—and, rather than merely instructing American managers, they assumed a dominant (often behind-the-scenes) role in running the plant. An advisor's authority over his American opposite number was complete and unquestioned. He set the American's agenda for the day and had to be consulted before even the most trivial decisions were made. In the summer of 1988, when a record-breaking heat wave pushed temperatures in the plant past one hundred degrees, a UAW representative walked into the office of one of Flat Rock's top American managers to demand that the company suspend its rule banning drinks from the shop floor so cold water could be brought out to the workers. The union official was shocked when the manager, who seemed genuinely sympathetic to the workers' situation, said that he would have to check with his Japanese advisor. My God, thought the union man. It's an oven in that plant, and this guy can't even get some water out there without asking the Japanese.

As part of his job as vice president of manufacturing, Pawley was supposed to review production and planning reports that came to Flat Rock from Hiroshima. Since these reports were written only in Japanese, Pawley had to depend on his advisor to tell him what was in them. This system was, Pawley realized, yet another way for the Japanese to limit his involvement in the management of the plant.

More and more often during his last year at Flat Rock, Pawley had begun to feel stifled and demeaned by having to work in the constant shadow of his Japanese advisor. "You more or less lived your day with your advisor," he recalled. "You would spend time in the morning talking about plans for the day, but it's almost like building a grocery list—here's what you [the Americans] have to go check and look at. Then we'd come back and discuss what we found and reach consensus about any actions we're going to take."

The Japanese, Pawley discovered, were not willing to give American managers a real voice in the consensus process. When an American made a suggestion, the Japanese would, he recalled, "sit there and smile and say yes, yes, yes—but nothing got changed." Of the *kaizen* changes implemented by the Flat Rock plant's upper management, Pawley would say: "Probably ninety percent of it is done by experienced Japanese."

The extensive network of Japanese advisors at Flat Rock created "two different [management] organizations" at the plant, according to Pawley. One organization—the Japanese advisors—held all the power and made all the decisions, and the other—the American managers—served as a conduit, communicating those orders to the plant's American workers. Pawley described how this system worked: "[Takashi] Itoh was my advisor, and I was the top American. Itoh had his crew of Japanese advisors working for him; he would communicate with them, then I would take what he communicated to me and I'd go to the American work force and say, 'Okay, this is what's going to happen.' "

In every department, the Japanese preferred to remain in the background and have their orders flow through American managers. They also liked to use the Americans as go-betweens when dealing with the media and local (American-owned) supplier firms. For example, in the purchasing department, said Pawley, "you have an American buyer, and you also have a Japanese head of the department in an 'advisory' capacity. The communication goes between the Americans at Mazda and the local supplier, but the true decisions are being made by the Japanese. . . . The suppliers sense that Americans don't have decision-making in their hands. Some people will adapt to that and live well within the system, and others won't. I've read articles to the effect that when Japanese come into America with their companies, they don't end up with all-stars. What they end up with is not the most aggressive American. They end up with good, hard, solid working Americans who will be more or less content to do what the Japanese say and be implementers."

An independent, shoot-from-the-hip manager for most of his career, Pawley found it impossible to remain at a plant where he would be permanently consigned to a supporting role. A former associate of Pawley's from General Motors who had left GM to become an executive with Otis Elevator had been after him to join the Connecticut company since the early 1980s. Once Pawley realized that he was destined for "a very stagnant career" if he remained at Flat Rock, he took his friend up on the Otis offer.

Before he announced his resignation, Pawley met with a group of Mazda's Japanese managers. The Japanese tried to convince him to remain at Flat Rock. "They obviously didn't want me to leave," he later said, since the company understandably feared the negative

publicity the departure of its top American executive was certain to create. But Pawley was unyielding. He had, as he would explain it, "tried extremely hard to understand Japanese ways," but as hard as he tried and as much as he understood, he could not become Japanese—and if one was not Japanese, one would never be admitted into the inner circle of power at Flat Rock. During his final meeting at the plant, Pawley gave the Japanese some advice on how to treat his as-yet-unnamed successor: "I shared with them [the] thought that they were going to have to let go more if they wanted to get a good broad-based American to stay; they'd have to share more responsibility with him."

Back in the fall of 1987, Pawley had been confident that the Japanese would make good on their promise to turn control of the Flat Rock plant over to American managers. Everyone at the plant expected it, he told the local media—besides, it was the only smart business decision for Mazda to make. Six months later he still maintained that allowing Americans to run the plant would be the wisest course of action, but he was convinced that Mazda would never entrust this responsibility to anyone who was not Japanese. When someone suggested that Flat Rock might one day have an American president, Pawley, by then with Otis, responded: "That job will always be a Japanese job—I'll be you every dollar I'm going to make the rest of my life on that." Pawley also believed that the two executive vice presidents at the plant would always be Japanese, and that every American manager would always have a Japanese advisor looking over his or her shoulder. "I think the Japanese will deny that, but look back [at the plant] in five years, and my guess is you'll still see advisors," he said in 1988. One thing that Pawley believes will prevent the transference of authority to Americans is the need to maintain close communication between Flat Rock and Hiroshima. "You almost have to have a Japanese head [at MMUC] just for communication," he explained. "I don't believe they would ever entrust that to an American. You can live with the Japanese and think you understand the Japanese and try to operate as you think the Japanese want you to operate—but unless you're Japanese you will never understand the Japanese."

Despite his problems with Mazda, Pawley would later insist that he left the company on amicable terms. He described his time at Flat Rock as "the two most rewarding years" of his career, observing: "I learned a great, great deal from the Japanese—I'll be forever thankful." He remained in touch with his former advisor after he left Mazda, calling Itoh "the brightest automobile man I ever met." He

had developed an unusually warm relationship with Itoh at Flat Rock, his resentment over the Japanese advisor system notwithstanding. The two men visited each other's homes and shared many long talks about car building. Pawley was especially impressed with his advisor's broad view of the automobile business. "Normally at GM you have a Roger Smith who makes all decisions from a financial standpoint, or an engineer who makes decisions from an engineering standpoint," said Pawley. "Mister Itoh—although he's an engineer—because of what he's learned and the teamwork he's utilized at Mazda in twenty-five years—has such a vast command and understanding of everything it takes to build an automobile. He's a manufacturing man who builds the car, but he's just so thoroughly understanding of everything else happening around him."

Pawley, who would later return to the automobile industry, taking a managerial position with Chrysler, also retained his admiration for Mazda's management system. The company was, he believed, vastly more efficient and better managed than any of the American automakers. After spending 21 years with General Motors, Pawley regretted to say that there was nothing in his experience that he could point to as an example of something GM did better than Mazda. Neither GM nor the other two members of the Big Three would, he believed, have been able to match Mazda's feat of building a major plant and having it up and running and producing two distinct products (the Probe and MX-6), in under two years. The key to the success of Mazda and other Japanese automakers was, thought Pawley, their absolute, "almost fanatical" commitment to planning. Every decision at Mazda was analyzed in minute detail before it was put into action on the shop floor. Pawley was certain that American automakers would be "a lot more competitive with the Japanese" if they followed the PDCA cycle, but he feared that the self-centeredness of American managers would always make true team planning impossible. "The Japanese spend a tremendous amount of time going into great detail [over] how they're going to do anything—I don't care if it's moving a box from one corner to another," he said. "Then, when the plan is done, that thing gets implemented. The plan isn't changed by emotion. . . . Nothing gets changed without data, so there's no guesses. American companies don't do that. In an American plant, you have political power plays—'I gotta look better than that guy, so my decision's gotta win.' In the Japanese system, it's a win-win type of situation—the individual isn't important. There's room for individualism in a Japanese company, but not if it comes at

the expense of the good of [the team]. Americans get their person-
alities tangled up into it. . . ."

The unit leaders who announced Pawley's departure on that cold
February morning had thus, in a sense, been correct. The highest-
ranking American at the plant was not leaving because he had lost
faith in the Mazda system. Pawley still believed in the team concept.
He could not, however, accept being a permanent bench player sim-
ply because he was not Japanese.

As for the workers who had debated the meaning of his resigna-
tion, Pawley believed that they would fare well at Flat Rock. They
were given at least some voice in running their work stations, some-
thing that had been denied to them at most Big Three plants, and
Mazda seemed to treat them with more respect than workers at
American companies. "In fact," said Pawley, "the hourly people [at
Flat Rock] might be happier than at any other plant. It's the higher
up you go in the organization [that] probably the discontent will
grow over time." James V. Higgins, the automotive writer for the
Detroit News, echoed this view in a March 1988 column about the
relationship between Japanese automakers—not only Mazda—and
their American managers. "Had you asked which auto industry job
is the toughest, the traditional answer would be the hourly assembler
forced to do endless repetitions of a boring job," wrote Higgins. "But
middle management in Japanese plants gets my vote today."[3]

Like Flat Rock, the other plants in the United States that were
wholly or partially owned by Japanese automakers in 1989 were
headed by Japanese nationals. The sole exception was Nissan's
Smyrna, Tennessee, plant, which had an American president, Jerry L.
Benefield, a former Ford executive. But the American parent com-
pany of the Smyrna plant, Nissan Motor Corp. USA, is headed by a
Japanese president, Katzutoshi Hagiwara. When filling middle- and
upper-level management positions, the Japanese often preferred to
hire Americans with nonautomotive backgrounds. Pawley estimated
that eight out of ten unit leaders at Flat rock were not only new to the
auto industry, but were just out of college with no job experience at
all when they were hired by Mazda. Scott Whitlock, the highest-
ranking American at Honda-Marysville, was an attorney with no
manufacturing experience when he was appointed senior vice presi-
dent and manager of the Ohio plant. Pawley suspected that the Jap-
anese hired inexperienced managers because they believed that these
Americans, not having manufacturing backgrounds, would be more
willing to sit on the sidelines and learn, and would not expect to

assume an active role in running the plant for several years. At the very worst, from the Japanese point of view, these novices would take longer than experienced managers like Pawley to become restless with their lack of authority.

The problems encountered by Pawley were shared by other American managers at Japanese companies, not only in automotives but in industries ranging from banking to home appliances. In contrast to most other multinational corporations, including those based in the United States, Japanese companies have rarely been willing to assign control of their foreign subsidiaries to local managers. American managers at Japanese plants and offices in the United States have frequently complained of being cut off from the decision-making process and being relegated to the role of passive bystanders. Many claim that they have been kept on at their companies largely for the sake of appearances. Others say they have often been patronized by their Japanese colleagues. A September 1988 article in *Business Month* magazine, entitled "A Matter of Control," painted a grim picture of the American manager's life at a Japanese firm: "There are now an estimated 25,000 American managers working for Japanese companies in the United States, and by and large they seem to be an unhappy and demoralized lot. The Japanese need American experts to sell their products in the United States and are willing to pay top salaries to get them. But in company after company, the Americans complain about a system of subtle and debilitating discrimination in which they are treated as necessary but inferior outsiders—without the authority to get things done and lacking upward mobility."[4]

A growing number of American managers have taken legal action against their Japanese employers over alleged discrimination. Edward Neubauer, once the highest-ranking American at NEC Electronics, the California subsidiary of Tokyo-based NEC Corporation, sued the company for $18 million in 1987, alleging that NEC had broken its promise to give him broad authority to run its American unit. Neubauer joined NEC in 1981 and had used his contacts in the American semiconductor industry to help the company establish its sales and marketing organization. Having successfully completed this task, Neubauer expected his authority to be increased but instead found his power usurped by new managers sent to the company from Japan over his objections. Neubauer would contend that he was frozen out of a position of authority at NEC because he was not Japanese.

Other Americans have claimed that their Japanese employers apply a double standard to protecting the job security of Japanese and

American employees. The commitment of Japanese companies in Japan to offering workers "lifetime employment" is well known. Japanese companies have gone to great lengths to preserve the jobs of their employees during market downturns or corporate restructurings, making huge cuts in executive salaries, eliminating stock dividends, and investing heavily in programs to retrain displaced workers. Mazda itself provided a heroic example of this lifetime employment commitment when it avoided laying off a single worker during its painful crisis following the Wankel engine disaster. Most Japanese firms, including Mazda, have intimated that they would be continuing the tradition of lifetime employment in the United States. Few, if any, have made concrete commitments to this effect. On the contrary, when American subsidiaries run into trouble or the marketing plans of the Japanese parent change, American employees are often let go while Japanese employees are transferred to new jobs either in Japan or the United States. In 1983 Toshiba decided to pull out of the calculator business. James Ristow, the head of the company's United States calculator operations, was instructed to dismiss the division's 41 American employees. Meanwhile, the division's Japanese employees were transferred to other Toshiba divisions. Ristow, a 14-year Toshiba veteran, was himself let go after he finished dismantling the calculator office. He brought a $1.6 million discrimination suit against the company but lost the case. "Americans feel that they are a vital part of the company, but when push comes to shove, they will not be figured into the equation," he complained.[5]

Mazda Motor of America, the automaker's sales subsidiary in the United States (a separate corporate entity from MMUC, the company's manufacturing subsidiary and the operator of the Flat Rock plant), also has laid off Americans, despite the company's widely publicized tradition (in Japan) of providing lifetime employment. In 1988 the Mazda sales subsidiary consolidated its eastern and western offices into a single national unit, laying off 70 American employees at its former East Coast headquarters in Jacksonville, Florida. Asked why the Jacksonville employees were being let go instead of reassigned to new jobs as Mazda's Japanese employees had been during the Wankel crisis, Yoshinori Taura, the president of Mazda Motor of America, could only say: "We feel very, very sorry for them, but we'll give them the best (separation) offer we can."[6]

For their part the Japanese have not been happy with the performance of their American managers. Products of a culture in which an executive is likely to spend his entire career with a single corporation,

the Japanese are put off by the tendency of American managers to jump from company to company in pursuit of better positions and bigger salaries. The Japanese often regard the job-hopping Americans as mercenaries who, because they have no real loyalty to the company, can never be fully trusted. To the Japanese the frequent job changes of Americans make the entire concept of lifetime employment meaningless. Why make the sacrifices necessary to preserve the job of an American during a crisis when chances are he will be leaving the company anyway in a few years? The Japanese also have been annoyed by the more casual work ethic of their American managers. Americans who balk at remaining at the office after five to wait for an important phone call, or refuse to come to the plant on weekends to work on a rush project, have increased the resolve of the work-driven Japanese not to turn over control of their American subsidiaries to local managers. "The American worker has been a pleasant surprise, but American managers do not work as hard as we thought," a Mazda dispatch complained to a visitor in 1988.

Unlike Denny Pawley, Jerry Healy did not have his departure from Mazda announced at team meetings throughout the plant. Healy, the Grand Rapids skilled trades worker who became a maintenance team leader at Flat Rock, left Mazda quietly on September 1, 1988, the day the plant celebrated the first anniversary of its official production start-up, and a little more than two years after his trip to Japan as one of Mazda's four hundred original American hirees.

Before he quit, Healy, like the growing number of other American workers who were leaving Mazda, had an "exit interview" with a representative from the company's labor relations department. Officially Mazda reported that seven out of every hundred workers at Flat rock were quitting, a turnover rate 40 percent higher than the company's original projection.[7] But in reality, many workers believed that the turnover problem was much worse, especially in physically demanding areas of the plant like the body shop. To learn why the plant's turnover rate was so high, Mazda began interviewing employees who quit. The labor relations representatives never tried to convince departing employees to stay with Mazda during an exit interview—theirs was purely a fact-finding mission. Why did you decide to leave Mazda? What were the things you liked about working here? What didn't you like? Is there anything that we could do differently to make this a better place to work?

Healy, a quiet and intense man, answered the interviewer's questions as honestly as he could. The main reason he was leaving, he told them, was not money, though he would be earning more at his new job with an American manufacturer. Nor was it the hours, even though his new employer did not require him to work the second shift, as Mazda sometimes did. He was leaving, he explained, because his job as a team leader at Flat Rock had "basically changed from what it was originally intended to be." When he started working for Mazda, Healy thought that as a team leader he would be coordinating the schedules of the workers on his team, assisting in the design of jobs, overseeing the team's supply of tools and spare parts, and rotating the members of his team into different job assignments. He assumed that as a *leader* he would be given the power and the responsibilities of a supervisor. For a brief period, this had in fact been the case. But over the course of his two years at the plant, Healy saw supervisory power steadily taken away from team leaders—who, like the workers under them, were hourly employees and members of the UAW—and placed in the hands of salaried (nonunion) unit leaders. Early in the plant's history, there were only four unit leaders for the entire maintenance department— two on the day shift and two on the afternoon shift. Most of the day-to-day supervision of teams was assigned to team leaders. But the legitimacy of the team leader's authority was never clearly established by Mazda. Charged with the responsibility of "running" the team and ensuring that it meets its production schedule, the team leader was given no authority to wield when carrying out that responsibility. Team leaders could not discipline workers by issuing written reprimands—this could only be done by unit leaders and other salaried managers. Nor did they have any discretionary power that could be used to back up their orders. Unlike unit leaders, for example, they did not have the power to accept or reject a worker's excuse for being late or absent. It was, recalled Healy, "a classic stress-type situation— being responsible for stuff, but not having authority to do [anything about] it."

Workers often balked at following orders from a team leader, saying, in effect, "You're just a union member like me, you can't tell me what to do." They were usually correct. The team leader who was confronted by a recalcitrant worker would have to summon a unit leader to enforce his or her authority. During break periods at Flat Rock, some teams are required to leave a worker behind to watch over the line. (These workers are then given a break at a later time.) When one team leader in the paint shop told a worker on her team

that it was his turn to remain behind, the man refused, saying he had an important phone call to make. The team leader repeated the order, but the man made an obscene gesture and continued walking toward the phones. Unable to take any disciplinary action against the worker himself, the team leader had to call in a unit leader from the break area to order the worker back to the line. This not only conveyed an image of weakness to other workers, it also created the impression that the team leader was simply a tool of upper management. Workers like Peter Barrow sympathized with the predicament of Healy and other team leaders. "Team leaders get yelled at if they don't get us to do what they say, but then we don't have to do what they say," the engine line worker observed in 1988. "Right now a lot of people won't touch the team leader job for nothing—because of the hassle, the pressure. You get it from both sides."

Many team leaders became demoralized as a result of their lack of authority and made only half-hearted efforts to supervise other workers. This made it necessary for Mazda to increase the role of unit leaders on the shop floor. By the time Healy left Flat Rock, the number of maintenance unit leaders at the plant had grown from 4 to 20.[8] "Once we got all these extra unit leaders," they became more involved in team meetings and started to take over a lot of scheduling stuff," he recalled. "That was a sore spot with me. One case in particular that upset me was when we [the team] got everything set up and figured out what we were going to do to implement this new manpower alignment. Then our unit leader comes in and says, 'Hey, we're moving these people to these other jobs.' By that time I was really fed up with it. I'd already been out on a couple of job interviews. Basically, I was back to being Joe Blow maintenance man. They took all of the supervisory things away." Unit leaders had assumed such a high profile on the shop floor by the fall of 1988 that they had completely taken over the running of team meetings. By then, the meetings could more accurately be described as "unit meetings," since they were attended by the members of several different teams. Workers no longer talked of belonging to a team of six to ten workers; instead they said they belonged to a unit of 20 to 30 workers, headed not by a fellow worker called a team leader, but by a management representative called a unit leader, who was assisted by two or three team leaders. The bigger meetings were less personal, they provided each individual worker with less of an opportunity to contribute to discussions, and, of course, they were now under the direct control of management.

Even as they were being supplanted by unit leaders, team leaders were still held responsible for the performance of their teams. The frustration inherent in this situation prompted some team leaders like Healy to resign; it led others to snap and lash out at workers, whom they often blamed for causing their role at the plant to be reduced. Soon after Flat Rock's production start-up in the fall of 1987, a team leader and a worker from a neighboring team got into a fistfight in the paint department. The worker had regularly helped himself to the work gloves that the leader had set aside for his own team. The team leader, who was held responsible for keeping his team supplied with tools and safety equipment, ordered the worker to stop poaching from the team's glove bin. Knowing that the team leader had no authority over him, the worker continued to help himself to gloves, which eventually led to the fight. Both men could have been fired immediately, but Mazda gave them a second chance, under the condition that they speak to teams throughout the plant about their fight and explain how it could have been avoided had they followed the non-confrontational problem-solving techniques that they had learned during their Mazda orientation.

Healy could sympathize with the workers who had given him and other team leaders such a hard time and indirectly contributed to their decline. The workers too were frustrated. Like the team leaders, and like Denny Pawley himself, they had not been given the authority that they had expected to receive at Flat Rock. Despite Mazda's orientation promise to involve workers in management decisions, team members were given no real voice in running the Flat Rock plant. Team members had expected to design their own jobs, but the programmed worksheets, which rigidly spelled out each step of every job, had already been written by Mazda engineers before the workers were even hired. Team members also believed that they would be consulted about the purchasing and positioning of tools and production equipment, but everything in the plant was already in place when most workers got there. The voice of workers was so weak that some skilled trades workers had to wait three weeks for management to respond to their request for screwdrivers. Workers in the trim and final assembly area were unable even to get a larger paper cup dispenser for their water cooler to keep it from running out of cups in the summer.

It was virtually impossible for team members to effect changes in the workplace, because—as Forrest Green and the other tool and die makers discovered when they wanted to repeal the helmet rule—not

even trivial changes could be made in the plant without being supported by exhaustively documented studies. Even then, a worker's proposal would still have to be approved at consensus meetings, first by American managers and then by their Japanese advisors, either of whom could reject it without explanation. Not surprisingly, few team members had the time or energy to undertake such speculative studies in 1988, once the plant started to produce cars full-time and they began working 60-hour weeks.

"Consensus makes it too hard to get things done," Healy would say two months after he left Mazda. "You've have to go through a lot of stuff to change something—more than in an American company. Now [at an American company], if I see something I don't think is working, I got the authority to change it." Workers became frustrated with Mazda's consensus process, according to Healy, because the Japanese refused to share power with Americans. "They try to put Americans in these positions to make it look like an American company, but it's not," he said of Flat Rock's Japanese managers. "If you see something you want to do, you got to have a meeting and get ten other people to clear it. The person who [ultimately] had to clear it was always Japanese. We'd have a meeting with Americans and Japanese attending—an American process engineer would suggest something, but the Japanese would have to approve. . . . The Japanese were flexible, sometimes. They would listen, sometimes."

An incident that occurred shortly before Healy left Mazda convinced him that, as an American, he could never expect to be given real authority at Flat Rock. Healy, who was interested in moving from a team leader to a unit leader position, had a meeting with a maintenance area leader to discuss the possibility of a promotion. The area leader said that he would like to promise Healy a promotion then and there, but he could not without consulting with his advisor who happened to be back in Japan attending a funeral. If Healy would wait until the advisor returned, they would see what they could do about the promotion. At that point, however, Healy began to wonder whether a unit leader's position would not be even more frustrating than his job as a team leader. He recalled thinking, "If [the area leader] is the number two man in all of maintenance and he hasn't got the authority to [offer the promotion], what am I going to do as a unit leader." As other Americans at Flat Rock had been, Healy was struck by the unlikelihood of creating a cooperative team system based on trust and mutual respect at a plant where the ideas and opinions of Japanese automatically carried more weight than

those of Americans. Not long after his conversation with the area leader, he was gone.

Phil Keeling also became frustrated with Mazda's team system. Keeling, like other workers at Flat Rock, had looked forward to having some say in the way his job was run. This opportunity was not provided at team meetings. Rather than serving as a forum for worker ideas, the meetings provided management with a convenient means of communicating new orders and assignments to workers. "Flexibility" at Mazda was really a one-way street, believed Keeling—the company did not have to be flexible when it came to listening to the idea of workers, but workers had to be flexible about having their job assignments changed and workloads increased. "What Mazda tries to pass off as giving us more input is basically just a way to dump more work on our laps—and more responsibility," he said.

Although team meetings were rarely, if ever, used for their ostensible purpose—to solicit worker input into the decision-making process—they did play a necessary role in Mazda's management system. The company needed daily team meetings to coordinate the activities of workers. Because Mazda's management system was so flexible, with few American-style work rules, the company was constantly changing job assignments, work schedules, and team sizes. Unlike his or her opposite number at an American plant, who performed the same job every day, a Mazda worker might install steering wheels on Monday and then be sent to the engine line on Tuesday. Workers were informed of such changes at team meetings. Attendance was also taken at the meetings, and the job assignments of absent workers were divided among those who were present. For example, of the worker who installed shock absorbers on the rear wheels of vehicles was absent, his job might have to be shared by two teammates.

By having workers fill in for absent teammates, Mazda created a self-regulating attendance system at Flat Rock, which relies on peer pressure to discourage tardiness and absenteeism. At a traditional Big Three plant, with its pool of reserve workers to cover for absences, the worker who shows up late or skips work altogether to go hunting does not incur the wrath of his fellow workers—for, although he has broken the rules, he alone must pay for his transgression. To his fellow workers he is the other driver, pulled off to the side of the road for speeding. His problems are not theirs. This is not the case at Mazda. The speeding driver is not ticketed on the side of the road,

but in the middle, forcing all traffic to come to a halt. The transgression of one team member creates problems for all team members. When one worker is absent, his teammates will have to work that much harder to pick up the slack. (The bulk of this burden will fall on the shoulders of the team leader, who, having been trained in all of a team's jobs, is often the first called on to fill in for the absent worker.)

Mazda's team system also encourges workers to pressure one another to maintain a rapid work pace. A worker's teammates must pay the consequences if he is too slow or mistake prone, since this will disrupt the flow of work through the team's station. This, in turn, will make it difficult for the team to complete its collective job assignment on time and will increase the likelihood that everyone will have to put in overtime to meet their production quotas. Because of Mazda's carefully synchronized JIT production schedule, the team's problems will quickly have a ripple effect on the next team down the line, preventing it from completing its work on time. The members of this team will then complain to their unit leader, who will then pressure the slow worker's entire team to move faster.

The result of Mazda's self-regulating team system is a plant where everyone minds everyone else's business. The rationale is simple: If we must bear the consequences of your actions, we have the right to demand that your actions conform to our standards. "People are pretty understanding," said one worker. "But if someone is goofing off or misses a lot of work, things get a little bit testy. . . . There's some guilt here about missing work for any reason, because you know it's going to hurt other people."

Team meetings at Flat Rock normally last less than ten minutes—the coordination of assignments and work schedules seldom requires more time. The Wednesday meetings are the exception. They last close to 40 minutes. At the Wednesday meetings, management reviews attendance records, safety problems, and quality control issues. It also introduces new job assignments and procedures that are too complex to be covered in shorter meetings. Mazda also attempts to drum up support for its management directives at the Wednesday meetings by giving them the appearance of group consensus decisions. Unit leaders have gone through the motions of soliciting worker opinions, just to make workers feel that they are contributing to the final decision, which, in fact, has already been dictated to the leader by upper management. . . . Okay, team, we have a problem—we need to cut the time it takes to assemble tires. Any suggestions on

how we can inflate them faster? After hearing ideas from three or four team members, the leader would suggest that the group try to reach a consensus decision. Then, through some gentle prodding and pushing and subtle arm twisting, he or she would steer the group toward the plan that management had already devised, passing it off as the workers' own. This made the plan a "consensus decision" on the part of the team, so everyone was supposed to agree with it—just as everyone was supposed to have worn caps "voluntarily."

This was meant to create enthusiasm for management directives among workers, enthusiasm that Mazda knew was critical if the workers were to have the commitment required to meet the demands of the plant's JIT work pace. In reality, the effect was quite the opposite. Workers felt patronized and manipulated at Wednesday meetings. It was as if management believed that if it repeated the words *teamwork* and *consensus* often enough, it could co-opt workers even while it blatantly ignored its orientation promise to involve them in the decision-making process. When asked how Flat Rock's team system was working, UAW Region–1A director Ernie Lofton (who later became vice president of the union's Ford department) said: "Mazda ain't walking like it's talking." The workers' anger over their lack of input into consensus decisions was soon felt on the shop floor. Many workers became less committed to meeting their JIT production schedules. As a result cars left the body shop without bumpers, and tires and plastic components failed to reach the final assembly line on time. In 1988 one of four cars came off the Flat Rock assembly line with at least minor defects. The defect rate exceeded the company's projections by 60 percent. Throughout most of the year, more than two thousand new cars waited in the plant's parking lot to have their flaws corrected in the reprocessing shop.[9]

Bob Ramp, the UAW representative, believed that much of the problem stemmed from the inflated expectations the company created during its orientation program. "I think some of the things that were stressed [during orientation] were maybe not some of the points that should have been stressed," he said. "You know, like for instance, 'We're going to have input'—and we do have input. But if Nobuto wants to put a new rug in his office, he's not going to call us. And I think some of the thing might have been misconstrued. People thought communication, input et cetera—because it was focused on—would be a larger part of the job."

"Phil Keeling was less diplomatic. "Sometimes I wish Mazda would just order us around instead of playing all those mind games,"

he said. "Believe me, they boss you around every bit as much as GM does, but they dress it up by calling it consensus. . . . Most people would rather be told, 'All right, do this,' instead of having all that happy-neighbor-how-are-you-today string pulling."

In a sense Keeling would get his wish. As the plant struggled to overcome its high defect rate and meet the demand for the Ford Probe in mid-1988, unit leaders, who by then had taken over most of the team leaders' responsibilities, found it more expedient to dictate orders without going through the pretense of consensus. Now workers often were not even informed of changes in their job routines until they attended team meetings on the morning the change was to go into effect. For example, when workers in side frame section 248 of the body shop returned to the plant from their 1988 Christmas holiday, they were told that the size of their team had been cut from six to five members as a result of a management *kaizen* plan, about which they had known nothing. The *kaizen* plan called for the team to perform the same number of tasks it had performed before Christmas, even though it now had one less member. This increased the workload of all the remaining team members, but one member—a worker who welded small components to doors—bore most of the added burden. Instead of welding parts to one door, as he had been doing, the worker had to perform his job—albeit with some modifications—on both sides of the vehicle. The redesigned job turned out to be so grueling that members of the worker's team, acting of their own volition, decided to rotate it among themselves every two hours. On the surface this represented the type of team-spirit consensus that Mazda had preached during orientation. But the workers' unit leader objected to this deviation from the programmed work routine. When the workers argued with him, the unit leader relented and allowed them to continue with their self-imposed job rotation. He could just as easily have issued them written reprimands for not following instructions. It was a matter of his own discretion.

Unit leaders were responsible for seeing to it that directions from upper management were carried out on the shop floor. They received orders from area leaders or other American managers (who in turn had received them from Japanese advisors), and they relayed those orders to workers. How unit leaders went about implementing management's orders often was left up to them. If a new job was added to a team's programmed work routine, the unit leader decided who filled it. If a team was assigned off-line janitorial work, the unit leader decided how it would be done and by whom. Like a field

officer in battle, the unit leader was given broad latitude to carry out orders received from headquarters. In a sense this made unit leaders the most powerful Americans at Flat Rock, since, unlike higher American managers, they were not constantly shadowed by Japanese advisors. As members of management, unit leaders also had the authority to back up their responsibilities, something that had been denied to team leaders. Unit leaders had the power to issue workers written reprimands, which, because of the union's reluctance to file grievances, were virtually impossible to rescind.

More important, as far as workers were concerned, unit leaders were given broad discretion to interpret work rules and enforce discipline. According to Mazda's employee manual, written reprimands were to be issued to workers who were late or absent without an acceptable excuse. Unit leaders had unchecked, unilateral power to accept or reject any excuse, even a written doctor's note. There were no written standards or formal guidelines that defined what constituted a legitimate excuse, and no rule mandating that a unit leader be consistent in evaluating the excuses of workers. A unit leader could, for example, excuse the absence of a worker who claimed to have a cold while refusing to accept the same excuse from another worker on the same team. The unexcused worker would not only be issued a written reprimand, but he or she would receive no sick pay (60 percent of base wage) for the missed day. It was also up to the discretion of unit leaders to grant requests from workers to use the restrooms or make phone calls during nonbreak work time. In addition to their power to enforce work rules, unit leaders had the authority to assign jobs and control the rotation of job assignments. Wayne Dodd, the former fast food worker who started out at Flat Rock in September 1987 installing struts, was rotated into more than twenty different jobs over the next two years. This variety, according to Dodd, has kept his job more interesting and helped him escape injury by allowing him to do tasks that emphasize different muscles. But other trim and final workers Dodd knows, who started at the plant about the same time he did, have been locked into performing the same job or two very similar jobs since they began. The difference, said Dodd, is in unit leaders—his believes in cross-training and job rotation; theirs do not. "So much depends on who your unit leader is," he remarked. "If your unit leader doesn't want to give you job rotation, you aren't going to get it."

Like many workers, Dodd believes that the unchecked discretionary power of Mazda's unit leaders has encouraged the type of cro-

nyism at Flat Rock that was prevalent in American auto plants prior to their unionization in the 1930s and 1940s. Team members who hope to get choice job assignments or have an occasional absence excused learn quickly to ingratiate themselves with their unit leaders. One way they can do this is by going along with everything their unit leader proposes at team meeting. (Needless to say this has made it easier for leaders to lend at least the appearance of consensus decisions to their orders.) Workers can also curry favor with their unit leaders by spying on fellow team members, reporting to the leader about those who have been taking shortcuts with the programmed work routine and those who have been complaining about the increased line speed. "It encourages snitching—people telling on each other to get in good with their leader," a black worker from Detroit said of Mazda's team system. As a member of a minority group, this worker was especially sensitive to the lack of protection offered workers against potentially biased unit leaders. "If a leader doesn't like you because you're black—or for any reason—he can cause you big problems. . . . There's a lot of cases where people have been late so many times and nobody writes them up. Then someone else is late once, and bam—they write him up." According to this worker and others at the plant, unit leaders have sometimes refused to accept written doctor's notes as excuses for the absence of workers who, for one reason or another, had fallen out of their favor. These workers were issued reprimands, and doctor's notes or not, there was nothing they could do to overturn their unit leaders' decisions.

Workers who do not actively seek to get on the good side of unit leaders have often come to regard them as objects of scorn. The unit leaders are, after all, the ones who pressure workers to keep up with the JIT work pace, who dictate new *kaizen* plans, who cut off worker input at team meetings, who play favorites when enforcing work rules. During Flat Rock's first full year of production, workers were more likely to blame the plant's problems on unit leaders than on upper management or Japanese advisors. One worker quoted in the *Detroit Free Press* on the first anniversary of Mazda's production start-up said: "The upper management is maybe not aware of what is going on now. They want the concept to work, but it's getting lost in the translation as it goes down. That's why I say maybe the unit leaders and the area leaders need a refresher course."[10] Adding to the resentment of workers was the fact that unit leaders often were younger and even less experienced in factory work than the team members they supervised. "Our unit leader, like many others, is a

little younger," Phil Keeling said in the fall of 1988. "He didn't come through a union shop. They look for these kinds of young, enthusiastic, rah-rah people for unit leaders. Experience does not count, thank you. Our unit leader, we had little trouble with him—he's not used to work rules and safety. He has a general lack of knowledge about electricity, but I think he's beginning to come around a little bit."

Yet some workers acknowledge that the unit leaders are themselves under tremendous pressure from Mazda's upper management. Unit leaders are directly responsible for having their units meet the demands of Flat Rock's JIT production schedule. Because the demands of this schedule are so rigorous and the number of workers available in each unit is relatively low, unit leaders have sometimes felt compelled to circumvent standard safety and quality control procedures, ordering workers to operate faulty equipment and not allowing adequate time for final safety inspections of repaired machinery. "People who were gung ho and would try to do everything the right way by the book were looked down on," said Peter Barrow. "My one unit leader tried to do everything the right way, and he got yelled at more than anyone else. If you do everything the proper way, things go slower—so now this guy's attitude is shot." There is also pressure for unit leaders to make sure the workers in their unit conform to Mazda's code of team spirit. Ostensibly voluntary activities like morning exercises were taken by upper management as litmus tests of a unit leader's leadership qualities—if the workers in your unit really respect you, they will want to exercise. Understandably, this has led some unit leaders to try to push workers into participating in voluntary activities, prompting a backlash from workers, who have viewed this as a violation of their privacy.

Not surprisingly, the way a unit leader goes about exercising his or her discretionary power has a lot to do with the way the workers in a unit view their jobs. In many instances workers in the same shop have been held to different disciplinary standards and received widely varying degrees of cross-training and job rotation, simply because they had different unit leaders. Greg Drudi, a mechanical skilled trades worker at Flat Rock, got to see many different areas of the plant as a result of his job repairing equipment and his activities as a union coordinator—a worker who serves as a liaison between other workers and the plant's official UAW representatives. A tough, wiry little man with a shrewd intelligence, Drudi described Flat Rock as "being like 50 different plants inside, because so much depends on

the unit leader." If a unit leader happened to be in a good mood, or had taken a liking to a worker, said Drudi, the worker "got the benefit of his discretion." But if a unit leader was a tough disciplinarian or regarded a worker as outspoken or militant, the worker received what Drudi called "the other side of the rag."

Drudi was 36 when he was hired by Mazda in 1987. A pipefitter by trade, he had spent most of his adult life working at construction sites in Florida and Michigan. He had come to Flat Rock "ready to buy into the Mazda philosophy," but because he was more seasoned than the plant's younger hirees, he had tempered his enthusiasm from the start. He saw the potential for abuse in a management system that took all the work rules that protected workers and replaced them with vague understandings that gave unchecked discretionary power to supervisors. Workers at Flat Rock would, he knew, be at the mercy of management unless their union was aggressive in protecting their rights. After a year at Flat Rock, Drudi had lost his faith in Mazda's orientation promises. The plant portrayed in the orientation center, with its open communication, worker input, and mutual trust and respect, was, he said, "the magic kingdom," a pure fantasyland that had nothing to do with the real plant he and three thousand other Americans went to work at every day. In reality Flat Rock was just another version of a General Motors plant, except that its workers tended to work harder—and to have fewer rights. "Let's face it—it's a place of work," Drudi would say of the plant in early 1989. "The candy-coated, pastel painting that they [gave] you during orientation built up a lot of false beliefs. . . . A lot of the younger people at the plant have gotten real disillusioned. It's like when you found out there was no Santa Claus. . . . What, you mean there's no Santa Claus? What, you mean there's no Mazda philosophy?"

Drudi hoped to change things at the plant by working through Mazda's union local. He became active in the local and attended union meetings every Sunday, taking detailed notes of the proceedings each time. It did not take long, however, for Drudi to become dismayed by the union's passivity at Flat Rock. He appreciated that this was supposed to be a team plant, one characterized by a new level of trust and cooperation between labor and management. And he certainly was not against the team system in principle: "The old traditional concept where you had to call a special guy in to mop up a puddle—maybe that didn't work so well either," he would later observe. But it was clear to Drudi that the union local had no intention of challenging the company, even in cases where Mazda was

obviously failing to live up to the spirit of its team plant philosophy. Whenever he or someone else at a union meeting voiced objections about the abuse of power by unit leaders, the lack of worker input into consensus decisions, or other problems, the union local's leaders gave the same vague, noncommittal answers. The union seemed to be doing all it could to avoid acting on worker complaints. "There's a fine line being walked," Drudi said of the union local. "It's close to nonrepresentation."

Drudi became a thorn in the side of the local's leadership. He argued with Local 3000 president Bill Judson and Region-1A director Ernie Lofton, who, though it was unusual for an official of his rank to do so, attended every Local 3000 meeting. Drudi, his finger jabbing the air for emphasis, would rattle off objections in a surprisingly powerful, somewhat nasal voice that increased in both pitch and volume as he became more excited. Why is the union in the same damn office as the company's labor relations reps? he would ask. Well, this is just something we thought we'd try to see if it works out. . . . When are we going to have elections for the plant's union reps? As soon as the local's bylaws are approved by the members. . . . When will this happen? As soon as the bylaws committee finishes writing them. . . . Drudi was becoming increasingly frustrated with the local. He was, in 1987–88, angrier with the union than with the company. Mazda had gone back on many of its orientation promises, but at least its actions were understandable. It was simply trying to maximize its profits at Flat Rock. But a union that refused to stand up for its members made no sense.

Forrest Green and the other workers on his tool- and die-making team were also frustrated with the union. They had complained to their union representative about a team leader who, they believed, was carrying out management's orders to aggressively. But the union rep, who rarely spoke to workers without his opposite number from the labor relations department present, had seemed to Green to be afraid to follow up on the complaint.

"We had a problem when area leaders and unit leaders wanted team members to . . . do some discipline—lean on a person if they were a little slow or didn't wear a helmet," said Green. "It put pressure on the team leader. . . . We called the union a number of times [about] different team leaders in our department, and we'd say, 'Hey, we don't think a team leader should be doing this. . . .' But [the

union] was in a very bad position. They tried [but] they were afraid—well, maybe not afraid—but they were careful."

Tensions continued to build in the tool and die shop, particularly between the team leader and Green, who were of very different personality types. The team leader was intense and high-strung, a man not given to frivolity. Green, large and heavyset, was the archetypal gentle giant. His movements were surprisingly nimble for his great size, since he still retained the reflexes of the high school hockey player he had been 25 years earlier. But his happy-go-lucky personality and the playful expressions that seemed to come naturally to his round, pleasant face did not project an image of burning intensity. This apparently upset the team leader, who, Green recalled, "had a real flash temper." One day that temper erupted against Green. "(The leader) and I disagreed on something," said Green. "He let loose, called me everything . . . he was ranting and raving. I said, 'Hey, let's go have some coffee and talk about it.' He kept screaming. My supervisor came over and took him away, and eventually we got together and he finally told me what was really bothering him—it had nothing to do with the actual action that had triggered the argument. It was something he'd seen in my working procedures that he didn't like. . . . I forg[e]t what he accused me of doing—he thought I was loafing; that was the bottom line. He gave me a job, and I couldn't go any further on it because of some reason, so he got all upset. But basically he thought I was too easygoing. I should show more intensity, which is not my personality."

Although Green would claim that he and the team leader resolved their differences during their discussion, he could never feel the same way about the Flat Rock plant after their altercation. Several weeks later, early in 1988, he left Mazda to take a job with an Ohio auto parts supplier. In his exit interview he cited a number of reasons for his departure: He could make more money at his new job; Mazda had failed to promote from within as promised; the company was not providing workers with adequate tools. Left unspoken was another reason—the realization that as Mazda–Flat Rock geared up to increase production in the spring and summer of 1988, the plant was becoming no place for anyone who did not share his team leader's intensity.

9

The Long Hot Summer

IT was Michigan's hottest summer on record. Temperatures in Detroit passed 85 degrees for 22 consecutive days in July and August 1988. During one 32-hour stretch early in August, when temperatures reached the upper 90s, five people in the city died from the heat. Appliance stores sold every air conditioner in stock, and when they had no more air conditioners to sell, they began running out of fans. The small farms and tall grass fields along the roads that led into Flat Rock from the west were parched brown from the heat and accompanying drought, giving the area a dust bowl appearance.

For Mazda's young American work force, the heat wave could not have come at a worse time. New to industrial work, most of the Americans were shocked by conditions inside the un-air-conditioned plant, where temperatures on occasion reached past 100 degrees. Only a year earlier, the idea of working in such temperatures would have been unimaginable to these workers, most of whom had been as naive as the young applicants in Mike Parker's assessment center group, who—in their prioritizing exercise—had ranked the question of whether to form a volleyball or bowling team as more important than the issue of dealing with uncomfortable heat conditions inside the plant. As they suffered through the heat, the workers faced a second, and in many ways, more vexing problem—they had to adjust to the very rapid acceleration of the plant's production pace.

During the summer of 1988 Mazda began the serious production of cars at Flat Rock. Before that time, the plant had been in a start-up mode, running a single production shift with volume kept purposely

low so bugs could be ironed out of the manufacturing process. But in June the company added a second shift and intensified the production pace, pushing the plant to grind out vehicles with Japanese-style efficiency. In May Mazda was making fewer than 10,000 cars a month at Flat Rock. By September the plant's monthly rate of production was 22,000 vehicles. The size of the plant's work force was not increased proportionately. In mid-May a few more than 2,990 American workers were employed at the plant; by late August the number of Americans had been increased only to 3,078.[1] In fairness this comparison is not completely accurate, since many of those employed at the plant in the spring were in training and not producing cars; nevertheless, the increase in the number of workers did not come close to matching the increase in the plant's workload. An American stamping and assembly plant producing 22,000 vehicles a month would have required a work force at least 15 to 20 percent larger than Flat Rock's.

Team members at Flat Rock discovered an inescapable fact of life during the summer heat wave, a fact that was rarely emphasized in the books and articles that praised the efficiency of the JIT-team system—and one that was never mentioned during Mazda's orientation program—a JIT plant is able to produce more cars with fewer employees because it works its employees harder. The process-engineering and *kaizen* refinements that constantly squeeze waste and inefficiency out of the JIT production process also eliminate any opportunity that workers have to pause and catch their breath. Unlike workers at Big Three plants, who enjoyed five- or ten-second breathers while they waited for cars to arrive at their stations or machines to complete their cycles, Mazda's team members were in near-constant motion. If a car was in a Mazda work station for 62 seconds, the worker at that station was given 62 seconds' worth of tasks to complete. If a unit leader or production engineer noticed that the worker was routinely completing his or her assignment with six seconds to spare, the worker would be given an additional task to fill up the time.

From a production engineering standpoint, there is an elegant beauty to a system that reduces the production process to its most elemental level to isolate and eliminate redundant motions and idle seconds. But production engineers do not work on the assembly line. To the workers who had to struggle to keep up with Mazda's relentless work pace, the company's JIT system not only eliminated waste, it eliminated rest—one man's evil *muda* being another's valuable

respite, depending on which side of the assembly line he found himself. Because workers at Flat Rock were actively engaged in their work for 57 seconds out of every minute, compared to the 45-second-a-minute average pace of the Big Three worker, a Mazda workday, in essence, included more work than a Ford or GM workday—12 seconds more every minute, 12 minutes more every hour, 96 minutes more every 8-hour day, and one 8-hour day more every 5-day week. On top of this, Flat Rock workers were paid wages below those of their opposite numbers at Big Three plants.

The heat and the 57-second-a-minute work pace took their toll on Flat Rock's young, inexperienced work force. This was evident in the small lines of fatigue that gathered around the eyes and mouths of workers and made them seem old beyond their years. "People say you can tell who works for Mazda because they look so tired all the time," said Phil Keeling. Many workers also saw their weight drop precipitously as their bodies adjusted to the JIT work pace. One man in trim and final assembly reported that he went from 280 to 200 pounds in his first 8 months at Flat Rock. Wayne Dodd, who stands 6 foot 1 inch, went from 210 to 180 pounds during his first year on the assembly line, most of the weight coming off during the summer. "We used to joke that the plant was a spa that paid you to join," he recalled. "A lot of us needed to lose some weight anyway, but now that we have, what's next? You can burn out pretty good at Mazda."

The JIT work pace was unlike anything Mazda's new workers had known in their previous work experience. At the restaurants where many had worked, customers would come in spurts. There would be a lunch rush at noon when everyone would work very hard, and then a lull at two when everyone would catch their breath. At the offices where others had worked, the typing and filing would be broken up by trips to the water cooler, phone calls, and errands to other offices. But at Flat Rock the cars kept coming . . . and workers had to keep moving at their 57-second-a-minute clip, without interruption, for 2-hour stretches between breaks. Mazda workers say it is difficult for anyone who has not worked at a JIT plant to appreciate the physical and emotional stress they experience performing boring, repetitive jobs at the company's accelerated production pace. Anyone wishing to approximate the feeling is invited to try the following exercise: Stand at a counter—as fast as you can—pick up a pen, write your name in a notebook, put down the pen, turn the page, and repeat the procedure for 57 seconds a minute over a 120-minute interval.

The idyllic image of the plant that had been presented to workers during their Mazda orientation made it even more difficult for them to accept the harsh realities of factory work. "I think Mazda shot themselves in the foot," Phil Keeling said, looking back on the company's orientation program in the fall of 1988. "People are getting real sick of that goody-goody teamwork stuff." Bob Ramp, the UAW representative, also believed that the unrealistic promises made by Mazda during the orientation contributed to the wave of discontent that swept through the plant during its first summer of production. "I'm going to be very frank with you," he told visitors in August 1988. "I think that throughout the orientation period some of this [the demanding production schedule] was sugar-coated. When I had the opportunity to speak in orientation, I tried to tell people, 'You know, when you get in the plant, it's the real world. You're going to work hard—it's not a country club.' I think there may have been some kind of misconception—[the workers] thought there wasn't going to be this strenuous work. . . . In the orientation process, input and interpersonal skills were touched on more than physical demands. If you worked somewhere else where the demands were not as great physically, it's quite a shock. . . . On some of the real hot days, we've had to explain to people why, since we're a new plant, everything is not up to what we expect—I don't know if a lot of people expected the plant to be air-conditioned."

But it was not only inexperienced workers (who accounted for over 70 percent of the plant's work force) who were disillusioned at Flat Rock. Those team members who had worked at American auto plants also were dismayed by Mazda's JIT work pace. More jaded than their younger teammates, the Big Three veterans had been skeptical about Mazda's orientation pledge to involve workers in the consensus decision-making process, so when the team system collapsed, they had taken it more in stride. They were accustomed to noble-sounding promises by management going unfulfilled. Nothing in their Big Three experience, however, had prepared them for the relentless grind of Mazda's 57-second-a-minute work pace. As one former General Motors worker at Mazda told the *Detroit Free Press* in August: "If I had my druthers, I'd rather work for GM. They don't fill up your time so much."[2] Sam Hill, a worker in Flat Rock's tire subassembly station who had come to Mazda from Chrysler's Jefferson Avenue assembly plant in Detroit, compared the work pace at the two factories: "What you did at Chrysler, you do here, plus they give you four more things to take care of. . . . We never had to run at

Chrysler, but we have to run at Mazda, because there's so much pressure to keep up."

The stress of working at Flat Rock was compounded by Mazda's programmed worksheets, the ubiquitous one-page documents that outlined every step to be followed when performing every production job in the plant. Workers were required to follow programmed worksheets to the letter. If the sheet said, Put down your spatula before you pick up your brush, the worker had to put down his or her spatula. If the sheet said, Drill in bolt A before bolt B, then bolt A had to be drilled in first. The worker who did not adhere to the sequence of steps prescribed in the programmed worksheet could receive a written reprimand at the unit leader's discretion. The sheets also prescribed the exact amount of time available to complete each step . . . two seconds to pick up this tool . . . five seconds to snap on that clip. Many workers complained that this locked them into a straight-jacket job routine that prevented them from changing their pace or varying the way in which they performed a job to relieve boredom and reduce the stress on specific muscles. Other than recognizing the distinction between left and right handers, programmed worksheets make no allowances for the physical differences that distinguish workers. A 6-foot, 2-inch, 240-pound Mazda worker and his 5-foot, 4-inch, 120-lb. teammate had to follow the same programmed work routine when installing mufflers or grinding A-pillars. Workers also complained that the time allotted on a programmed worksheet to complete each step of a job was often insufficient for the average person, being based on the performance of factory olympians like the young trunk installer who had impressed Bob Ramp during his tour of Mazda's Hofu plant. Any worker who persistently failed to keep up with the pace specified in his or her programmed worksheet was likely to be written up.

To labor activists like Mike Parker, the programmed work system employed at Flat Rock and other JIT-team plants represented a return to the scientific management theories of Frederick Taylor. Like Taylorism, the programmed work system seeks to reduce each job in a plant to a series of minute steps, so it can be standardized and performed by workers with minimal training. Under both systems, the individual skills and talents of workers are de-emphasized, according to Parker, making factory jobs less personal and more routinized for the sake of increasing efficiency. Programmed work is, if anything, even more severe than Taylorism in imposing a strict regimentation on workers, because unlike Taylor's scientific manage-

ment, which relies exclusively on external rules and supervision to enforce its prescribed work routine, programmed work has an added means of enforcement—it is part of the self-regulating JIT system. Since the work routine that is spelled out in a programmed worksheet is usually the fastest way to complete a job, the worker who strays from this prescribed path will fall behind the production schedule. With no cushion of spare parts to draw upon in a JIT plant, this will quickly disrupt the flow of work through the worker's entire team station, making it all but impossible to hide the transgression from supervisors. Although they complained about the routinization of their jobs, Mazda workers rarely deviated from their programmed work routine, because it was the surest way to keep up with the plant's production pace. "They're ridiculously rigid," Judy Wilson said of her programmed worksheets. "They'll have a picture of a little man walking over to pick up a wrench: 'Then you take the wrench in your right hand.' Every single movement is spelled out. It's sort of insulting. I deviate from it sometimes, I'm sure everybody does when no one is around. . . . But we do follow them most of the time, because you get the job done faster when you do."

Yet despite the regimentation of programmed work, many American industrial engineers have welcomed the Japanese JIT-team concept as a major advance over the scientific management traditions of U.S. manufacturers. If Japanese workers are more motivated and more productive than their American opposite numbers, the team advocates argue, then surely Japanese manufacturers must have come up with a better way to manage people. Among those subscribing to this view are former labor secretary Ray Marshall, who told a management conference that the NUMMI team plant managed by Toyota in Fremont, California, had "done away with Taylorism."[3]

Advocates of the team plant concept like to argue that the Japanese team system is more enlightened than scientific management because it not only allows but encourages workers to contribute to the design of their own jobs. This is supposed to tap the creative and intellectual resources of workers and free them from the mind-numbing routine of factory work. Unfortunately, workers at Flat Rock, NUMMI, and other team plants have rarely been given the opportunity to experience this involvement. As American workers discovered when they joined Mazda, most jobs were designed by management before the plant opened. Workers like Forrest Green, who wanted to implement changes at Flat Rock, found their paths blocked by the rule requiring that they conduct detailed documented

studies. When a unit leader in Mazda's material handling section was asked, two years after the Flat Rock plant opened, for an example of a *kaizen* change implemented by workers in her unit, she thought carefully and then responded that workers on one team had decided to use wire rather than string to affix their cards to the carts they used to deliver parts to the final assembly line.

Team plants were also supposed to distinguish themselves from their scientifically managed predecessors by giving workers the power to act as their own quality control inspectors. "If you spot any quality problems or are having trouble keeping up with the line, pull the yellow cord and your team leader will come running," workers had been told during their orientation. But by the summer, when the plant was struggling to reach full production—and at least three out of ten cars coming off the Flat Rock line had flaws of some kind—workers who pulled the cord to report a defect found themselves upbraided by their team or unit leaders, who, being under pressure themselves to meet production quotas, were in no mood to stop the line to find the cause of a quality problem. "We've got something like two thousand cars sitting here waiting to go to reprocessing," said Phil Keeling in November 1988. "People see this and say, 'This isn't what they told us in orientation—and they told us that they were going to stop the line and fix the car' . . . now if you pull that yellow cord they want to know why. Everytime some poor bastard pulls the [cord] now, you get a [written report] on it. . . . He's just asking for trouble."

Workers who pulled the cord because they were having trouble keeping up with the JIT work pace were treated even more harshly. Unit leaders often accused them of loafing and threatened them with written reprimands unless they finished their jobs on time. One worker who pulled the yellow cord several time during a shift to request help found a group of Mazda engineers with a video camera at her work station the next morning, ready to conduct a time study on her. Nervous under the glare of the camera and the stone-faced engineers, the woman slipped off her work platform and broke an ankle.[4]

Products of the JIT tradition, Mazda's Japanese managers were committed to keeping their American work force as small as possible. The pressure to hold down labor costs was especially intense at Flat Rock, because six out of ten cars produced at the plant were Ford

Probes, vehicles that—since they were sold by Ford—were less profitable for Mazda than the company's own MX-6. Because the plant's work force was so small, even normal absenteeism had a devastating effect on productivity at Flat Rock. This problem became especially severe in the summer, when the ranks of the plant's work force were already thinned by vacations. Upper managers pressured unit leaders to improve attendance in their units. As a result, the leaders became more strict in their interpretation of attendance rules; some announced to their units that they would no longer accept any excuse for absences, even a doctor's note. Some leaders also decreed that workers would only be allowed to use the restrooms during their morning and afternoon breaks and at lunch. When two workers complained to their union representative about this policy, he noted sarcastically that "some people have already wet their pants," and implied that they should consider the same course of action if they lacked self-discipline to wait two hours to use the restroom on their break.

The union local, with its Sunday lectures on the need to reduce absenteeism, cooperated with Mazda's tougher attendance policy. This put the union out of step with its rank and file, which was growing more resentful almost by the day during the summer over the stricter interpretation of attendance rules by unit leaders. Phil Keeling typified the darkening mood of the workers: "What they call a problem with attendance is you miss one day a year. The problem is not absenteeism, but not enough people to run the plant."

Because the size of its work force was small, Mazda had to schedule overtime on virtually a daily basis during the summer, as it struggled to bring Flat Rock up to full production. Almost no one worked a five-day week at the plant between May and September. Six-day weeks were the norm for hourly workers, not only during the summer but throughout the second half of 1988. Under the terms of their contract, workers were required to accept sixth-day overtime assignments. Seven-day workweeks were voluntary, but some workers went most of the summer without taking a day off because they were afraid of falling behind their production quotas. Invariably the workdays themselves also included overtime and lasted between nine and ten hours, excluding a half hour lunch. As a result Mazda workers usually spent more than 60 hours a week at the plant. At least one ambitious worker spotted an entrepreneurial opportunity in the long workweek. Not bothered by the extra work himself, he sold his vacation days to teammates (usually for $25 to $50), allowing the

teammate to take the day off while he filled in. His unit leader went along with this arrangement, apparently unaware that cash payments were involved.

According to its contract with the UAW, Mazda was required to give workers advance notification of mandatory overtime—one day's notice of daily overtime, two days' for Saturday overtime, and 30 days' for Sunday overtime. These requirements were routinely ignored. The company usually told workers that they were being required to work daily overtime less than an hour before a shift was scheduled to end. The uncertainty created by this practice was a major grievance among workers. "One of my biggest gripes is why can't they let us know what time we're getting off when we come to work," said Peter Barrow. "The team leaders and unit leaders don't know when we're getting off either—the only ones who know are management. It [the overtime announcement] comes over the microphone; they tell us what our build is. Each line has a microphone, and the unit leader grabs the microphone as we're working and says we're going to have to build this many more cars. Usually it takes us one or two hours of overtime."

Workers complained to the union local about the lack of overtime notification, but the union could not help them. A provision of the contract that the UAW signed with the Mazda allows the company to ignore the advance notification rule with impunity. The provision, Article XVI, Section 1, states: "It is understood and agreed by the Union that certain instances, such as equipment breakdown, material shortages, process bottlenecks, and conditions beyond the control of the Company, may cause the Company to schedule daily overtime on the same day it is required."[5] The "instances" cited in this provision, particularly "process bottlenecks" and "conditions beyond the control," are sufficiently vague to allow Mazda to disregard the notification requirement at will. It is as if the company is telling workers, "Trust us, we will not spring overtime on you unless we have a good reason." In Japan, where hourly employees and their managers share a strong group identity, extending this trust to the company would seem natural to workers. But Mazda's American workers, products of a society in which the rights of individuals—both inside and outside the workplace—are protected by clearly defined written regulations (be they the laws of a government or the rules of a contract), were uneasy with an overtime provision that asked them to place so much trust in management's good intentions. The workers' uneasiness deepened, turning into resentment, during

the summer heat wave as Mazda piled more and more overtime on them. "The overtime problem is making people feel like they are just parts in Mazda's just-in-time system," said Phil Keeling.

Mazda circumvented the 30-day-notice requirement for Sunday overtime by posting announcements throughout the plant in the summer that declared that Sunday overtime was scheduled for the remainder of the year. This did not mean that the company's employees would be working on Sundays for the rest of 1988, only that all workers were eligible to be called in at the company's discretion.

Vacations were another sore spot with workers. The UAW-Mazda contract entitled employees with 1 to 3 years' seniority at Flat Rock to 10 vacation days. (First-year employees were allowed between 1 and 3 days.) But because the plant was attempting to reach its full production schedule in the summer with a work force that was already stretched very thin, upper management sought to discourage workers from taking their vacations. This request would not have been unusual in Japan, where the average number of vacation days taken by workers a year is 6.3, compared to 19 in the United States, and where workers often refuse to take all their vacation days as a sign of loyalty to the company.[6] But American workers recoiled at the suggestion and continued to take their vacations. This prompted an angry public criticism from president Nobuto, who chided the workers for deserting the plant during this critical phase in its history. In the Japanese view, the worker who went off on a personal vacation while his plant was trying to reach full production was almost equivalent to the adult child who deserts his elderly parents in their time of need. To minimize the loss of workers to vacations, the company issued an order (later modified) that only one worker per unit could take a vacation at a time. Since a unit often consisted of 20 or 30 people, if this order had been implemented as originally intended, it would have kept as many as half of the workers in a unit from vacationing during the summer months.

Although worker resentment and union protests compelled Mazda to allow more than one vacation per unit, the company had acted within its rights under the vaguely-worded UAW contract when it issued the original vacation order. The contractual provision covering the scheduling of vacations gives the company sweeping unilateral power to rule on vacation requests. In Article XVIII, Section 3, of the contract, Mazda declares that it "recognizes the importance and desirability of providing employees the opportunity to take their full vacation entitlement, and to do so at the time(s) they desire, so

long as that does not jeopardize the efficiency of operations." The contract does not specify the conditions that would pose a threat to the plant's efficiency. (Is it when two workers from the same unit take a vacation, or three?) This judgment is left entirely to management's discretion. A later provision in the contract describes how vacation requests are to be prioritized: "In the event more employees have applied for time off for a particular period than can be spared and still maintain efficient operations, team consensus will be the basis for determining priorities."[7] The contract allows seniority to be used to determine vacation schedules only if a consensus decision cannot be reached. By calling for vacation requests to be decided by the consensus process rather than the more impartial seniority system used at American plants, the Mazda-UAW contract transfers yet more power to the already-powerful unit leader. The same unit leader who can unilaterally decide to accept or reject a worker's excuse for being late or absent, allow or forbid him to use the restroom, rotate him to a new job or consign him to the same repetitive task, can also—by influencing the consensus process—determine whether or not the worker will be able to have a summer vacation.

The pressure of meeting its JIT production schedule forced Mazda to restrict the amount of training it gave new employees in the summer of 1988. The elaborate three-month training program that had been the source of so much favorable publicity only a year earlier was quietly scrapped. New employees were now rushed onto the understaffed line with only two or three days of "training," most of it consisting of filling out insurance forms and other paperwork for the plant's labor relations department. Gone entirely were the interpersonal problem-solving exercises and inspirational speeches of the old training program. With rumors beginning to filter out of the plant about widespread worker discontent, continuing this team-oriented training would have appeared ludicrous. Besides, Mazda's upper management had, by the summer, come to agree with Bob Ramp and others who argued that the lofty promises made by the company during its 1987 training program had contributed to the morale problem at the plant by creating unrealistic expectations among workers. James Korowin, a former Chrysler plant manager who replaced Denny Pawley as the highest-ranking American at Flat Rock, admitted to *Automotive News* that the company's early training was "probably too philosophical." Korowin told the trade magazine that he made sure all new workers understood "it's a bear out there" on the shop floor.[8]

A large share of the new employees hired at Flat Rock in the summer of 1988 were support member pool workers (SMPs), temporary employees, who, in theory, were hired for specific job assignments for a limited length of time. SMPs were not part of the regular Mazda work force. They occupied the lowest stratum in the plant's caste system. Even their uniforms set them apart from everyone else, being drab, loose-fitting work pants and shirts of the same blue, rather than the snappier blue-and-khaki combination worn by *real* team members. Reflecting their lower status, the SMPs were paid 15 percent less than regular Mazda workers, who themselves were paid 15 percent less than Big Three workers. SMPs could be fired at any time without explanation, since they had no access to the plant's normal grievance procedure, though they did pay union dues. An offense that got a regular worker reprimanded would usually result in an SMP's dismissal. (Like so many decisions at Flat Rock, this was up to management's discretion.) Many of the two hundred SMPs who worked at the plant in 1988 were applicants who had successfully completed Mazda's five-step screening process a year or two earlier. These workers, like other Mazda job applicants, had been put through the exhaustive screening process even though the company had already identified enough acceptable applicants to fill all available jobs at Flat Rock. The future SMPs were competing, unknown to them at the time, for temporary rather than permanent positions at the plant.

Most SMPs at the plant labored in the hope of one day being granted permanent worker status. Not surprisingly, they went out of their way to please their unit leaders, knowing that a recommendation from a unit leader was necessary to make their dream of a real Mazda job come true. SMPs were almost always the first to volunteer for an undesirable job, and the first—and the loudest—to support the unit leader's ideas at a consensus meeting. By the summer almost all permanent Mazda workers had stopped participating in the plant's voluntary morning exercises—some as a sign of protest, others because they were too tired from the JIT work pace. But at 6:45 every morning, there were the SMPs, bending and stretching with unit leaders, plant engineers, and Japan advisors. Soon after the SMPs were made regular workers and completed their 90-day probations, they too invariably stopped exercising.

Permanent Mazda workers resented the presence of so many SMPs at the plant. In their eagerness to please management, the SMPs moved at a breakneck pace, especially during their first three

or four weeks on the job. This increased the intensity of the plant's production pace and made it more difficult for regular workers to keep up. The regular workers found themselves in the position of boxers who, after every round, are forced to fight a new—and fresh—opponent. Even more distressing to the workers was the psychological leverage given unit leaders by the presence of so many SMPs. "If you complained about your job, the unit leader would just point and say, 'If you don't like it, leave—there's plenty of other people waiting on line for your place,' " recalled Wayne Dodd. The fact that there were so many workers vying for Mazda jobs was not, Dodd believed, a reflection on working conditions inside the plant. It was, instead, a reflection of how much a $13-an-hour job meant to desperate Downriver workers. This was a distinction that Dodd, who had been making $18,000 a year at Burger King, could appreciate. "It's sad when you see how the SMPs are treated. How desperate they are for a good-paying job. Management keeps leading them on with the hope that they'll be hired [as regular workers]. There's some [SMPs] in trim and final who've been there six or eight months and they're still not considered permanent employees," he said in the spring of 1989.

In its UAW contract Mazda promised to consider an SMP assignment a "permanent opening" once the assignment exceeds 90 days in length. This led many workers—both SMPs and regular team members—to believe that an SMP automatically became a permanent employee after working 90 days at the plant. Nothing could have been farther from the truth. Because the contract covered SMP *assignments* rather than individual workers, Mazda was able to circumvent this implied promise simply by rotating SMP employees to new job assignments every 90 days. Once vacated by an SMP, an assignment could be filled by a regular worker, even if only for one day, to avoid its being reclassified as a "permanent opening." By constantly reshuffling SMPs and regular team members through different job assignments, Mazda thus kept individual "temporary" employees (with their 15 percent lower wages) on its payroll indefinitely. By contrast, American automakers, who use fewer temporary employees to begin with, must grant permanent employee status to their temporaries once the workers have been on the job for a specified period of time.

Regular team members might have been more accepting of SMPs, had Mazda hired enough temporaries to fill all the plant's manpower needs. But even with the addition of two hundred SMPs, many workers still felt their units were stretched too thinly. "If Mazda made all

of the SMPs permanent, and no one was ever absent for a day, there still wouldn't be enough people in this place," said Phil Keeling.

The union local was sympathetic to the workers' complaints about the plant's thin work force and Mazda's apparent abuse of the SMP provision of its contract. The union representatives could see for themselves when they walked through the plant during the dog days of summer that the workers were having trouble keeping up with the line's car-a-minute pace. "I think one of the biggest problems was that we didn't have enough people to start this place," Bob Ramp, the UAW representative, would recall. Even Local 3000 president Bill Judson, who normally was eager to defend the company against criticism, had to admit that the plant was understaffed. Judson promised the beleaguered workers that reinforcements were on the way. "We are and have been trying to get Mazda to hire more people," he declared. But Judson and the union local lacked any contractual leverage either to pressure Mazda to hire more workers or convert more SMPs to permanent employees. Nor could they exert public pressure on Mazda through the news media, since this would have run counter to the union's larger goal of creating a "cooperative image" with other Japanese automakers in America. Despite the local's efforts, Mazda did not budge. The company refused to accelerate its hiring schedule. One year later, in the summer of 1989, Flat Rock had not expanded the size of its work force beyond its original projection of 3,500 (a figure that included management and administrative employees). The union, meanwhile, agreed to accept an expanded role for SMPs at the plant, because, as Judson explained, "We had trouble maintaining line speed and salaried personnel were working on the line."[9] The fact that Judson seemed more concerned about management's ability to maintain line speed than the need to curb the excessive use of SMPs typified what many workers believed were the union's inverted priorities—priorities that seemed to place the needs of the company over those of the worker. "Sometimes it seems that the union wants to make itself more attractive to management than to its own members," said Phil Keeling.

But there were many in the union local who felt uneasy about what was going on at Flat Rock. Publicly they continued to describe the plant and its Japanese management system in positive terms, emphasizing the union's role as a valued member of the Mazda team. Problems at the plant were typically blamed on an isolated American manager or two who had brought over some bad habits from Ford or GM and had not yet got in step with the Japanese system. Sometimes,

as Bill Judson explained, the Japanese philosophy "[wore] thin with American managers."[10] Privately, though, many union officials were angry and frustrated with Mazda, and appalled by the treatment of workers under the company's production-driven JIT system. "A lot of people have lost a lot of sleep over what's gone on over there," said a union official closely involved in the Mazda plant. "You've got to turn your head away from a lot of things."

The shortage of workers at Flat Rock made it virtually impossible for Mazda to continue cross-training employees once it began its drive toward full production in the summer of 1988. With scarcely enough team members to meet their units' most basic requirements, even those unit leaders who were committed to cross-training in principle were unwilling to pull a worker off the line and send him or her to a training crib two hours a day for instruction only to put up with a slower rate of production later, when the worker began his or her learning curve at a new job. "Its difficult to cross-train everyone while you're trying to attain line speed," Bob Ramp explained in 1988. "It's true employees feel that they haven't been cross-trained as they thought they would, but I think that's coming. We've addressed that issue with management. They know they're going to have to cross-train. Our contract will provide the impetus to cross-train."

But even those workers who had been cross-trained often were not given the opportunity to use their new skills. In the body shop's 1987 four-week training program, new employees learned spot welding, mig welding, carbon dioxide gas bracing, and metal finishing. Yet, two years later, most body shop employees had only done spot welding, the one skill required to perform the majority of jobs in the shop. "We have a lot of people who have done nothing but hold a spot gun for two years, and they're pretty upset. They keep asking themselves, Why did Mazda put me through all this training if all they wanted me to do was to be a spot welder?" said one body shop team member. According to this team member, workers in the body shop and other areas of the plant could not use all the skills they had acquired because Mazda was not providing the degree of job rotation it had promised. Like many in the plant, he blamed this on the JIT production pace. In its drive to attain greater and greater productivity, the company was reluctant to rotate a worker experienced in one job to a new one in which he or she would have to start the learning process all over again. Besides, most workers were naturally better at one job than others, and the company wanted each worker to stay at the job he or should could perform most efficiently. "A lot of people

are frustrated, because Mazda said we'd have job rotation, but you can't have job rotation when you're pushing cars through the plant so damn fast," complained the body shop team member.

Kaizen changes implemented by management made it even more difficult for workers to keep up with the production pace. Mazda production engineers, unit leaders, team leaders, and Japanese dispatches were constantly studying the line in search of wasted steps and idle time that could be kaizened out of the production process. Special *kaizen* teams looked for ways to rearrange job assignments so a worker's position could be entirely eliminated from a team. Workers were encouraged to participate in the *kaizen* process and promised cash incentives for ideas that were adopted. *Kaizen* was the only area in which Mazda remained true to its promise to invite worker input. The required documented studies and other obstacles that usually blocked the implementation of workers' suggestions to increase their own comfort or safety, were never used to impede *kaizen* ideas that showed the company how to get a job done in less time or with fewer workers. In the early phases of the plant's history, workers eagerly contributed suggestions for increasing productivity, welcoming the *kaizen* process as a creative outlet that relieved the boredom of factory work. Later, when it became obvious to the workers that their suggestions were only increasing their own workloads, enthusiasm for *kaizen* all but disappeared. "*Kaizen* creates more pressure," said Peter Barrow. "You might figure out a way to get your job down from a minute to thirty seconds, but then they find you something else to do [for] thirty seconds." As the work pace in the plant became more intense, other workers took an even dimmer view of *kaizen*. "What [kaizen] means is you get seven people to do the job of eight people," remarked Greg Drudi. "Honest to God, some of these people [already] don't have the time to put a stick of chewing gum in their mouth."

As they struggled to keep up with Flat Rock's JIT production pace, team members often became resentful toward fellow workers who increased their workloads by making *kaizen* suggestions. In 1988 a pregnant team leader, who because of her condition could no longer work her regular job, was told to kaizen the waxing station of the paint shop, where protective sealant is applied to vehicles. By redistributing job assignments and combining redundant operations, she was able to reduce the number of workers in the waxing station from ten to eight. But because the station's collective job was essentially unchanged, the workloads of the remaining eight employees

increased substantially. Much of this increase fell on the shoulders of the team member who operated the ALC machine. A complex piece of equipment, the ALC machine sends vehicle bodies into the waxing booth and thus indirectly controls the rate at which cars go through the final assembly area. Running this machine requires that the operator be familiar with elaborate sequential instructions that may vary slightly from car to car. If the operator pushes the wrong buttons at the wrong time, the production pace of not only the paint shop but the entire final assembly line can be thrown off. In Mazda's original job design, the ALC operator was responsible only for running the machine. But as a result of the pregnant team leader's *kaizen* plan, the operator was given the added job of installing jigs in the engine and trunk hoods and wax-spraying back panels. The expanded job assignment caused an increase in the number of ALC operator errors, which prompted unit leaders to issue a general warning that operators would be "written up" if the mistakes continued. "It's a difficult pace to keep up with since the *kaizen*," recalled a former ALC operator. "In the beginning, we all made mistakes. I once pushed some wrong buttons on the ALC machine, and all of a sudden I had three Japanese . . . standing behind me. They didn't say anything, just kept looking over my shoulder. Then I got real flustered and messed up some more. . . . I threw the final assembly line off by twenty minutes. . . . I kept thinking about the team leader who kaizened our operation; she never worked on the ALC machine in her life. She doesn't know what it's like. How could she do this to her peers, other union members?"

A *kaizen* plan implemented in one area of the plant often created pressure for another area to speed up its production. For example, if the workers who installed gas tanks had their jobs kaizened so they could complete their tasks five seconds faster, the subassembly team that supplied the assembly line with gas tanks would be pressured to shave five seconds off their job cycles as well.

Mazda's JIT system intensified this pressure by depriving workers of spare parts cushions to draw on when they fell behind the production pace. The gas tank subassembly team, for example, would not be allowed to build up a reserve of tanks by working on breaks or putting in overtime. They would instead be forced to struggle to keep up with the more efficient tank installers on the assembly line— the theory being that the pressure of trying to keep up would force the subassembly team to kaizen their operation; whereas allowing them to create a spare parts reserve would make them soft and

complacent, taking away the quality that Mazda training literature describes as "the will to kaizen."

Even without the imbalances created by *kaizen*, Flat Rock's thin-stretched JIT inventory levels kept the workers who supplied components to the line under constant pressure. JIT is unforgiving of even the smallest mistakes. It is a one-strike-and-you're-out system. If the worker fabricating metal components in the body shop or building parts in a subassembly operation missed 20 or 30 seconds of production, the effect was soon felt on the main assembly line. Sam Hill, the former Chrysler worker who became a team member in Mazda's tire subassembly station, described the pressure of supplying a JIT assembly line: "We have to jump over a moving conveyor about two-to-three feet high—actually we jump on it and walk across it. If you walk[ed] around it, instead of jumping, you lost a minute, which means you lost eight tires' production . . . which we can't afford to do. . . . They don't yell at you, but the pressure is on you to keep the tire pool full. Between subassembly and the line, you need thirty to forty tires at all times. . . . If you run low on tires, you miss your lunch and break—instead of a break at nine o'clock, you'll get a ten o'clock break." During his first eight months in the tire subassembly station, the 5-foot, 10-inch Hill went from 185 to 155 lbs. There were days in the summer when he felt almost too exhausted after work to walk to his car.

Mazda's fragile JIT system was frequently beset by problems during the summer, frustrating both workers and managers alike. The main assembly line was running out of tires so often (primarily because of equipment failure in the tire subassembly station) that the company, departing from its JIT philosophy, allowed the subassembly station to maintain a 20 to 30 minute "safety stock" of spare tires to cover emergencies. In the stamping shop, workers were having trouble filling the "pull demand" for fenders from the body shop. Management refused to allow the workers to create a backup supply of parts, and instead had the cars run through the body shop without fenders. Since the cars could not go to the next step in the production process (the paint shop) fenderless, management would pull the cars off the line and have the fenders installed at a separate work station when they arrived.

Mazda also used JIT principles to control its supply of tools at Flat Rock. The company kept the number of tools available in the plant at a bare minimum. "There's a tremendous shortage of tools," said Greg Drudi. Both skilled trades and production workers had

their horror stories about the lack of adequate tools in the plant—the requested wrench that took two weeks to arrive, the lathe that had to be shared by 30 skilled trades workers, the electrical sockets that had to be taped to extensions. "Mazda will squeeze every penny it can," said Phil Keeling. "The plant's roof leaks—it leaks like crazy, because they were so concerned about cutting corners when they built the place, they couldn't do it right the first time."

For their part, the Japanese were disappointed in their American workers and managers. Nobuto's criticism of workers who took vacations while the plant was reaching full production was only one of many Japanese grievances. As the summer wore on, the Japanese became more and more disturbed by the plant's high defect rate. They complained about what they believed was the lack of commitment on the part of Americans to maintaining quality standards and meeting production schedules. When Americans complained of fatigue and muscle aches from working on the line, the Japanese often viewed them as "sandbaggers." This impression stemmed from what union representative Bob Ramp believed was a difference between American and Japanese attitudes toward the individual worker's personal comfort. "I couldn't say . . . but I get the impression that the Japanese would work through a lot of injuries," noted Ramp. "I'm not saying that American workers are babies or anything, but—yeah— the Japanese might try to overcome some of that on their own."

The Flat Rock plant's problems wore on President Nobuto, who appeared tired and drawn. Unlike most Japanese executives in the United States, who present a quiet, diplomatic image, the Mazda–Flat Rock president was not reluctant to express opinions critical of American work habits and quality standards. In his 1988 speech to the Ann Arbor automotive conference, Nobuto criticized Mazda's American suppliers for their lax delivery standards. "All of you are familiar with just-on-time delivery, and these words are very popular in the United States auto industry," he told his audience. "Yet we find that the commitment to delivery as promised—whether it is furniture for the office or drawing changes requested of a supplier— is much more flexible among Americans than among Japanese. Perhaps it is a cultural difference, but I frankly hope it is one that we can help to change. . . . I regret to say that our purchasing staff spend many hours just following up and making sure that deliveries will take place as scheduled."[11]

Nobuto felt uncomfortable with the Americans' independent, shoot-from-the-hip style. He wondered how workers with this free-wheeling attitude could be molded into successful team players. "Basically, I believe the American people are rather individualistic, which means respect for the individual but at the same time they do not want to be interfered with by other people," he said. "That makes it more difficult to work as a team. . . . That tends to result in delay in the delivery of work and so on."[12]

When looking for a replacement for the outspoken Denny Pawley, Flat Rock's Japanese managers wanted someone who was less ambitious, less independent—or, as they would have preferred to describe it—a more cooperative team player. In either case they found what they were looking for in James F. Korowin. A one-time high school teacher of physical education and American history, Korowin was 47 when he was named vice president of manufacturing at Mazda–Flat Rock in April 1988. He had begun his automotive career 23 years earlier, leaving his teaching job to become a receiving inspection clerk at the Ford assembly plant in Wixom, Michigan. By 1978 he had worked his way up to become manager of the Wixom plant. Six years later he left Ford to join American Motors as director of manufacturing operations in charge of plants in Toledo, Ohio, and Kenosha, Wisconsin. Korowin's responsibilities were curtailed after AMC was acquired by Chrysler in 1987. He was replaced at the Kenosha plant and was, in essence, demoted to plant manager of the Toledo Jeep factory. But all accounts Korowin was a competent detail man at Ford and AMC, but in contrast to Pawley, he was not the kind of manager who led a plant with the force of a dominant personality. He was instead a consensus builder, a manager who sought advice from all quarters before taking action. He was not the kind of man who would impale a brand new car to get an assembly line moving. As one union official at Flat Rock noted, Korowin seemed to operate on a lower flame of intensity and ambition than did Pawley.

Mazda's Japanese managers were also troubled by the negative image that the Flat Rock plant had in the Downriver community. Many people in the area began to feel betrayed when the new auto plant failed to create the promised number of spin-off jobs. "Expectations about attracting Mazda suppliers have dimmed considerably," concluded a study of the plant and its economic impact on the community conducted by Michigan State University researchers Richard Child Hill, Michael Indergaard, and Kuniko Fujita.[13] Japanese supplier

firms did not follow Mazda to Michigan in the numbers promised by state politicians eager to sell workers on the Mazda incentive package in 1985. By the summer of 1988, fewer than ten Japanese firms had built, or announced plans to build, factories in the Detroit-Downriver area directly because of Mazda. None of the new plants employed more than four hundred. Most had payrolls of less than one hundred. State officials stopped talking in terms of ten to fifteen thousand Mazda spin-off jobs. Realistically, the officials thought that Michigan would be fortunate if Mazda created half that many jobs, either by attracting new supplier firms or by increasing the volume done by the state's existing parts factories.

The spin-off jobs that were created were not free. Every supplier that followed Mazda to Michigan demanded and received its own incentive package. Lenawee Stamping, a joint venture by Mazda and two suppliers, which employed 350, received tax breaks and training incentives worth $328,500. Delta USA, the American subsidiary of Mazda's Hiroshima seat supplier, employed 180 and received $553,000 in state and county incentives. Penstone, a 55-employee glass supplier, was given almost $100,000 worth of incentives.[14] A high-level executive with one Japanese supplier firm expected more than an incentive package; during discussions with a county official, he asked if the official could arrange to keep the UAW out of his company's plant for a specified number of years. When the official refused, pointing out that such an arrangement would be illegal, the Japanese supplier said that the mayor of a city in another, competing, county was willing to extend such a guarantee. (The supplier firm located in the official's county anyway, without the promise to keep out the union.)

Mazda's Flat Rock plant itself did not turn out to be the provider of jobs that many Downriver had expected. The hiring of out-of-state skilled trades and production workers angered local residents who had been turned down for Mazda jobs. The company's image as an economic white knight was also tarnished by the complaints of local suppliers and service firms, which charged that Mazda's preference for dealing with Japanese vendors made it difficult to do business with the Flat Rock plant. Mazda claimed that the "local content" (the value of components made in the United States) of its Flat Rock cars was 50 percent in the summer of 1988, a figure substantially below the 60 percent or more local content claimed by Toyota, Nissan, and Honda for their American-made cars. But the Japanese automakers all count the cost of American labor, as well as the cost of shipping and storing

Japanese components, when calculating the local content of their ve-
hicles. According to a study conducted by the General Accounting Of-
fice (GAO) in 1989, the local content of cars made at the U.S. plants
of Mazda, Honda, Toyota, and Nissan averaged 38 percent if only the
actual value of parts was considered. By contrast, the report noted that
the American-made content of cars produced at Big Three plants was
88 percent. Citing the GAO report, Senator Lloyd Bentsen (D., Tex-
as), chairman of the Senate Finance Committee, claimed that though
Japanese-owned plants in the United States produced a record
794,000 vehicles in 1988, their heavy reliance on imported parts re-
sulted in a net loss of 25,000 American jobs.[15]

Nowhere was disappointment over the Mazda plant's limited
economic impact greater than in Flat Rock itself. Only two small
supplier firms had followed Mazda to the city. Plans to build a one
hundred acre "mixed use" office-industrial park across the street
from the plant were postponed. The 100 percent property tax abate-
ment left Flat Rock ill-prepared to handle the increased costs of
police protection, road repair, and other city services associated with
the plant. Only emergency grants totalling $500,000 from the state
kept Flat Rock afloat financially in the two years following the ap-
proval of the Mazda abatement. Flat Rock voters blamed Ted Anders
for the city's problems. They voted their five-term mayor out of office
in favor of a candidate who accused him of "giving away the store to
get Mazda."

Mazda's image problems in Flat Rock grew worse during the
summer heat wave of 1988. At taverns, lunch counters, and dough-
nut shops, workers told locals of the brutal conditions inside the
plant. It was one hundred degrees in there, but Mazda refused to
slow down its drive to full production. The Big Three were cancel-
ling, or at least curtailing, shifts during the worst of the heat wave;
Mazda was still running nine- and ten-hour shifts, with overtime.
Only on two of the hottest days did the company relent and lift its
overtime requirements so workers could go home after eight hours.

Not only was it like a furnace inside the plant, the workers told
townspeople, it was sometimes impossible to get a cold drink until
lunch. Throughout most of the heat wave, Mazda had refused to
relax its rule banning beverages from the shop floor. For weeks the
union had to plead with management to get permission to take juice
and ice out to workers on the line. Otherwise workers had to wait
until their breaks to get a drink—but this was never guaranteed. To
save money Mazda had installed bottled-water coolers, rather than

piped-in water fountains, in off-line break areas. The coolers often ran out of water. Or, more frustrating still, they ran out of paper cups. When this happened, said Wayne Dodd, workers would "cup their hands or use a piece of cardboard to make a funnel, to get water into their mouths. It was degrading."

Dodd, like other workers at Flat Rock, was angered by Mazda's refusal to put fans on the shop floor as Big Three automakers did in their plants. "It would have been a lot more comfortable to get some air circulating in the plant with fans," he said. "With all Mazda's talk about respecting the worker's dignity, you think they would have done this for us—but they didn't. . . . We started asking our union rep to get us some fans in May. He told us then, 'The fans are on order.' Whenever we asked him, that's the answer we got—'The fans are on order.' We heard it all summer, but we never got fans."

Conditions were especially uncomfortable for workers in the paint department, who were required to wear nonporous nylon dust suits, even during the hottest days. "It felt like you wrapped yourself up in cellophane—within a few minutes you were soaked," said a paint shop worker. "It got so hot, you felt tired after ten minutes, but you had to stay there working for ten hours." The workers accepted the need to wear the protective suits in the spray booth and other areas where there was a risk of freshly painted car surfaces being damaged by dust particles from clothing. But they did not understand why the suits were required in areas behind the paint ovens, wet sand areas, and masking stations, where there was no exposure to wet paint. It was, they were told, Mazda's policy that dust uniforms be worn in all areas of the paint shop—and Mazda, a company that believed in the supremacy of the process, was not about to allow inconsistency to creep into its uniform policy. Some of the paint shop's skilled trades workers, who, because of their specialized skills had more bargaining power with the company, began to ignore the dust suit rule on their own. "I talked to people about getting away from dust suits in the oven area—that wasn't a dustproof area anyway," recalled Jerry Healy, the former maintenance team leader who left Mazda in September 1988. "I talked to quite a few people— they'd say, 'Yeah, I can see a big problem with [wearing the suits in the heat], but I just can't say, okay you can [take them off].' We were back into this meeting situation. . . . Probably for about the last three months I was there, I didn't wear my dust suit back by the oven. I told my guys, you take your suits off; if anyone says anything, I'll take responsibility for it. We never had a problem with it."

At the height of the heat wave, day-shift workers in the trim and final assembly area (the area of the plant with the largest number of employees) began to protest conditions at Flat Rock by "walking to the wall" during their morning and afternoon breaks. Rather than going to their designated break areas, the workers congregated at the plant's exit doors. Had they walked past those doors, the workers would have been technically out of the plant. This could have resulted in their immediate dismissal under Mazda's work rules, which prohibited employees from leaving the factory on break time. Unit leaders copied the names of the protesting workers in their notebooks, warning the protesters that they were literally two steps away from being fired. At first only a small group of workers walked to the wall. But support for the protesters spread quickly—within days, almost half of the 550 workers on the trim and final A-shift were crowding against the exit doors, demanding fans and a reduction in working hours, threatening to take those two final steps en masse. The unit leaders were rapidly losing control of the situation. Bill Judson was summoned from his office in the administration building. The union local president did not mince words when confronting the protesters—if they left the plant, he warned, they would be "looking for a job" tomorrow; the company would fire them, and the union would not stand behind them. Judson's warning frightened the workers from walking out, but for many of the protesters the local president's actions were yet another indication of where their union's true allegiances lay. Judson had acted, the protesters thought, more like a member of management than a representative of workers.

In October 1988, long after the summer heat wave had ended, the UAW paid for a group of Mazda workers to go to the union's Black Lake lodge in northern Michigan. The workers were union coordinators like Greg Drudi, sent to Black Lake for a weekend educational seminar. After classes at the Walter and May Reuther Family Education Center, the coordinators, who came from different areas of the Flat Rock plant, met for drinks. Talking into the night, they exchanged what Drudi called "Mazda war stories." Drudi was impressed by how much the different stories overlapped. The problems he had seen with unit leaders not accepting doctors' notes in the paint shop were repeated in the body shop and the trim and final area. . . . Unit leaders in the stamping area were showing just as much favoritism in assigning choice jobs as their opposite numbers were in the

plastics department. . . . Tools were just as scarce in one area as they were in another. . . . No one had fans or water coolers. . . . Everyone complained that the work pace was killing them. The coordinators had all known that conditions at the plant were bad, but prior to the Black Lake meeting many of them had wondered, believed Drudi, if perhaps they were being unfair, viewing normal start-up problems in the worst possible light. The *real* Mazda plant that Drudi and the other coordinators worked in every day was almost the exact opposite of the storybook team plant depicted in the company's orientation program. This had lent a bizarre, unreal quality to the experience of workers at Flat Rock, where what was said rarely bore any relationship to what was done. Mazda talked about involving workers in the team process, as it gave unit leaders the unchecked power to dictate decisions. The company talked about treating workers with dignity and respect and making everyone part of the Mazda family, while it refused to give them fans and cold drinks on 90-degree days. For the coordinators, hearing one another's war stories cut through the fog of disbelief and made the events of the summer seem more real. It was, recalled Drudi, as if everyone started saying to himself, "I haven't been crazy all along—something is really wrong at that plant."

After Black Lake the coordinators continued to get together informally at a Flat Rock pizza restaurant to discuss conditions at the plant, which, despite the cooler temperatures, had not, in their view, got any better since the summer. Mazda had yet to provide the promised cross-training and job rotation. Unit leaders still wielded dictatorial power. As a result of the continued kaizening of the production process, the JIT work pace was more intense than ever. But the anger and frustration of the coordinators was often directed more against the UAW than Mazda. As coordinators they served as liaisons between their teammates and the plant's official representatives. Regular Mazda workers, the coordinators were elected to their positions by their peers. The Mazda-UAW contract allowed the coordinators to devote two paid hours per week to union business.* Most of this time was spent gathering complaints and grievances from teammates and relaying them to union representatives, who often appeared either unable or unwilling to take any action on behalf of the workers. The coordinators realized that the union had what one

* Coordinators cannot subtract the two hours of union service from their normal work week. They can attend to union business only during break periods and before or after shifts.

worker called "a toothless contract" with Mazda, but they were certain that the union local was not pushing hard enough to represent the interests of its members. Even in areas where the contract gave the union some power—such as in the filing of grievances—the local leadership seemed reluctant to exercise that power if it meant upsetting management.

In December the coordinators formed a coalition to challenge Bill Judson and the incumbent local officers in the Local 3000 election that was to be held at a still-unspecified date in 1989. Holding their first meeting in the basement of Greg Drudi's home in the rural town of LaSalle, Michigan, the workers called their coalition New Directions, naming it after the union dissident movement started by former UAW officer Jerry Tucker in the union's Region 5, based in St. Louis. An outspoken critic of the team plant concept, Tucker ran a successful campaign for the directorship of UAW Region 5 in 1988, becoming the first successful candidate not backed by Solidarity House to win a seat on the union's powerful 22-member executive board in more than 25 years. Although the Flat Rock dissidents had no connection to Tucker's group, the Local 3000 incumbents would seize on their choice of the New Directions name to brand them "radicals and leftists." This bothered the union coordinators and their small group of supporters, most of whom considered themselves salt-of-the-earth midwestern moderates on most issues.

"Maybe we should have chosen a different name, I don't know," Drudi would later acknowledge. "But if going to work in the morning and knowing when you're going to get off in the afternoon is radical, then I'm radical. . . . If being able to file a grievance is radical, then I'm radical. . . . If wanting a consistent attendance policy is radical, then, yeah, we're all radicals."

10
Safety and Health

A LARGE and rather plain-looking concrete building stands in the southwest corner of Mazda's Flat Rock complex, not far from the main stamping and assembly plant. The building is all that remains of the Michigan Casting Center, the troubled foundry that was closed by Ford in 1981. Mazda demolished two million of the Casting Center's three million square feet after purchasing the foundry, leaving this section to survive as a "multiple-use structure." Part of the building has been turned into sales offices for Mazda's North American marketing division. Part has been converted into a subassembly station, where air-conditioning units are put together for the cars built in the main plant. Part has become an employee training center, and part a warehouse.

The remainder of the former foundry, about 90,000 square feet of building, has been given new life as the Mazda Fitness Center, the first indoor health and recreation facility built by a Detroit automaker for the use of hourly workers. With its running track, weight machines, tennis courts, and putting greens, the center has many of the amenities of an executive health club, though its concrete floors and old foundry support beams create a setting that is clearly more spartan.

When the fitness center opened in November 1987, it was viewed by many in the local media as yet another indication of how Mazda's Japanese team system was leveling the barriers of perquisite and privilege that had long separated management and labor in the United States automobile industry. But to Don Kricho, Flat Rock's director of safety and health, the center was far more than a simple recre-

ational perk granted equally to managers and hourly employees. A big, deeply tanned Missourian, Kricho saw the center as an integral part of Mazda's "total wellness program." "It's much more than a recreation center," he said at the facility's official opening. "Employees who are fit both physically and mentally will feel better about themselves and be able to fully participate in our team environment."[1]

A 20-year veteran of General Motors' safety and health department, Kricho was the safety director of GM's Hamtramck, Michigan, plant in 1985 when he was hired by Mazda. His first reaction to the Japanese automaker's job offer was, "No thank you, I'm very happy where I am." Then a dinner with Mazda representatives changed his mind: "I started listening and it grabbed me, because the concepts Mazda was talking about were basically everything I had been thinking about or tried to do myself and gotten beaten up with over the years by managers who wanted no part of [total wellness]," he recalled.

General Motors had, believed Kricho, followed a negative approach to worker safety. Like the two other U.S. automakers, it viewed safety almost entirely in terms of problems that were to be avoided—the exposed machine that mangled a worker's arm, the car that fell off the assembly line and injured a group of assemblers. As long as such incidents did not occur frequently, the American safety engineers considered their programs successful. But Mazda was different. As Kricho learned from his dinner companions, the company would be taking a proactive approach to the safety and welfare of the Flat Rock plant's workers. The avoidance of injuries, though important, would not by itself be enough—Mazda was going to make positive contributions to the physical and emotional well-being of its American team members. The idea, as one American manager would later describe it, was that, "Somehow, from working at Mazda [the team member's] health is going to be enhanced."[2]

In May 1988, as the Flat Rock plant was being readied to begin its second shift and the drive to full JIT production, Kricho explained the company's total wellness program to interested visitors: "If you had come to me at GM and asked, 'What do you base your safety program on?' I would probably have said, 'Respect for human life.' But if I only respect human life, there's an implication that I can get away with a whole bunch of other things as long as I'm not endangering life."[3]

Kricho then asked his visitors to consider how he would answer the same question at Flat Rock—"respect for *human beings*." Here,

he explained, the safety program was not just concerned with "life or the physical body," but with "the way a person thinks—everything." He described how Mazda was developing programs to improve the safety awareness of workers and encourage them to adopt healthier personal life-styles. His own personal goal was one day to create a system for determining the actual physical ages of all Flat Rock employees (as opposed to the "chronological ages" listed on their drivers licenses) and then, through the proper dietary and exercise regimen, lower the average physical age of the entire work force. For example, the program would take a worker who, though 25, had the body of a 35-year-old and, by getting him into shape, bring his physical age down so it more closely approximated his chronological age. This would, claimed Kricho, increase the plant's productivity by giving it what in essence would be a younger work force. At the same time, it would result in happier and healthier workers.

At a traditional Big Three plant, this involvement in the personal lives of workers would have been viewed as paternalism. But workers at Flat Rock did not view the company's total wellness program in this light, said Kricho. One important difference between Mazda and paternalistic American automakers like Henry Ford was that Mazda allowed workers to have input into the development of its total wellness program. An even more important distinction, though, was that Mazda cared about the well-being of its workers in a way that few American manufacturers ever had.

Accidents involving team members, regardless of how insignificant, were called "disasters" by Mazda, said Kricho, explaining that unlike "accidents," which may be regarded as unavoidable and thus acceptable, disasters are less likely to be tolerated as an inevitable part of factory life. "We're the first plant in North America to even consider the idea of implementing a zero-accident safety process," he said. "We believe that no injury or illness caused by occupation is ever necessary—it's not acceptable, pure and simple. . . . It's a disaster when someone gets a cut here that requires a couple of sutures. There's a massive investigation that immediately takes place [to] find out why it happened and come up with countermeasures [that can be] spread through the rest of the plant. . . . Some managers [at U.S.-owned plants] take the attitude, 'You're in an industrial environment, you're going to get hurt.' They accept that as part of doing business. I'm telling you that Mazda won't accept that as necessary. Here, there is truly a totally different attitude toward people."

Early in Flat Rock's production history, Mazda appeared to have

"zero tolerance" for accidents. If not a disaster, every accident was at least treated like a major crisis. Safety engineers were called in to study the accident, detailed reports were written about it, special team meetings were held to discuss how it could have been avoided. In the spring of 1987, one worker who was cleaning a work station rested his broom against a car that was on the assembly line while he took off his safety gloves. The line started moving before the worker had removed his second safety glove, and when he reached for the broom with his exposed hand, is palm caught the sharp metal edge of the unfinished vehicle. After receiving several stitches, the worker was brought before President Nobuto himself to explain the accident. Later, he went around the plant lecturing teams on the importance of wearing safety gloves.

Like many of Mazda's broader ambitions, however, total wellness and zero-accident tolerance were swept into oblivion by the company's relentless drive to reach full production during the summer of 1988. The accelerated rate of production that began with the start of the second shift in June brought with it an alarming increase in worker injuries. The rate at which Michigan Occupational Safety and Health Act (MIOSHA) recordable injuries were occurring at the plant increased by 50 percent between June and September.[4] A total of 1763 workdays was lost to occupational injuries and illnesses at Flat Rock during the plant's first year of two-shift production (June 1988 to May 1989). This factors out to a rate of 42.6 days lost for every 100 workers. By contrast, the lost workday rate at all Michigan motor vehicle and car body assembly plants as reported by MIOSHA was 33.9 in 1987, the last year for which statistics were available at the time this book was completed. The number of MIOSHA recordable "incidents" that resulted in lost workdays at Flat Rock during the first year of two-shift production was 152, or 3.7 per 100 workers. This also compares unfavorably to other auto plants in Michigan, which had an average MIOSHA rate of 2.4 lost workday incidents per 100 workers.[5]

Rather than representing a new, more enlightened approach to safety and health, as Don Kricho had believed and Mazda's Japanese managers had promised, the Flat Rock plant became the focus of negative publicity as a result of its high injury rate. In a February 13, 1989, front-page story, "Injury, Training Woes Hit New Mazda Plant," *Automotive News* reported on Flat Rock's widespread safety problems, declaring in its opening sentence, "The number of injuries among workers at the plant raises fundamental questions about the

much-heralded team system." The trade journal quoted an unnamed source at the Michigan Bureau of Workers Compensation in Detroit who noted, "They've got a problem down there," referring to the "recent rash" of disputed injury claims at the Mazda plant.

The *Automotive News* report was picked up by local newspapers, which ran stories with headlines like, "Injury Rate Higher Than Normal at Mazda Plant," and by wire services.[6] Mazda management moved to contain what would later be described in an internal company memo as the "financial risk and negative public exposure for the corporation as these relate to occupational injuries/illness."[7] Mazda planned to do this by publicizing the positive benefits of its fitness center and its employee assistance program (EAP). Through EAP workers could obtain counseling for drug abuse, alcoholism, and emotional problems. The company also tried to counter the negative publicity it had received by dismissing the rash of injuries at the plant as a temporary problem—a glitch that resulted from starting second-shift production with a young, inexperienced work force. That this was exactly the kind of work force that Mazda had searched for so methodically in its five-step screening process was never mentioned by company spokespersons when they attempted to reassure the media in the winter of 1989 that the plant's injury rate had declined significantly now that the second shift start-up bugs had been worked out of the production system. Injury statistics from the plant do not suggest such a decline, however. Although there was a peak of injuries in August and September of 1988 when the plant reached full production, records for the plant's first 12 months of two-shift production (June 1988 to May 1989) show no significant drop in the injury rate. The monthly recordable injury rate for June 1988 was 35.4; for January 1989, 37; for April 1989, 34.6. In the last three months of 1988, 70 workers were injured at Flat Rock. In the first three months of the new year, when the company was claiming that most injuries had been the result of now-solved start-up bugs, the number of workers injured was 71.[8]

As part of its plan to prevent further "negative public exposure," Mazda prohibited workers from speaking to the news media. In February 1989, the month the *Automotive News* article appeared, the company added a special insert to its "MMUC Employee Handbook (For Team Leaders and Team Members)." The newly inserted page N 3 of the handbook informed workers that, "Whether you know it or not, you are a public relations representative for Mazda Motor Manufacturing (USA) Corp. . . . Positive comments contrib-

ute to strengthening your organization. Negative comments or un-informed comments only weaken the organization and damage the environment we work in."

The insert reminded workers of Mazda's "sensitive" position, being the first Japanese automaker in America's Motor City. "All the national media have journalists in Detroit ready to report on every aspect of the car business. Because MMUC is a subsidiary of a Japanese firm, located in the heart of the domestic auto industry, what it says and does will receive quick, often intense, scrutiny. MMUC's location in the Detroit community places an extra burden of responsibility on each of us to project the best image of MMUC, its philosophies, its policies, and its people."[9]

Apparently, the way for workers to contribute to this positive image was to avoid talking to the media. Under a subsection entitled, "When The Media Calls," the Mazda insert cautioned employees, "It is MMUC's Policy that *all* inquiries from the media or other organizations *must* be referred to public relations, *before any* comments can be made [italics are the company's]. . . . MMUC and Mazda Corporation have people on staff who are responsible for handling such inquiries. These types of contacts should immediately be referred to them."[10]

But many Mazda workers who were New Directions members ignored the N 3 insert, freely granting interviews to the media. New Directions also distributed flyers criticizing the company and the incumbent union representatives for Flat Rock's high rate of injuries and other problems. Crude and homemade in appearance, the flyers nevertheless stirred emotions at the plant, often dramatizing the hardships caused by the JIT system in the sardonic style of the hardened factory veteran: "Brother Jim, a team leader in stamping, has asked to be able to give up his team leader position because of a hardship. Brother Jim's wife is pregnant. She is also paralyzed from the chest down. Under his present schedule it is almost impossible [for Jim] to do his banking and other chores that are necessary to run a household under these conditions. But more importantly, he is having a great deal of difficulty finding someone to stay with his wife while he is at work. As a team member Jim would be able to work on days and stay with his wife in the evening and ease this situation considerably. . . . The Union and the Company with 'respect for the family' and in the 'spirit of teamwork' have decided that Brother Jim does not have a 'hardship,' and will have to continue to struggle alone."[11]

From the handful of workers who met at Greg Drudi's house

before Christmas, New Directions grew to become a powerful force within the plant by the winter of 1989. The coalition's meetings, by then held in the basement banquet room of a Flat Rock restaurant, drew as many as 50 active supporters. By March, 500 of the plant's 2,800 hourly workers had signed a platform endorsing the New Directions challenge to the incumbent union committee and the UAW's "cooperative" relationship with Mazda. This challenge was led by Phil Keeling, whom the dissidents nominated to run against Bill Judson for president of Local 3000 in the upcoming union election. Keeling, the tall, angry, and intense West Virginian, attended his first New Directions meeting in January, about a month after the group's official beginning. His immense, Viking-warrior appearance and fiery southern oratory attracted an immediate following among the dissidents. Greg Drudi, his friend from the paint shop, urged Keeling to run for the presidency of the local.

In his campaign Keeling lashed out at the company for disregarding the safety of members in its pursuit of production goals. The majority of injuries at the plant stemmed either directly or indirectly, he believed, from the excessive demands made on workers by Mazda's JIT system, a system that stretched human and material resources at Flat Rock to the breaking point for the sake of increased efficiency. "People are suffering at that plant because there aren't enough workers," he said. "When you have seven people trying to do the job of eight, and then you kaizen it down to six, you're going to have problems."

Team members who were pushed to the point of physical exhaustion to keep up with the JIT production pace were, said Keeling, more likely to sprain a muscle or injure themselves through careless mistakes. Workers found it difficult to keep their minds focused on their jobs after nine hours of 57-second-per-minute motion. This explained why the worst accidents seemed always to occur near the end of a shift, believed one worker, whose teammate suffered a concussion in 1988 after another worker, struggling to meet a production goal just before quitting time, inadvertently swung an air tool into the teammate's head.

The most common safety complaint from Mazda workers involved cumulative trauma injuries (CTIs), most notably carpal tunnel syndrome, a painful, sometimes debilitating inflammation of the tendons in the hands and wrists caused by excessive repetitive motions, particularly those accompanied by vibrations or resistance (for example, the operation of powerful hand tools). When the inflamed

wrist tendons swell, they push against the carpal tunnel of bones and ligaments that carries the main nerve to the fingers and flexing tendons. This causes the tunnel to narrow, leading to numbness, pain, and an inhibition of finger movement. Approximately 5 percent of those diagnosed with carpal tunnel syndrome require corrective surgery, about 1 percent end up with permanent injury, and the remainder recover completely by resting and eliminating stressful motions.

Carpal tunnel syndrome and other CTIs occur at all automobile plants, as well as other industrial facilities, and are clearly not a problem unique to Flat Rock. A study cosponsored by the National Institute for Occupational Safety and Health, the Ford Motor Company, and the Motor Vehicle Manufacturers Association found the incidence of carpal tunnel syndrome to be as high as 5.1 percent in certain industrial jobs.[12] But what surprised many health professionals about Flat Rock was the rate at which workers appeared to be developing the disorder at the Mazda plant. Detroit physicians who specialized in the treatment of hand and wrist injuries were accustomed to seeing autoworkers with CTI complaints. But most of the CTI cases from Big Three plants involved workers who had been working in factories for years, since the "cumulative" injuries usually took time to develop. The Mazda workers, by contrast, were young; they were new to factory work; and they were employed at a plant that had not even been making cars a year and a half earlier. A Detroit industrial hygienist quoted in the *Automotive News* article remarked: "It's been said in the [local] medical community that there's a mini-epidemic of carpal tunnel syndrome [at Flat Rock]."[13] This contention was supported by Walter Crowley, the president of Michigan Injured Workers, a federally recognized non-profit advocacy and support group that received 64 calls from Mazda workers complaining of hand and arm injuries (mostly CTIs) during Flat Rock's first five months of full production (September 1988 to January 1989). "I've never seen as high an intake of workers compensation claims as we're getting from Mazda. It's well beyond the Big Three rate," Crowley said. In 1988 Mazda's Flat Rock plant recorded 97 CTI incidents; by comparison, Chrysler's Sterling Heights, Michigan, assembly plant, built a short time before Flat Rock and not operating under a JIT system, recorded 54 CTI incidents over the same period, even though it had longer hours of operation and a much larger work force.[14] (The Chrysler plant ran two shifts at full production for all of 1988 and employed 3,500, while Mazda did not add a second shift until June and employed fewer than 3,100.)

Not surprisingly, Mazda denied that Flat Rock had a "carpal tunnel syndrome problem." The company's managers officially maintained that CTI incidents occurred no more frequently at Flat Rock than they did at Big Three factories. "To the extent that we are encountering carpal tunnel syndrome and other cumulative trauma disorders in our work force, we believe we are no different from the rest of our industry," Osamu Nobuto asserted in a letter to the editor responding to the *Automotive News* article.[15] This declaration of parity with other automakers was in sharp contrast to the we-have-a-more-enlightened-attitude-about-worker-safety posture that Mazda had assumed with the media prior to the appearance of stories about the plant's high injury rate.

Despite Mazda's denials, New Directions critics like Phil Keeling and Greg Drudi continued to believe that the company's accelerated JIT production pace sped up the onset of carpal tunnel syndrome and other CTI problems. They argued that because Mazda team members were kept busy 57 seconds a minute—as opposed to the 45-second-a-minute Big Three pace—workers at Flat Rock were forced to repeat the same hand and arm motions with greater speed and frequency, putting a greater strain on muscles and tendons. Not only did Mazda workers have to perform their repetitive tasks faster and more often, they had to do so over longer stretches of time without rest, because almost all idle moments or "waiting *muda*" had been kaizened out of their work routines. This, too, increased the strain on muscles and tendons by denying workers the chance to rest overused wrists and arms for brief periods.

The risk of developing a CTI was compounded for team members who had to use hand-held power tools when performing their repetitive jobs. A study of 652 workers at 7 different industrial sites by the University of Michigan's Center for Ergonomics and School of Public Health in 1986 concluded that carpal tunnel syndrome was "strongly associated with high-force, high-repetitive work and to a lesser extent with high repetitiveness alone, irrespective of other factors. High force combined with high repetitiveness appears to have more than a multiplicative effect, increasing the risk more than five times than that of either factor alone."[16] Early in 1989, every worker on a five-member team in Unit 24 of Flat Rock's trim and final assembly line (all of them SMPs) were put on medical leave or restriction because of CTI problems. The injured team members had been required to work with an air tool, which, because of its configuration, had to be triggered with the pinky finger. They had to flex their

pinkies against the resistance of a trigger hundreds of times a day.

The physical intensity of the Mazda work pace and its role in contributing to CTIs is evident in the work routines followed by two team members during the summer of 1988. Like virtually all Mazda workers, these team members were at the Flat Rock plant between 9.5 and 10.5 hours a day, 6 or 7 days a week, throughout the summer. Their workdays were punctuated by a 30-minute unpaid lunch and 52 minutes of paid breaks (a 15-minute break in the morning, a 10-minute break at lunch, a 15-minute break in the afternoon, and a 3-minute break for every half hour of overtime). They were actively engaged in work activities for almost all the remaining time.

The first team member installed engine mounts in the trim and final assembly area. In performing his job, this worker had to use an LB-46 air gun, a three-foot-long tool, with a torque so powerful it could lift an automobile engine two inches off its frame. His *one-minute* job cycle consisted of the following nine steps: (1) separate the accelerator cable and cruise control cable; (2) pull the EMI harness up from below the automatic transmission cable; (3) place the engine mount in the car; (4) push two bolts through the mount; (5) position washers and nuts on each bolt; (6) using the air gun, tighten the washers and nuts on each bolt; (7) install the bracket bolt; (8) pull off the engine jig; (9) push the radiator hose down in preparation for radiator installation at the next work station. During the course of a ten-hour workday, he often had to complete this routine, without variation, more than four hundred times. After less than a year on the job, he began to notice sharp pains in his wrists, aggravated by repeated jolts from the powerful air tool. Eventually the pain became so intense that he was forced to take a three-month medical leave, receiving 60 percent of his base pay.

The second team member worked at a welding booth in the body shop, where he was responsible for grinding and smoothing welds on either the driver or passenger side of vehicles. He had to perform the following eleven steps during a job cycle that lasted less than four minutes, using very powerful (up to 12,000 rpm) sanders and grinders: (1) install brackets on fenders; (2) using a hammer-and-punch tool, raise the weld on the post connecting the roof to the body in the front of the vehicle (this post is called the A-pillar on the driver's side and the B-pillar on the passenger's); (3) use the grinder to grind off the top of this weld; (4) use the same grinder to grind off the top of the "mig weld post" connecting the roof to the body at the rear of the vehicle (C-pillar on the driver's side, D-pillar on passenger's); (5) use

the belt sander to sand down the five gas braces on the side and rear of the vehicle; (6) replace the belt sander with a grinder and work on the same gas braces; (7) again, take the belt sander and work on the hinge pillar inside the door; (8) take a rough hand sander and work on all the aforementioned welds and gas braces; (9) take the hammer-and-punch tool used in step one and raise the mig weld; (10) using a fine sander, smooth the mig weld finish; and (11) using an oscillating tool, remove sander marks from the mig weld post.

Like all team members at the welding booth, the worker had to perform this job cycle on 12.25 cars every hour, leaving him with "no time to rest, except during breaks." Because the job, with its frequent use of powerful hand tools, was so physically punishing, he and his teammates were rotated through it on two-hour shifts. During the summer he was in the booth for two hours before lunch, two hours after lunch, and for one or two hours' overtime. By August he had developed large bulges on his wrists and was experiencing considerable discomfort. He was transferred to another part of the body shop for a short period of time, and the bulges and pain went away. But soon after he returned to the welding booth, the numbness in his hands and wrists returned. The company's medical department gave him wrist plates to wear to bed, which were supposed to improve circulation to his hands by keeping him from bending his wrists during sleep. "My muscles are built now, so it's easier, but it's a tough job, because you're working with power tools all day, and they fight you like crazy," said the worker in 1989, shortly before he transferred out of the body shop permanently. A large, powerful man in his twenties, the worker doubted that many people over 40 could handle the welding job on a daily basis.

Workers who were injured trying to keep up with this intense work pace were often ridiculed and harassed by Mazda managers. Many of those who complained of cumulative trauma pains were denied permission to visit the plant's medical department by suspicious unit leaders who accused them of feigning their injuries to avoid work. "Whenever we saw [a worker] walk by with a clipboard [a sign that he was on a restricted work routine], we would holler out insults like 'Medical Mary,' " said the engine mount installer whose work routine has just been described. "The unit leaders didn't come right out and tell us to say these things, but they really encouraged it in a way by telling us things like, 'You guys would be able to rotate [jobs] if it [weren't] for people like that not doing their fair share of work.' "

The intense pressure placed on unit leaders to meet JIT production schedules created a built-in antagonism toward injured workers. "Even the unit leader who starts out as a decent human being is going to get cold hearted as a result of all the pressure," said a skilled trades worker. One Mazda production worker who was placed on a medical restriction that excused her from using hand-held power tools was ordered to use an air gun by her unit leader the day she returned to work. When the worker refused, saying she had a medical restriction, the unit leader told her, "Just do it. If you want to keep your job, do it."[17] The worker continued to refuse and was fired. She later filed suit against Mazda for wrongful discharge and eventually received an out-of-court settlement.

The hostile reaction of unit leaders was part of a corporatewide antagonism toward injured workers at Mazda. Workers who went to the plant's medical department reported that they were treated coldly by the staff, which regarded their injury claims with suspicion. "Their attitude when I went there was, 'We're more interested in protecting the company than taking care of you,' " said one former team member, who claimed to have carpal tunnel syndrome from her job in the body shop.

Mazda contested the majority of compensation claims filed by workers during its first two years of production. According to Walter Crowley of Michigan Injured Workers, the advocacy group, the company's response to worker injury claims followed a predictable pattern: "At first they say that the worker is faking it. Then once it's medically established that he or she is in fact injured, they'll turn around and say, 'Well, it's not really a serious injury,' or failing that they'll claim that the worker's injury couldn't have been job-related anyway. I've heard of Mazda changing its defense in the middle of a workers compensation argument. . . . Their opposition to workers' compensation is so entrenched that I have to think the company made a conscious corporate decision to oppose every claim no matter what." The Big Three "certainly aren't princes about workers' compensation," said Crowley, but he believed they were far more flexible than Mazda. "About seventy-five percent of the workers' compensation cases in Michigan are settled before they ever go to court," he said. "It's still early in the history of the plant to tell how they'll ultimately compare to that, but I'd be very surprised if it's favorably."

The company's response to workers' compensation claims amounted to a "starve-them-out defense," believed Crowley. "Sim-

ply by contesting a worker's initial claim, the company can buy six months [the amount of time needed to schedule a mediation hearing on a workers compensation dispute]," he explained. "Since the mediation is nonbinding, the company can reject an unfavorable decision and insist on a court trial, which can take an additional two years to schedule. Then, by appealing an unfavorable court decision, they can easily drag the case on for another three, four, or five years. Meanwhile the worker who has lost his job and his medical insurance becomes desperate and either drops the case or agrees to some ridiculously low settlement." Mazda had a strong incentive to follow this strategy, believed Crowley, because its work force was so young. "It's dealing with a lot of twenty-five-year-olds who have young families to support and want to get on with the rest of their lives. They aren't going to have the patience of a fifty-three-year-old whose kids are already grown," he explained.

Mazda denied that it ever systematically obstructed workers' compensation claims, insisting instead that it simply fulfilled its responsibility "to protect employees and the company" by investigating the legitimacy of every claim.[18] But many workers alleged that the company persisted in opposing their claims even after its own doctors determined their injuries to be serious and work related. Charles Palmer, an attorney who represented more than 35 injured Mazda employees in suits against the company, observed: "I've been handling workers' comp cases for ten years, and I've never seen anything like it. Mazda has sent people to doctors, specialists in hand injuries, and they have called the injuries work related, but the company still refuses to reach a legitimate settlement. When this sort of things happens to the Big Three, they settle. I honestly couldn't tell you what Mazda is thinking—it doesn't make sense."

The relative lack of skilled trades workers at Flat Rock also contributed to the plant's safety problem. Since Mazda's skilled trades work force was roughly half the size of its opposite number at an American auto plant, skilled trades workers at Flat Rock had trouble keeping up with the volume of repair and maintenance jobs. As a result regular production workers often tried to repair faulty equipment themselves, rather than "waste" valuable production time waiting for the appropriate skilled trades worker to fit the machine into his or her overcrowded work schedule. Not adequately trained to perform skilled trades jobs, the production workers often failed to

follow proper safety procedures. Production workers did welding without wearing welding masks, applied caustic sealants and other chemicals without proper safety gloves, opened wire mesh gates and entered the safety envelope of equipment that was still in operation, and climbed on moving assembly lines while working on machinery. Unit leaders, pressured to meet tight production schedules, often encouraged workers to take these safety risks. "Almost every day we see safety infractions that we try to point out to those involved. But the people involved have been told what they are doing is safe, or they have seen unit leaders or trainers doing it," a group of skilled trades workers wrote to the editor of a Mazda employee newsletter.[19]

Not surprisingly, the poor quality of the skilled trades work done by inexperienced production employees often created safety hazards itself. Untutored line workers welded brackets directly onto building columns, a clear safety hazard, since the heat from the welding gun changes the molecular structure of the building's I-beam and creates a weak bond. A former Mazda worker repeated a story that became legendary around the Flat Rock plant: "Back when we had just started production, a skilled trades guy noticed a very bad weld that had been done by a guy in the body shop and got real upset. He called over someone from safety and let him have it, telling him that the weld was no good and would never hold. The safety man looked over the weld, and said, 'It doesn't seem so bad to me.' This got the skilled trades guy really steamed, so he just reached out and yanked the [welded] bracket right off, . . . handed it to the safety man [and] said, 'Here, I'm telling you it's not good.' "

Because Mazda's shallow pool of skilled trades workers could not keep up with the influx of safety-related repair jobs in 1988–89, malfunctioning and potentially hazardous machinery was kept in operation for days or even weeks before it was finally attended to. The task of the overburdened skilled trades worker was complicated further by the meager supply of spare parts and components available to him or her as a result of Mazda's bare-bones JIT inventory system. Skilled trades workers sometimes had to wait for needed parts to arrive from outside vendors before they could begin a repair job.

On Saturday, March 4, 1989, a metal arm lift that automatically fed tires to installers on the final assembly line began to malfunction. Normally the lift would follow the worker along a track that ran parallel to the assembly line. When the worker took a tire off the lift, it would retract to its home position to retrieve a new tire. But on this particular Saturday, the lift started acting up, following the worker

for about five or six feet and then, for no apparent reason, whipping into reverse at high speed. "If you happened to be grabbing the tire at the time this thing took off, it would tear your arm off," recalled a trim and final worker. "On Monday, I told my team leader that this lift was really dangerous; he said they were aware of the problem, but [they] hadn't gotten around to it yet. Later, a few maintenance guys came over and they couldn't fix it. . . . When I left work on Tuesday afternoon, it still wasn't fixed. Then on Wednesday, the other lift [on the opposite side of the conveyor] started doing the same thing. This one knocked a worker on the arm and bruised him up pretty good, but it was never entered as an injury report because he didn't lose any time [from work]."

In other instances, needed equipment repairs were postponed, and safety shortcuts taken, because unit leaders were reluctant to stop the production process to allow skilled trades crew to work on machinery. This was especially true of the subassembly stations, which, because no back-up inventory was permitted under Mazda's JIT system, were under constant pressure to keep the main assembly line supplied with parts. The tire subassembly station, where tires are automatically mounted on metal wheels and inflated, provided a vivid example of how safety was sacrificed for the sake of production. As a safety precaution, the station's tire-mounting and -inflating equipment was designed with a conducting cable running across the wire mesh gates that seal off its safety envelope. This guarantees that anyone wanting to open the gates to service the equipment will first have to unplug the cable and thereby cut off its power. Although this feature offers obvious safety benefits, ensuring that workers do not get their hands mangled by moving parts, it also increases the time that must be spent on service calls by placing an added obstacle in the path of the repair technician. In late 1988, when the equipment began to experience frequent mechanical problems, someone removed this "obstacle" by repositioning the connecting cable so it could run along the floor, while the wire gates were left open permanently. As a result technicians could not only gain faster access to the equipment, they were also able to work on it while it was in operation, allowing tire production to continue but increasing their own risk of injury. Safety procedures were compromised further when production employees were required to reach in through the open gates about ten inches to the operating machinery and align tires and wheels by hand, after the "electric eyes" that did this automatically began to malfunction. The tires and wheels had to be

aligned manually as they traveled along a moving conveyor, less than two feet from a powerful metal arm that wedged the tire under the metal wheel lip. "If you slip up, you can get hurt," said a team member. "We have to do this [manual alignment] a lot, because the equipment that's supposed to do it automatically is always going down. Sometimes we've operated manually three or four days in a row. . . . If they find the [automatic equipment] can't be fixed without stopping the line, they'll let it go until lunch or after the shift ends."

Mazda's pressured JIT system also made it difficult for workers, once injured, to readjust to Flat Rock's intense production pace when they returned to work. At a traditional Big Three plant, the worker recovering from an injury could always be eased back into the work routine by being assigned to an off-line janitorial job or other less-demanding task. But few such jobs existed at Flat Rock. Under Mazda's JIT system, with its emphasis on maintaining the smallest possible work force, all of the easier support jobs were either incorporated into the work routines of regular production workers or hired out to low-cost subcontractors. This often left the company with no place to put the recovering worker but back in a full-paced production job that was likely to reaggravate, and even worsen, the original injury.

Darryl Williams was one of many injured workers in 1988–89 who alleged that Mazda forced them back to full production work before their recovery was complete. One of the elite group of four hundred original hirees sent to Japan for special training, Williams was a team leader in the paint shop. In the summer of 1988, he was climbing off the conveyor after removing a hood jig from a car when he slipped on a patch of cleaning solution and twisted his back. The plant's medical department placed Williams on medical restriction, exempting him from on-line production work. But, as Williams would later tell it, his unit leaders, pressured to meet their JIT production schedules and having few off-line jobs available, pushed him to return to the line. In October Williams was working the line, when he received a call on his two-way radio that a solvent line had broken at the end of the paint booth. Running to the booth, he felt a pop in his back, followed by a pain that almost took him off his feet. Williams later visited his personal physician, who recommended that he be put on medical disability, excusing him from work until December 1. But in early November, Mazda ordered Williams to see the plant's doctor, who, after sending him to a local hospital for tests,

declared him fit enough to follow a restricted work routine. Returning to work, Williams began to experience severe back pain after four hours on the paint line. He asked to see the plant doctor, but his unit leader refused him permission. When Williams said that he could no longer continue working, the unit leader informed him that if he left his work station he would be issued a written reprimand. Williams decided to take the reprimand and went home. For the next two weeks Mazda tried to find less strenuous off-line jobs for Williams, but apparently no such assignments were available. He ended up spending two or three hours a day in the plant's labor relations department, drawing stick-figure cartoons for the department's publications and doing other "busy work."

Finally, after Thanksgiving, Williams was sent back to the paint line and put to work masking cars, a job that required him to raise his hands above his head, aggravating his back pain. The labor relations representatives who observed him saw that the stretching was causing him considerable discomfort, so they moved him to another job, grinding the stone guard on the bottom of cars. The six-foot-three Williams had to sit on a footstool and lean forward to perform this task. After lunch he was given the job of wiping cars in the primer booth at the full production speed of 480 cars a day. At the end of the day, he went to the plant's medical department to receive heat treatments for the knifing pains in his back.

The next day Williams was again sent to the primer booth. After 25 minutes of stretching over the hoods of Probes and MX-6s, the pain in his back became unbearable. He called the labor relations department and said that he could not continue wiping cars. A group of labor relations representatives came to the primer booth and, after telling him that the job was within his medical restrictions, ordered him to continue. At this point Williams exploded. "I told them off," he recalled. "That was it. Hell, I'm in pain, and they're screwing with me."

Mazda fired Williams for "refusing work and disruptive behavior." In January 1989 the former team leader filed a workers' compensation suit against the company in Wayne County Michigan Circuit Court. A myelogram administered by an outside physician in March showed that Williams had an enlarged ruptured disc, a condition that eventually required him to have surgery.*

* Williams later won his job back from Mazda after the UAW filed a formal grievance against the company. His workers' compensation claim against the company was still pending in January 1990.

The absence of relatively easy off-line janitorial and support jobs at Flat Rock has raised an uncomfortable question for many at the plant—where will Mazda put its young workers, most of whom are still in their twenties and early thirties, when they are no longer able to keep up with the JIT production pace? "There are no easy jobs [at Flat Rock] for old guys," said Greg Drudi, who occupied the second spot on the New Directions campaign ticket, behind Keeling, as a candidate for chairperson of the plant's bargaining committee. "What are you going to do with this guy when he can't put in a catalytic converter? The easy jobs like driving finished cars to the loading docks and sweeping up, that they hire out now, should be held for old guys."

As a UAW representative, Bob Ramp also worried about the issue of older workers. "Some of the [workers] out here have asked me, 'Bob, you know I'm able to cut it now, but what happens in three or five years down the road if my body won't take this anymore?' It's an interesting question—and I don't have an answer for them."

In Japan Mazda was able to ease its older employees into less physically demanding positions at its six-story Hofu training center, its company dormitories and stores, and its national network of car dealerships, or with one of the supplier firms with which it shares a familial closeness. But no such off-plant network of potential jobs exists in the United States for older Mazda workers.

The availability of these off-plant jobs has also made it easier for Mazda to implement its JIT system in Japan without incurring the high injury rate it has encountered in the United States. In Japan, Mazda can assign workers who are recovering from injuries to softer jobs at the Hofu training center to allow them to regain their strength, thereby minimizing the risk of reinjury. Mazda's Japanese workers, typically hired directly out of high school, receive much more extensive cross-training than do their opposite numbers in America. This has allowed the Japanese to enjoy more frequent and more significant job rotation, which appears to reduce the risk of CTIs by distributing physical stress over a wider variety of joints and muscles. The traditional stoicism of the Japanese worker also would tend to obscure any injury problem at Mazda's Japanese JIT plants—a worker who is hurt and suffers in silence will never be recorded. The lifetime employment policies followed by Mazda and other Japanese manufacturers have encouraged workers to remain silent about injuries. Since workers are confident that their company will be taking care of them for life, they do not feel the need to protect themselves by

reporting their injuries to a government agency. But in recent years, as Japanese workers have become more willing to speak out, it has become more apparent that they, too, have paid the price of keeping up with the JIT production pace. On November 27, 1988, Japan's Ministry of Labor issued the results of a survey of fifteen thousand workers in eight thousand firms that showed that 82.7 percent of Japanese workers complained of some form of physical ailment, notably stiff shoulders and necks as well as back and hip pains.[20]

The UAW local was sympathetic to the injury complaints of Mazda's American workers. The union's leaders were also angered by the company's intransigence in dealing with worker injury claims. A union official told *Automotive News* that the UAW was "not satisfied with either the rate at which injuries are occurring [at Flat Rock] or the relief provided to workers who are injured."[21] Local 3000 president Bill Judson and Region 1A Director Ernie Lofton also told visitors in August 1988 that they were dissatisfied with the level of cross-training Mazda was providing workers, something that the union believed contributed to the plant's high injury rate.[22]

Yet, even though the UAW was aggressive in helping some injured team members like Darryl Williams pursue their grievances against Mazda, the union was reluctant to confront the company over management policies—such as the decision to maintain a lean work force—that workers believed contributed to the plant's high injury rate. Nor did the UAW seem willing to challenge management over clear-cut safety violations. Workers in the tire subassembly station complained to the union about the open safety gates, just as workers on the trim and final assembly line complained about the erratic tire feeder. But, in each case, the workers received the same noncommittal response: "We'll see what we can do." Nothing ever was done, because the union was, the workers believed, too afraid of offending management.

Judson and Lofton were candid about the plant's problems. They acknowledged that Mazda had not "been walking like it's talking." The injury rate was too high. The number of workers at the plant was too low. There were not enough training and job rotation. But even as they spoke of these problems, the union's leaders continued to praise the "Mazda philosophy" for its "innovations" and the "dignity and respect" it accorded workers. The union was, they insisted, working diligently to improve conditions inside the plant,

applying behind-the-scenes pressure on Mazda to modify its JIT management system. Judson and Lofton were confident that this cooperative, low-keyed approach would work with Mazda. If it did not, the union was prepared to become more aggressive. "I can assure you that the [UAW's] nonadversarial position will become adversarial," Lofton said in the summer of 1988, when asked what the union would do if Mazda failed to implement the promised level of job rotation.[23] Until then, patience would be the UAW's watchword. The union would not pressure the company by publicizing the plant's problems as the New Directions dissidents were doing. On the contrary, the union's leaders seemed intent on shielding Mazda from public criticism. The plant was still new, and any problems were probably the result of start-up bugs, they explained. The overwhelming majority of workers still believed in the Mazda team system, said the union, despite the noisy protests of a few dissidents. Even as more and more Mazda team members began showing up at the plant wearing the New Directions buttons that the dissidents had begun distributing in the winter of 1989, the union's leadership continued to believe that most workers shared their willingness to be patient.

11
The Divided Union

THE woman from trim and final assembly sat near the door of the restaurant's basement banquet room. Short and plump with a round face, she snuffed out her cigarette on the gold foil disposable ashtray and tapped her fingers, thick with broken nails, on the table. It was her first New Directions meeting. She was not sure she should be in this stale, windowless room, filled with blue-and-khaki-clad Mazda workers clustered in large, noisy groups waiting for the meeting to begin. Her father, a retired autoworker, had often told her about how bad things used to be in the "old days," when the union and company were constantly at war with one another, fighting over every petty rule and job assignment. It took forever to get things done back then. If workers and managers had not stopped fighting, there would have been nothing left to fight over, her father had told her, because all the jobs would haved moved overseas. Her father did not approve of this, the woman said, gesturing toward the room full of dissident workers. But she had seen too much at the plant—team members being forced to work hurt, unit leaders playing favorites—to accept her father's view of the dissidents as irresponsible rabblerousers. She did not know if she would join the New Directions coalition; she was not even sure she would vote for its candidates in the upcoming union local election. She was there on that Monday night in March 1989 to listen.

Had she come to the meeting expecting to hear the dissidents discuss their ideology, she would have been disappointed. There would be no speeches attacking the company's team system, no re-

counting of Mazda war stories, no complaints about safety violations and broken orientation promises. The time for such talk had long since passed. The dissidents were of one mind about the inequities of Mazda's team system, and there was no point preaching to the converted.

Nor did the dissidents spend time discussing how they planned to deal with the company should they win the upcoming election. This too had already been decided upon, at least in general terms. The dissidents admitted that there was a limit to what the union could do at Flat Rock, regardless of who led it, because of the weakly worded Mazda contract. No one could demand that the company adhere to rules that did not exist. Real changes at the plant would have to wait, they knew, until 1991, when a new contract would be negotiated. Since the coming election was for a one-year term, the candidates who won would have to be reelected in 1990 to have an impact on the new contract. Until that time, though, there were steps the dissidents promised to take, if elected, to change things at the plant. They would be more aggressive in filing grievances on behalf of workers. They would complain more loudly—to the media if necessary—about safety violations. They would pressure Mazda to hire more workers and provide more cross-training. They would begin acting more like a worker's union than a company union, moving the union representatives into their own office, away from the labor relations department, and starting a union newsletter (none existed at the plant) to inform members of their rights and publicize grievances.

But none of these plans was discussed on that March night in the basement of Fiorelli's. Instead, with the election for Local 3000 president, bargaining committee members, and Mazda plant representatives scheduled for April 19, a little more than six weeks away, the meeting was given over to the small, mundane details of running a union election campaign, something at which the dissidents clearly lacked experience. Phil Keeling called the meeting to order, rising from his seat in a corner of the room and reaching a tree-limb arm up to pound on a ceiling support beam. Unlike most of the other workers in the room, who were wearing blue-and-khaki Mazda uniforms, Keeling was dressed in jeans and a red plaid shirt. He asked if there were any newcomers at the meeting who wanted to introduce themselves, emphasizing that such introductions were completely voluntary and that everyone would understand if a visitor wished to protect his or her anonymity. One worker stood up, gave his name, and said

he had come "to check things out." The woman from trim and final assembly remained silent.

Keeling then introduced Greg Drudi, who, in his role as rcording secretary, read the minutes of the previous Monday's meeting. Drudi also gave an account of the group's finances, telling the members how much money had been raised at the last meeting (under two hundred dollars) and how it had been spent—mostly on the purchase of campaign buttons that read, "I support New Directions Coalition," and the printing of flyers. The group had found a new, less-expensive button supplier, Drudi said, so buttons should become more plentiful. Even so, Keeling broke in, since buttons cost a lot and the coalition's funds were running low, members should be more careful when they distributed buttons.

An older worker, a large man in his early forties, stood up and took a collection, walking silently from member to member with an upturned Mazda cap, the kind that had been at the center of the mandatory-voluntary cap-wearing controversy during the plant's start-up phase eons ago.

After the collection the workers scheduled assignments for passing out New Directions flyers at plant gates during the upcoming week. The scheduling involved a great deal of give-and-take—one worker agreed to come to work early on Wednesday and Thursday to hand out flyers, provided that someone cover for her the following week. The consensus problem-solving techniques the workers had learned during their three-month training program were being put to use.

The plant's security force had been good about allowing them to distribute flyers. Most of the uniformed guards had even been friendly, exchanging greetings with the dissidents as they waited outside the plant gates in the chilly predawn March mornings for the morning shift workers to arrive. Inside the plant, though, the attitude toward the dissidents was less cordial. The dissidents claimed the New Directions campaign was being harassed by Mazda unit leaders and labor relations representatives. Unit leaders had, they said, confiscated New Directions literature from team members, warning the offending workers that support for the dissidents was considered a sign of disrespect for the company. Because of the broad discretionary power wielded by unit leaders, the dissidents were certain that these threats would discourage many sympathetic workers from showing their support for the New Directions coalition.

An undercurrent of fear was present whenever the dissidents

spoke of the unit leaders. The dissidents knew that they had crossed the Rubicon by joining New Directions. From that point on they would be marked as "troublemakers" in a plant that prized team players. Unit leaders would be gunning for them, eager to write them up for even minor infractions, pushing them into the worst assignments and refusing to excuse their absences or tardiness. Their union, which regarded them as traitors, would never support them in a dispute with the company. Many worried that, should their side lose the upcoming election, unit leaders, with the tacit cooperation of the union local, would be able to force them out of their Mazda jobs, either hounding them until they quit in frustration or finding excuses to fire them. As much as they disapproved of the way things were done at the plant, few of the dissidents had thought of working elsewhere (although some had begun to look for nonfactory jobs). The reason they wanted to stay at Mazda was financial. No job within their reach could come close to matching the $35,000 to $45,000 a year they earned at Flat Rock. According to UAW statistics, the majority of displaced autoworkers take new jobs that pay at least 16 percent less than auto factory work, and nearly one-third of them end up earning more than 25 percent less at their new positions.[1]

Although Mazda professed to be neutral in its plant's union election—as indeed it was required to be by law—the dissidents believed that the company was clearly favoring the incumbents. This had become obvious to the dissidents early in their campaign, when the labor relations department tore down the New Directions flyers they had posted on the plant's "public" bulletin boards. When the dissidents protested, the labor relations representatives told them that any notice must be approved by the company before it could be posted. But prior to the New Directions campaign, workers had been free to use the bulletin boards to advertise used cars and karate classes and announce the formation of bowling leagues and fishing expeditions without receiving company approval.

Mazda also tried to stop workers from wearing New Directions buttons, citing the rule that prohibited jewelry, patches, and buttons on uniforms. But throughout 1987–88, the company had frequently relaxed its prohibition against buttons. "We always had people wearing buttons," said Greg Drudi. "People wore University of Michigan buttons. . . . When we had a United Way drive they wore United Way buttons. . . . They wore little smiley-face buttons. . . . I personally always wore a UAW pin. No one ever said anything. . . . But

when New Directions came along it was, 'No buttons can be worn on uniforms.' "

The dissidents believed they found a loophole in the button rule. At a meeting with labor relations representatives to discuss the button prohibition, one of the dissidents pointed to the white turtleneck the woman was wearing under her Mazda work shirt. "What about that?" he said. "Is that part of your Mazda uniform?" The labor relations representative admitted that technically it was not. "Well, then, since turtlenecks and undershirts are not part of the uniform, it should be okay if we wear our buttons on them." The labor relations representative was uncertain how to respond to this assertion. So, too, it seemed, was everyone else in Mazda management. The company refused to take an official position on this new interpretation of the dress code. Once again unit leaders stepped in to fill the vacuum created by the absence of clear written guidelines. Some unit leaders did nothing when New Directions buttons began to peek up over uniforms on T-shirt collars and over breast pockets on the tops of pens (held in place by adhesive tape). But other unit leaders refused to bend the button rule, threatening to write up any worker who wore a button to work, regardless of whether it was technically attached to the uniform or not.

At the New Directions meeting in March, several members complained to Keeling that they were being harassed by unit leaders for wearing buttons on their T-shirts and turtlenecks. Some of the members expressed fears about being fired. "I can't tell you what to do," Keeling said. "I can't honestly tell you that there's no way you can get fired. All I can say is I've been wearing my button, and no one has bothered me yet. But this is something [you've] got to decide for yourself. . . . One of the things we want to change in the plant is this kind of inconsistency." New Directions had contacted the National Labor Relations Board (NLRB) about the harassment the group had received from Mazda, Keeling reminded the members. If the NLRB found that the charges had merit, as Keeling was sure they would, they would file a formal complaint against the company.

The anger the dissidents displayed when they talked about Mazda deepened into a darker, more visceral contempt when they discussed the UAW establishment. Mazda had broken its orientation promises, but in the end the company had acted in a way these sons and daughters of working-class America expected any employer to act: When faced with a choice between squeezing an extra ounce of profit out of its plant or protecting the interests of workers, it invariably

chose the former. The dissidents felt Mazda had let them down by being just like any other company. By contrast, they believed that their UAW local had betrayed them by being unlike any other union. The UAW had, they said, turned on its own cause, ignoring the interests of workers at Flat Rock for the sake of currying favor with Japanese automakers—collecting dues from more than three thousand new members in the process.

Despite all of the problems at Flat Rock, many of the dissidents believed that the Mazda team system could still live up to its promise, if there were a powerful union at the plant. "We don't want to go back to the old confrontational ways," said Keeling. "We aren't against the team system and cooperation . . . and we certainly aren't against anything that will improve quality. What we want is for workers to be treated with the respect and dignity they were told they would receive." Mazda could not be relied on to police itself and make sure that it kept its own promises, argued the dissidents. A strong, independent union was needed to keep the company honest.

The dissidents were also angry over what they considered to be the deliberate distortions in the campaign run against them by the incumbent union officers. They accused the incumbents of trying to mislead workers into believing that New Directions was a radical fringe group that did not belong to the UAW. "A lot of people have been led to think that this is an election between the UAW and this other union called New Directions," said one dissident. "I've gone to hand out flyers to people, and they'll say, 'No thanks, man, I'm going to stick with the UAW.' I tell them, 'Hey, we are the UAW too,' and they don't believe it because they've been told all these lies."

This insider-outsider distinction was reinforced by the incumbent union officers' campaign literature, which was printed to look like official UAW flyers. (Like the company, the UAW was legally required to maintain an official position of neutrality in union elections. For example, union funds and facilities could not be used to aid the cause of any candidate, although individual union officers could endorse and assist any candidate they chose.) On the morning of February 10, workers reporting to the plant were given flyers with a large UAW seal on top. The flyers began by reporting on a bylaw meeting that the local had held the previous night, but this quickly led into an attack on the New Directions candidates, who were described as "individuals that are trying to take advantage of you." The flyers warned workers not to be misled "like sheep to the slaughter in the wrong direction." Their identity as campaign literature by then

clearly established, the flyers concluded by asking workers to "vote USA all the way" in the upcoming election, a reference to the United Solidarity Administration caucus, the name under which Bill Judson and the other Local 3000 incumbents were running.

On March 9, 1989, the NLRB, responding to the allegations made by New Directions, filed an eight-count complaint against Mazda, charging that the company's ban on buttons, its rule requiring bulletin-board notices be approved by management, and other practices discriminated against the dissidents' campaign. A total of 26 Mazda managers, including James Korowin, the vice president of manufacturing, and Penny Morey, the labor relations director, were named in the complaint, which was upheld at a subsequent hearing. Mazda refused to comment directly on the NLRB complaint to the media, but the company insisted that it had not interfered with "the rights of . . . employees to express their opinion."[2]

The NLRB's action emboldened the New Directions dissidents. No longer fearing company reprisals, at least not in the short run, they began to wear their buttons more openly and distribute their campaign flyers more freely. The basement banquet room at Fiorelli's became more crowded as new volunteers turned up for each dissident meeting. Articles about the dissidents began appearing in local newspapers, which until then had largely ignored the New Directions campaign, giving the coalition's candidates greater credibility with workers.

This surge in the dissidents' popularity roused the USA incumbents out of the complacency that had characterized their campaign throughout the winter. Aside from the occasional potshot lobbed against New Directions, attacking the alleged radicalism that separated the coalition from the "real UAW," the incumbents had dismissed the dissidents' challenge to their authority. This had surprised the dissidents, who could feel the groundswell of support building beneath them and knew firsthand the depths of the workers' alienation from Mazda's team system. To some of the dissidents, the complacency of the incumbents was a sign of how out of touch with the mood of the workers the local leadership had become. To others it was indicative of the arrogance that characterized the UAW hierarchy, which was not accustomed to having its authority challenged.

The USA incumbents stepped up their criticism of their opponents' motives, accusing the New Directions candidates of not only

being radicals who sought to disrupt the plant but of being oppor-
tunists, who, in Bill Judson's words, were "trying to get into office to
better their own position versus actually having the interest of the
membership at heart."[3] The dissidents countered by accusing the
UAW leadership of nepotism, complaining that Penelope Dawkins,
the daughter of Ernie Lofton, the Region 1A director, had been
appointed union benefits representative at the plant despite her lack
of experience. New Directions candidates also objected to Lofton's
direct involvement in Sunday afternoon local meetings, noting that it
was unorthodox for a regional director to attend every meeting of a
local. But Judson defended the director's actions, claiming that Lof-
ton attended the meetings only because he was genuinely concerned
about the success of the UAW's first local at a wholly-Japanese-
owned plant.

The USA caucus incumbents admitted that there were problems
at Flat Rock with the way in which the JIT/team system was being
implemented. But they reassured the workers that these problems
were minor and temporary and promised to continue using quiet
diplomacy to pressure Mazda to increase the amount of cross-
training and job rotation and provide more off-line jobs for workers
recovering from injuries. The incumbents never specified, however,
how they were going to persuade the company to make these changes.
Nor did they explain how these changes could be made without
undermining a JIT/team system that the company believed realized
its competitive advantages by keeping a thinly stretched work force
in perpetual motion. In contrast to the New Directions candidates,
the USA incumbents were careful not to blame conditions in the
plant on the JIT/team system itself—only on the failure of American
managers to implement it properly. The incumbents thus found them-
selves engaging in the newspeak that had become common at Flat
Rock, where few people in positions of authority walked like they
talked. At the same time they praised the "Japanese philosophy" and
criticized isolated American unit leaders and area leaders for carrying
over bad habits from Big Three plants, the USA incumbents acknowl-
edged that because of the Japanese commitment to eliminating "wait-
ing *muda*," workers at Flat Rock would always be kept busy close to
60 seconds a minute. At the same time they insisted that the physical
demands made by Mazda jobs would become less intense once the
work pace at the plant stabilized, the incumbents refused to criticize
kaizen, which, through its constant refinement of the production
process, ensured that such stabilization would never take place. At

the same time they criticized the plant's high injury rate, the incumbents praised Mazda's more caring attitude toward people. Even as they moved to appeal to disenchanted workers at Flat Rock, the plant's incumbent union officers still were restrained by the UAW's larger goal of improving its image with Japanese automakers.

Included in the incumbents' campaign was an appeal to the deepest anxiety of American autoworkers—the fear of seeing their jobs forever eliminated by a plant closing. If the dissidents had their way, claimed the incumbents, productivity at the plant would be sapped by archaic and inefficient work rules. It would take five hours more to build a car. Everything on the line would have to come to a stop while the unit leaders tried to figure out who was authorized to do what job. Costs would rise and the plant would become less competitive. Mazda would begin shifting production to other plants in other countries, laying off workers at Flat Rock. Eventually, if the radicals continued to have their way, Mazda would decide it was no longer feasible to build cars in America's industrial heartland. The plant would close and the workers would go back to flipping hamburgers at half their Mazda pay.

Of all the attacks made on New Directions by the USA caucus, this was the one the dissidents feared most. Many of them had themselves recently come from low-wage jobs in what had once hopefully been called the "service sector." None wished to return. Although they thought it highly improbable that Mazda would desert a new $550 million plant rather than deal with a more militant union local, they worried that the fear of layoffs—if not a complete plant closing—would compel many workers to vote for their USA opponents. The dissidents went out of their way to emphasize that they supported labor-management cooperation and did not wish to return to the confrontationalism of the past. In a newsletter entry entitled, "NDC [New Directions] Wants This Plant To Be Successful," the dissidents declared: "We challenge anyone to show where NDC has made unreasonable demands or statements concerning our goals. *The Company is not going to shut down* because its workers insist on the basic rights entitled to them under the collective bargaining agreement and the fulfillment of commitments made by management and the Union [italics newsletter's]." But in the heady days following the NLRB action in March, the dissidents believed that if the USA incumbents beat them, it would only be because the workers feared that a New Directions victory would result in the loss of jobs.

Apparently the UAW administration, which supported the USA

caucus, believed that the threat of a plant closing would be enough to win the Flat Rock election for the incumbents. Solidarity House paid little attention to defeating Keeling and his ragtag group of inexperienced supporters, thinking that they did not pose a threat to Judson and his USA ticket. Besides, in the spring of 1989, Solidarity House had its hands full dealing with a more serious challenge to what, until recently, had been the union establishment's unquestioned authority. Jerry Tucker, the founder of the New Directions movement, was involved in a bitter and widely publicized campaign for the directorship of UAW Region 5, an eight-state region based in St. Louis. The former assistant director of the region, Tucker broke ranks with the UAW administration in the mid-1980s over his opposition to the cooperative programs the union was developing at the time with American automakers. A fiery and outspoken critic of the team system, which he believed required workers to surrender most of their rights and contractual protections while giving them very little in return, Tucker ran for the directorship of Region 5 in 1986 against incumbent Kenneth Worley. He lost by less than half of one vote. But in 1988 U.S. District Judge Richard F. Suhrheinrich ordered a new election, after the U.S. Department of Labor found irregularities in the 1986 vote, including the improper use of union funds to support the Worley campaign and the intimidation of Tucker supporters. Tucker won the special election to fill the last year of the three-year term begun in 1986, becoming the first dissident to gain a seat on the union's powerful 22-member executive board in over a quarter century.[4]

The UAW administration was busy working on plans to defeat Tucker in his bid for reelection in early 1989, when the union was confronted by another unexpected challenge to an incumbent member of the executive board. Donny Douglas, president of UAW Local 594 at the GM Truck and Bus Plant in Pontiac, Michigan, was making a serious bid to unseat incumbent Bob Lent as director of UAW Region 1-1B north of Detroit. Like Tucker, Douglas was a dissident critic of cooperative union-management team programs. By March, when only about one-third of the union locals in Region 1-1B had elected delegates to the UAW's triannual convention, Douglas had already accumulated over 400 of the 558 delegate votes needed to become director.[5] (Each union local in a region has, depending on its size, a specified number of delegate votes. The workers at each local elect delegates who are committed to the regional director candidate of their choice. The delegates then formally elect the director.)

Confronted by this challenge to its authority on the regional level,

the UAW establishment engaged in a little hat-passing of its own. In February, the union's 800 paid staff members were asked to make voluntary $500 contributions to the "Friends Social Club," a special fund headed by Richard Shoemaker, the chief administrative assistant to union president Owen Bieber, set up to finance the incumbent campaigns against Tucker and Douglas.[6] Such "flower funds"—so named because the money raised ostensibly went to buy flowers for sick union members and funerals—have been used historically by American unions to get around laws that prohibit the use of official union funds in labor elections. Armed with its four-hundred thousand-dollar war chest, the UAW establishment unleashed an aggressive campaign to discredit Tucker, Douglas, and the entire dissident movement. UAW president Bieber made campaign appearances on behalf of the dissidents' opponents. Like the USA candidates at Flat Rock, Bieber and other campaigners from Solidarity House portrayed the New Directions candidates as reckless radicals who would endanger the job security of members by returning the American auto industry to the confrontationalism of the past. Not surprisingly, the auto companies themselves were sympathetic to the UAW administration's efforts to crush the dissidents. At one General Motors plant in Region 1-1B, management stopped the production line so workers could hear a Bieber speech urging them to vote for delegates committed to the incumbent Lent.

Former UAW presidents Leonard Woodcock and Douglas Fraser, and retired vice presidents Irving Bluestone, Pat Greathouse, and Ken Bannon, lent their collective prestige to the fight against the dissidents. The five former leaders, all proteges of the late Walter Reuther, wrote a widely publicized open letter to Reuther's brother, Victor, who at 77 was one of the New Directions movement's most prominent spokespersons. "In his speeches around the country, Victor repeatedly commits factual errors, makes unfounded claims about the union's history, and makes false charges concerning its current actions," stated the letter. Among the false charges Victor Reuther had made, according to the letter, was that the UAW granted concessions to Japanese automakers to induce them to allow the union into their American plants. The letter also accused Reuther and the dissident movement of hurting the union's efforts to organize Japanese-owned plants in America by creating a divisive image of the union. This charge was repeated often by the Bieber administration, which blamed the dissidents for the union's continual failure to organize Nissan's Smyrna, Tennessee, plant.

Reuther, an early union organizer and a member of the UAW staff until his retirement in 1975, dismissed the administration's charges with a shrewd observation: "[The UAW's] campaign for Nissan was a failure before I said anything about it," he contended. "[Workers] don't need the UAW for [a team system] when the Japanese are going to give it to them anyway."[7]

By April the Bieber administration's attack on the dissidents was beginning to take its toll. The Tucker and Douglas campaigns had lost their momentum. The final delegate votes needed to win the regional elections, votes that had once appeared to be well within the grasp of each dissident, became more and more elusive. The Bieber-backed incumbents caught up with Tucker and Douglas and eventually pulled ahead, ultimately defeating both dissidents. (Tucker and Douglas would later file complaints with the U.S. Department of Labor charging the union with unfair campaign practices.)

But things were not going as well for the Bieber adminsitration at Flat Rock, where the New Directions campaign continued to gain momentum as the April 19 election approached. Crowds at the dissidents' meetings continued to grow larger. New Directions buttons were appearing on workers more frequently. The dissidents themselves could see that they were reaching more people just by looking in the trash cans by the plant gate. In early winter, when they had passed out campaign literature, a good number of the flyers wound up in the trash cans, thrown away by workers as soon as they were out of the dissidents' field of vision. Now there were hardly any New Directions flyers in the trash—workers were holding on to the campaign material to read it.

On April 12, 1989, exactly one week before the Local 3000 election was to take place, it was canceled without warning by Owen Bieber, who gave no date for its rescheduling. (A short time later, it was announced that the election would be held on May 9.) The UAW claimed it canceled the election to correct a mistake made by Bill Judson that deprived Mazda's SMP workers of their right to seek office in the union local. At a Sunday afternoon Local 3000 meeting, Judson informed an SMP that her temporary status at the plant prevented her from becoming a candidate for the local's presidency. The SMP wrote a letter to Solidarity House, arguing that under the union's constitution, she had a right to seek office. This, said the UAW administration, is what prompted Bieber to cancel the election. But to Keeling and the other New Directions candidates, the postponement was a thinly veiled stalling tactic, intended to break the

momentum that they had built up since the NLRB complaint and provide the USA incumbents with a chance to launch a counterattack. "When they realized they were going to lose, they looked for an excuse to cancel the election," Keeling said of the UAW administration. "Bieber had the letter in his drawer for almost a month before he canceled the election. They waited, because they wanted to make sure that we spent all our campaign money before they scheduled a new election date. The SMPs can't file a grievance if they're fired or disciplined; they're on probation the entire time they're here, and they have no guarantee that they'll be called into work tomorrow— but the president of the UAW canceled the election so one SMP could run for office? If that doesn't sound like the union's scared, then please explain to me what's going on." Keeling and the other New Directions dissidents were quick to point out that the SMP whose complaint prompted the postponement had not been employed at the plant in more than six months (since September 1988). The woman, who allegedly injured herself on the job, spent a total of less than two weeks working for Mazda. Ernie Lofton, the UAW Region 1A director, was present at the Sunday union meeting when Local 3000 president Judson told the SMP that she could not run for office. According to the dissidents, Lofton appeared to agree with Judson's decision. In any event he certainly did nothing to dispute the local president's ruling.

As they had after the NLRB action, the USA incumbents picked up the tempo of their campaign following Bieber's postponement. USA flyers began to appear more often, coming out daily in the week leading up to the May 9 election. The flyers also became harder hitting, focusing more sharply on the alleged radicalism of the dissidents.

At the head of the USA ticket, Bill Judson became a more aggressive campaigner. Until the final weeks of the campaign, Judson had refrained from handing out flyers himself, delegating this task to lower-ranking union officials. But, with his chance of victory slipping away, the Local 3000 president began turning up at C gate, the busiest entrance to the plant, every morning to distribute campaign literature. Judson stood shoulder to shoulder with New Directions volunteers, most of whom had been handing out flyers at C gate since the early winter. The dissidents were on a first-name basis with many of the workers, bantering and exchanging small talk with them. By contrast, Judson distributed his flyers quietly. "We used to kid Bill and tell him, 'The reason you're going to lose is you don't know

anyone at the plant,' " recalled one dissident. "After that, he started getting more outgoing."

As the Tuesday of the election drew near, the dissidents, like a boxer closing out the final round of a fight that has clearly been won, became concerned with avoiding the roundhouse knockout punch thrown by a desperate opponent. Phil Keeling was worried that the USA caucus would make a last-ditch effort to defeat New Directions by coming out with a flyer filled with outrageous new accusations against the group. Even if the accusations were patently false, they might, feared Keeling, scare workers away from New Directions, unless the dissidents had the chance to respond to the charges. Since the dissidents' funds were almost depleted, they decided not to print a new flyer on the Friday before the election, saving their money so they could issue a counterattack flyer on Monday, should the USA caucus make new charges that called for a rebuttal. But the incumbents' Friday flyer included no such charges. So on Saturday Keeling locked himself up in his Flat Rock apartment and wrote the dissidents' final campaign flyer. It was, as one New Directions member would later say, "a wrap-up of what we stand for . . . enforcement of the contract—even though the contract we have is a poor one—more flexibility on the part of management, and a bigger voice for workers in the way things are done at the plant."

There was a steady drizzle on election Tuesday. Despite the weather, long lines of workers formed at the polling places that had been set up in trailers at the Mazda plant's three main gates. Many of the workers were made uncomfortable by the media attention that was being focused on the election. That morning's *Detroit Free Press* had called the election "a test of [the] Japanese concept" and quoted industry experts who predicted that what happened at Flat Rock would be "very crucial to other Japanese transplants." The *Detroit News* had headlined the election, "UAW Leadership Faces Test," and noted that: "The balloting has been described as a referendum on the Japanese manufacturing process in U.S. auto plants."[8]

The workers walked up the metal steps of the polling trailers and marked their choices on paper ballots that were then dropped into dark containers the shape of janitorial cleaning drums. Representatives of an outside accounting firm were in each trailer to monitor the voting. Ernie Lofton had wanted the union's own election committee to supervise the balloting, but members of Local 3000 had, at a

Sunday union meeting, voted for an outside firm to assume this responsibility.

At eight o'clock that evening, an officer of the accounting firm and a UAW election official walked into the first polling trailer, locked the cylindrical ballot box shut, and put it in their car. As they drove across the plant parking lot to the next trailer, the two were followed by a caravan of more than a dozen cars filled with New Directions candidates and their supporters. The dissidents continued to follow the two officials, determined not to lose sight of them or their cargo, as they stopped at the final polling place and then turned out of the Mazda lot and headed north for the UAW Region 1A headquarters in the Downriver suburb of Taylor.

Less than 20 minutes later, the two officials, with the dissident caravan close behind, arrived at Region 1A headquarters. The locked ballot boxes were brought into a meeting room and opened, their contents spread out over large tables so representatives from the accounting firm could begin the task of counting votes. Only the candidates themselves and representatives from the union's election committee were allowed in the room to observe the vote count. Supporters of the dissidents had to wait in the lobby outside the meeting room. Every few minutes, a New Directions candidate would emerge from the room to update the supporters on the races. The first report came soon after the ballot boxes were opened. When the ballots had been spread across the tables, the dissidents had immediately scanned the president's column—Xs seemed to appear much more frequently by the name "Keeling" than "Judson." "It looks like Phil's got it," the dissidents were told not more than 15 minutes after their caravan had arrived. A short time later there was more good news—"Keeling's way ahead . . . Drudi's winning too." Any doubts the dissidents had about their impending victory were dispelled when they saw Ernie Lofton march out of the ballot room and into his private office, pausing to shoot a cold, hard stare at the dissidents milling about in the lobby. "You could see Ernie was really bent out of shape, so we knew it was all over for his side," said one of the dissidents.

Phil Keeling was not in the caravan that sped past the hamburger restaurants, doughnut shops and motels that bore names like Oasis and Ventura Inn on Telegraph Road, Downriver's main north-south thoroughfare, on its way to the Region 1A headquarters. Keeling had gone back to his Flat Rock apartment after the polling trailers closed to shower and change out of his Mazda uniform. By the time he got to the regional headquarters, it was already clear that he and most of

the other New Directions candidates, including Drudi, had been victorious. Soon after his arrival, Keeling ran into Bill Judson in the lobby. "Well, Bill, it looks like I got you," he said, extending his hand. "We don't know that yet," Judson responded, staring at the hand extended before him. Later, at around midnight, when the final vote was counted, Judson came over and congratulated Keeling on his victory. The defeated president promised to work with his successor to make the transition of power as smooth as possible. But first, said Judson, he needed a few days' rest. Keeling said he understood. As the two men stood there shaking hands, they looked, in the words of one dissident, "like they had gone the full fifteen rounds."

The dissident victory was impressive. Keeling defeated Judson 54 to 35 percent in the presidential race, with the remaining votes divided among two other candidates, including the SMP whose complaint had prompted the postponement of the original election. She received less than 1.4 percent of the vote. In addition to winning the presidency, New Directions candidates were elected to the chairmanship of the bargaining committee, the second vice presidency of the union local, six out of ten seats on the local committee, both of the local's UAW International Convention delegate positions, and one out of two alternate delegate positions.

The UAW administration publicly dismissed the dissident victory at Flat Rock as a product of "local politics and personalities." The election was not, UAW spokespersons said, a reflection of worker dissatisfaction with the cooperative relationship that had developed between the union and management at Flat Rock. According to Solidarity House, workers had voted the dissidents into office because the New Directions candidates were more popular personally than their USA caucus opponents. The same Mazda workers who had walked to the wall the previous summer to protest conditions in the plant, who had complained openly and bitterly about the high injury rate, the treatment of injured workers and the lack of cross-training and job rotation, who had lamented their weak and vague union contract had not, the UAW insisted, voted against the team system as much as they had voted against individual Local 3000 incumbents.

By portraying the defeat as a rejection of local officials rather than the team system, the Bieber administration apparently hoped to minimize the damage to the union's campaign to organize other Japanese-owned plants. If the Mazda election was seen as a repudiation of the cooperative labor-management relationship, it would only reaffirm the fears of other Japanese automakers about militant

UAW workers and stiffen their resolve to fight union organizing efforts. The UAW could not afford to have this happen in May 1989, only two months before workers at Nissan's Smyrna, Tennessee, plant were scheduled to vote on the question of union representation after a long and bitter organizing campaign.

Some staff members at Solidarity House did concede that in their desire to defeat Jerry Tucker and Donny Douglas, they had perhaps not paid enough attention to Flat Rock. "We bungled this thing," one staffer lamented.[9] Had they been more involved in the Local 3000 election, the staff members could, they believed, have kept the young, inexperienced Mazda workers from being "misled" by New Directions. Many workers who had not been swayed by the person-alities of the candidates had voted for New Directions anyway, ac-cording to the UAW staff members, because in their naïveté, they had believed the unrealistic campaign promises made by the dissidents. Analyzing the New Directions victory, one union official reminded the *Detroit Free Press* that the workers at Flat Rock were "new people who don't really understand the procedures."[10] To the Bieber administration, Flat Rock's young workers did not yet understand that their only strength lay in maintaining solidarity with the rest of the union. They did not yet appreciate that concessions such as those the UAW had made to Mazda were necessary to preserve jobs in today's competitive world market. Nevertheless, the UAW adminis-tration promised to cooperate with the new leaders of Local 3000. "Being a democratic union, we will do everything we can to work in the best interest of the membership," said the same union official.

Mazda's public reaction to the dissident victory was similar to the response of the UAW administration. The election of the New Di-rections candidates, like the reports of the high injury rate earlier in the year, had made the Flat Rock plant the focus of unwanted media attention. Once again, the company tried to deflect this attention by downplaying the significance of the events that had transpired at its plant. Just as it had insisted that Flat Rock's injury rate was "no different" than those of other automakers, Mazda now portrayed the dissident victory as an internal union matter, one that had no bearing on labor-management relations at Flat Rock, and one that was cer-tainly not indicative of worker discontent with the team system. "Our contract is with the UAW and not individuals. The election doesn't change that. . . . We take issue with those who say that this reflects on the cooperative union-management relationship," Mazda spokesperson Jim Gill remarked after the election.

But despite Mazda's attempt to maintain an unflappable, business-as-usual appearance, the company's managers, especially the Japanese, seemed to many workers to be clearly upset by the dissident victory. Some of the Japanese, uncertain about what to expect from the new, more militant leaders of the union local, sought reassurance from their American managers: Would it be possible to work with the dissidents? Would they make unreasonable demands about modifying the JIT system? Doing away with *kaizen*? The American managers, though disappointed about the dissident win, were hopeful. The new leaders of Local 3000 were young. They had not come of age in a contentious American auto industry, as Tucker, Douglas, and other older dissidents had. Their military would be less entrenched. Besides, all the local dissidents, including Keeling, had repeatedly said that they were not opposed to the team system in principle.

Some Mazda managers had sought to explain the dissident win by using the same argument they had used to rationalize Flat Rock's high injury rate—the plant had a young and inexperienced work force. (As they had in the winter when defending Mazda's safety record, they again neglected to mention that youth and inexperience were two of the qualities the company had screened for in its elaborate hiring process.) Robert Leadbetter, who had replaced David Merchant as vice president of personnel at the plant—after Merchant had joined the exodus of American managers from Mazda in late September 1988, taking a job with a Canadian stockbrokerage firm—dismissed the suggestion that the dissident victory was a repudiation of the team system as practiced at Flat Rock. Echoing the view of the UAW official quoted in the *Detroit Free Press*, Leadbetter explained the dissident victory with the observation: "What we see here is a young, inexperienced work force, in many cases involved in their first union election."[11]

But Mazda's American workers, though still young, were no longer inexperienced by May 1989, when they cast their votes for Keeling and the New Directions dissidents. They had been building cars for close to two years, often working six- and seven-day weeks, and ten-hour days. The last remnants of innocence they had about factory work had been swept away during the heat wave of the previous summer. Few workers in America had as much experience working under a Japanese management system. Their decision to replace the cooperative, "procompany" union incumbents with more militant leaders was not the product of youthful naïveté. Unless, of

course, it was "naive," as some of the dissidents suggested, for the workers to have believed the promises that were made to them during orientation. By the spring of 1989, Mazda workers viewed factory work with a cold, hard realism. They knew what could reasonably be expected from an employer. They did not expect to be consulted about management decisions. They did expect to be taken care of when they were injured on the job.

Phil Keeling was a more charismatic candidate than Bill Judson. But if this was an advantage for the dissidents, it was more than offset by the wariness that Keeling's "radical" image aroused in many Mazda workers, who, after all, had been carefully screened for their cooperative attitudes during the hiring process. Keeling and the other New Directions candidates also had to overcome the widespread fear among workers that a dissident victory might ultimately cost them their jobs by making the plant less competitive.

The Local 3000 election was not a popularity contest. It was a battle between two sharply different views of labor-management cooperation. Throughout the campaign, the USA incumbents had, in the name of teamwork and cooperation, defended a contract that awarded virtually unlimited discretionary power to management. The dissidents, though they did indeed support "the team system in principle," were less trusting. The gist of their message never varied— management could not be counted on to look after the interests of workers. For true teamwork to take place, the dissidents argued, workers must have a strong and independent union to counter management's power.

The results of the Local 3000 election were, then, if not a repudiation of the Japanese team system, clearly a warning that the system was not working as advertised at Flat Rock. Despite the magazine articles and television specials that praised the Japanese system for treating workers with dignity and respect, and despite the noble promises made by Mazda during its orientation, workers at Flat Rock were not happy. Rather than dignity and respect, they had found a dehumanizing management system at the plant that pushed them harder and harder in pursuit of unattainable production goals and then abandoned them when they became worn out and injured. Having come to mistrust Mazda, the workers sought protection instead from union representatives who promised to place their interests above those of the company.

12
Shaping the Third Culture

ON May 10, 1989, one day after the Local 3000 election, Phil Keeling and Greg Drudi took a "victory tour" of the Flat Rock plant. Symbolically, the newly elected president and bargaining committee chairperson of the Mazda local wore personal clothes rather than their blue-and-khaki company uniforms. They hoped, through this gesture, to send a message to the plant's managers and workers alike—they would not be part of the "Mazda team," accountable to the company as the old union officers had been, but independent representatives of the plant's work force, accountable only to the workers who had elected them.

During their tour Keeling and Drudi were approached by James Korowin, the vice president of manufacturing, who stuck out a thick, steady hand—"Phil, Greg, I don't believe we had the chance to meet— I'm Jim Korowin." Keeling was charmed by Korowin, whom he described as "a real smooth guy—meet him in a bar and you'll love him." Because of this, he was extra cautious that Friday (May 12), when he and Drudi held their first formal meeting with Korowin and the vice president of personnel, Robert Leadbetter. The two Mazda managers were very friendly, acting, Keeling thought, as if there had never been any real differences between the company and the dissidents, just some silly misunderstandings, blown way out of proportion by the media, trivial things that weren't even worth mentioning now that they were

all on the same side pulling together for the good of the company and its workers. "I read all your literature and I don't see anything I can't agree with," Korowin told the New Directions leaders. Keeling and Drudi smiled politely. *That's just great Jim, then we should have no trouble getting along.* A short time later, Leadbetter came up with an offer, "We got to get your guys to Japan as soon as possible." The new union leaders declined the invitation, explaining that they intended to maintain their independence from the company. Nothing personal, they reassured their hosts, but they wanted to keep their professional distance from managers at the plant. They wouldn't be getting together after hours for drinks the way some of the previous union officers had. "The last thing we wanted to do," Keeling would recall some months later, "was take a company trip to Japan."

The week after their meeting with Korowin and Leadbetter, Keeling and Drudi were invited for tea with Osamu Nobuto and other Japanese managers. Keeling did not know what to expect from the plant's president. The first time he had seen Nobuto after the election, a chance encounter in the plant, the Japanese manager had averted his glance and abruptly walked away. But Nobuto was sincere and cordial. Wearing a neatly pressed Mazda uniform, the trim and rather elegant plant president looked like an officer in an elite aviator corps. Over tea he questioned Keeling about life in West Virginia. As the mood of the meeting became more relaxed, Nobuto admitted that the dissident victory had caused him some concern—from what he read in the papers, New Directions was against programs to improve quality. This was not true, Keeling assured him; New Directions was not opposed to improving quality or productivity, the dissidents just wanted the workers to get a fair shake. Nobuto could appreciate that. Before the meeting ended, one of the Japanese managers had a question for Keeling. He had noticed that the dissident's picture was on the "kaizen board," a wall display Mazda had made to recognize employees who suggested valuable *kaizen* ideas. Keeling had got on the board for his suggestions for improving maintenance procedures on equipment in the paint department, particularly the fluidized sand bed-stripping unit, a machine that uses swirling hot sand to remove paint that has dried on the floor gratings of paint booths. The Japanese manager was confused; how could Keeling be participating in *kaizen* if he was against the team system? Keeling shrugged: "I'm not against worker involvement or improving quality, and I wouldn't make a suggestion that would take away someone's job."

The first real test of the New Directions pledge to stand up to management came on the Friday before Memorial Day 1989. Early in the afternoon, an announcement came over the public address system of the trim and final assembly area that two hours of overtime would be added to the day's production schedule. Since Friday is payday for Mazda's A-shift employees, this meant that the workers would not be able to get to the bank in time to cash their checks before the three-day weekend. The workers, especially those who had no credit cards or ATM cards, were incensed: Being without cash for the entire weekend all but ended their plans for the first holiday of summer. A murmur of hostility traveled down the assembly line after the announcement. Those who had been on the line a year earlier believed that the mood of the workers was as menacing as it had been in the summer of 1988, when half of trim and final had walked to the wall. Later in the afternoon, Ernie Lofton, the Region 1A director, who was soon to leave his post to become a UAW vice president, and Bob King, the man who had been named Lofton's successor as regional director, took a tour of the plant with Keeling.*
Having been in a meeting all afternoon, the three men were unaware of the overtime announcement. When the union leaders walked though trim and final, the workers shouted at them. Unable to hear what the workers were saying over the din of the production equipment, Lofton apparently assumed they were giving him a final cheer. He smiled and waved like a presidential candidate at a friendly campaign stop. After Lofton and King left the plant, Keeling returned to trim and final. This time there was no doubt what the workers were saying: "We have to stay here until five-thirty—what are you going to do about it, Keeling?" "Let's see you stand up for our rights now."

Keeling went to the open office area and called the manager of the trim and final section out of a meeting. He demanded that the manager rescind the overtime and reschedule it for Tuesday, when the workers returned to the plant. The manager explained that the company couldn't do this—it had a production schedule to meet. "Look, these people have been waiting a long time for this weekend, and now you're screwing it up because of your overtime. They aren't going to be able to get to the bank with their paychecks. They'll stay here, and they'll put parts on cars, but they're probably not going to be too careful about how they do it, so come Tuesday you may have

* In one of his last official acts as Region 1A director, Lofton appointed Bill Judson, the defeated Local 3000 president, to the position of UAW quality representative at the Mazda plant.

a hundred new cars in the reprocessing shop that need to be fixed. Why not wait until after the holiday so we can get it done right the first time?" When the manager said that he would go out and talk to the workers on the line, Keeling warned him, "I wouldn't if I were you. They're in a mean mood. They almost killed me, and I'm in their union." The trim and final supervisor left to confer with other Mazda managers. When he returned, he told Keeling that the company had relented—the overtime would be rescheduled for the following week.

The Memorial Day overtime rollback was followed by other early accomplishments that increased the standing of Keeling and his administration. By June the new union local had had more than 60 large fans installed at the plant. The new union representatives were also more aggressive than their predecessors in pressing grievances, initiating more than 10 cases during their first 60 days in office. This aggressiveness on the part of the union pressured Mazda to correct the more blatant safety violations in the plant and discouraged some of the flagrant abuses of power by unit leaders. Safety gates on production equipment in the tire subassembly station were no longer left open. Faulty equipment was turned off and repaired more quickly. Managers were less likely to pluck sky cards from machines.

But New Directions did not deliver on all its campaign promises. Despite the criticism they had leveled against Judson and the union incumbents for sharing an office with the company's labor relations department, the dissidents did not move to new quarters once they were elected. After their initial demand for a separate office was turned down by the company on the grounds that no space was available, the new union leaders dropped the issue. But they did open a new UAW Local 3000 headquarters about a mile from the plant in a former movie theater in downtown Flat Rock. (Before this, the local had no outside office.) Local 3000 also, for the first time, established its own bank account, rather than taking funds directly from Region 1A headquarters, and began publishing its own newsletter. To Keeling the lack of independent local finances and a publishing arm—two features found in all UAW locals—had been indicative of the passive role the union had played at Flat Rock.

The power of Keeling and his administration to make serious changes in the plant was, of course, limited by the vague and weakly worded UAW-Mazda contract. Almost every commitment seemingly made by Mazda in the contract came with a convenient loophole, through which the company could unilaterally decide to ignore its promises. Keeling could complain to management about unan-

nounced overtime, reason with them about it, threaten them about it, and sometimes, as on the Friday before Memorial Day, he might even succeed in getting the company to rescind an overtime assignment— but, in the final analysis, there was no binding contractual provision he could use to force management to stop the practice. Nor were there any contractual provisions that could be called upon to force Mazda to slow its work pace, add more workers to its thin-stretched work force, design less-demanding jobs for workers recovering from injuries, or provide team members with the promised cross-training and job rotation. New union leaders or not, workers at Flat Rock still found themselves at the mercy of Mazda's good intentions. "We desperately need a new contract," Keeling told a visitor in the summer of 1989.

Keeling was not certain that he would be around to participate in the negotiation of that contract. Solidarity House would not forgive or forget his successful challenge to an administration-backed incumbent, he said, and he was afraid the union hierarchy would work hard behind the scenes to defeat him. Already, after the UAW convention in June, one of New Directions' former leaders, Ed Schmitt, had turned against the coalition. Schmitt, who had been elected to a UAW convention delegate seat on the New Directions ticket in May, had publicly changed his allegiance, becoming a backer of the UAW administration. Keeling feared that Schmitt's defection would be the first of many, and he worried that the administration was priming Schmitt, an articulate skilled trades worker, to run against him in the next election.

The workers were also beginning to grow impatient with New Directions in the summer of 1989. Despite the improvements that the new leaders of Local 3000 were able to make in the plant, the major sources of worker grievances remained unchanged: The work pace was still too fast, the injury rate was still too high, and Mazda still fought virtually every injury claim. "Some people are getting mad at Keeling, because things are about as bad as they always were," said one New Directions supporter. "They see changes, but not big changes."

This criticism of New Directions, which had been building up all summer, came to a sudden stop in September 1989, when the union local and Mazda, after several weeks of secret negotiations, reached a new agreement on the use of SMP workers. Effective immediately, all SMPs who had been at the plant 90 days or more—even those who had been rotated to different job assignments—were granted

permanent employee status. In one fell swoop, the number of permanent workers at the plant was thus increased by 135. Mazda also agreed to restrict its use of SMPs in the future, limiting SMP assignments as much as possible to Mondays and Fridays. Henceforth if individual SMPs had to be employed at the plant on every scheduled full production day (Monday through Friday, and often Saturday too) over a 90-day period, the company would, if promised, make them permanent employees, regardless of any job rotations.

Although the SMP agreement improved the lot of temporary workers, providing them with job security and lifting them out of the second-class status to which they had been relegated at the plant, it did little to change working conditions for those who were already permanent employees. The Flat Rock plant still had the same number of workers struggling to keep up with the JIT production pace. Mazda did not expand the true size of its work force; it simply granted permanent employee status to 135 "temporaries" who had been working at the plant on a regular basis for over three months.

A second agreement reached between the new leaders of Local 3000 and Mazda in September 1989 had a much greater impact on the work lives of Flat Rock's team members. The plant's first uniform attendance policy—one not subject to the discretionary power of unit leaders—would be implemented on a one-year trial basis beginning in October 1989. Under the plan, a worker's first four absences would be excused automatically as personal/sick days, and the worker would be allowed to receive 60 percent of his or her base pay. After an employee had missed four days of work "free and clear," he or she would automatically be issued a verbal reprimand for the fifth absence. From that point on, throughout the rest of the year, the employee would automatically be issued a written reprimand—and receive no pay—for every alternate day of missed work. For example, the employee would be reprimanded on the seventh absence, the ninth, and the eleventh, while even-numbered absences (sixth, eighth, tenth, and so on) would remain free and clear. After the fifteenth day of missed work, the employee would receive a fifth written reprimand, giving the company the right to terminate his or her employment. Workers who received reprimands for other reasons would be allowed fewer absences before they reached the point of losing their jobs. (Those employees who suffered from long-term illness or serious injury were covered by a separate agreement in the original UAW-Mazda contract.) Employees who had perfect attendance for the year would, under the new policy, be entitled to a $1,500 bonus.[1]

The new attendance policy promised to ease the physical strain on Mazda workers, allowing them to take an occasional day off to nurse a flu, have a tooth extracted, or care for a child with the measles. Just as important to many workers, the new attendance policy took a major disciplinary weapon out of the hands of unit leaders and moved the plant a step closer to achieving the consistency that New Directions had advocated. Individual unit leaders still had broad, unchecked discretionary power to discipline workers, make up schedules, and rotate job assignments, but at least they could no longer play favorites by selectively enforcing attendance rules. Although it was only an experiment—one that could easily be discontinued—the uniform attendance policy was seen by team members as a hopeful sign that Mazda–Flat Rock was becoming a fairer place in which to work.

But the new policy did not change fundamental working conditions at Flat Rock. Workers were still pushed to the breaking point, locked into rigid programmed worksheet routines that spelled out every step of a job and offered no opportunity to rest. As Mazda managers had repeatedly emphasized, the 57-second-a-minute JIT work pace and the *kaizen* process that wound it ever more tightly would not be negotiated out of the plant.[2] Safety stocks of back-up inventory would not be increased to relieve the pressure on workers struggling to meet the JIT-pull demand for components. The work force would remain thin stretched, with workers being required to fill in for absent teammates in addition to performing their normal jobs. Cross-training and job rotation were still sporadic: A long-promised apprenticeship program, intended to provide production workers with the opportunity to become certified in a skilled trade, was open to only 12 team members when it began in the summer of 1989.

The September agreements, though they did not make jobs at Flat Rock any less demanding, did create a more democratic work environment at the plant. By agreeing to hire all SMPs, Mazda eliminated what had in fact become a two-tier labor system at Flat Rock, with a permanent underclass of "temporary workers" relegated to receiving lower wages and fewer benefits and enjoying fewer rights. The new attendance policy, with its removal of unit leader discretionary power and its implementation of uniform standards for all workers, regardless of their standing with supervisors, was also more consistent with democratic notions of equality and fair play. By extending greater protection to the rights of individual workers, and restricting the unchecked authority of managers, the September agreements

moved the Flat Rock plant closer to the cultural values of Americans, away from those of the more hierarchical, authoritarian Japanese.

New Directions leaders and their supporters pointed to the September agreements as proof of how a tough and vigorous union local could effect important changes in the plant. They were, to a large extent, correct, but Mazda managers were responding to many factors, not just the pressure exerted by the new union leaders, in the early autumn of 1989, when they began to modify their management system to accommodate cultural differences between Japanese and American workers. Flat Rock's higher-than-expected turnover rate, its persistent problem with defects, and its walks to the wall appeared to have persuaded the Japanese to adopt a new, more tolerant approach toward dealing with American workers, even before Keeling defeated Judson in the May 9 election. On the day before the Local 3000 election, Norimasa Furuta, who had succeeded Kenichi Yamamoto as president of Mazda Motor Corporation in Japan, acknowledged the need to make Japanese managers at the company's American plant more attuned to the cultural sensitivities of the workers under them. "Since this Flat Rock operation was the first real experience for Mazda interfacing with American workers on a large scale, we could have done more in terms of training—in language, about differences in culture, different lifestyles—so [Japanese managers] could more easily understand any signs of strain or possible problems."[3]

But despite their eagerness to improve relations with U.S. workers, there were limits to the lengths to which Mazda's Japanese managers were willing to go to accommodate the Americans. Late in the afternoon of Wednesday, October 11, 1989, one day after workers at the plant voted to approve the new attendance policy, Mazda announced the resignations of MMUC vice president of manufacturing James Korowin and vice president of personnel Robert Leadbetter. News of Korowin's and Leadbetter's departures took Americans at the plant by surprise. "It's extremely shocking that both major executives would resign at the same time," Greg Drudi told a local newspaper reporter.[4]

There was speculation in and out of the plant that the two Americans had been forced out of the company by Japanese managers, who blamed them for failing to defuse the new union leaders' campaign for a standardized attendance policy. The *Wall Street Journal* quoted a "Mazda spokesperson," who said that the company was "dismayed" with the way Korowin and Leadbetter handled the ne-

gotiations on the new attendance policy. But at Flat Rock, Jim Gill, Mazda's chief spokesperson, downplayed any connection between the resignations and the attendance agreement. "I recognize the timing was bad," he acknowledged, before going on to "emphatically" reassure the press that the sudden departure of the two top Americans had nothing to do with the change in the plant's attendance rules.[5] Phil Keeling viewed the resignations with characteristic wryness. "I'm not privy to management's decisions," he said, "but it would seem to be quite a coincidence that they just happened to resign at this point."

In the immediate aftermath of Korowin and Leadbetter's departure, when everyone at the plant seemed ready to speculate about the reasons behind the American managers' resignations, little thought was given to the issue raised by the appointment of their successors. When announcing the resignation of Korowin and Leadbetter, Mazda also introduced their replacements. Although the positions of vice president of manufacturing and vice president of personnel at Flat Rock had implicitly been regarded as "American posts," the men who would succeed Korowin and Leadbetter were both Japanese.

The issues faced by workers at Flat Rock are certain to confront, in one form or another, a growing number of other American workers in the 1990s, as Japanese manufacturers continue to establish plants in the United States. Already in 1990, there are approximately 640 plants in this country owned or partially owned by Japanese, employing some 160,000 workers. More than one hundred new Japanese-American plants are expected to begin operation by 1991. This, of course, does not include the Japanese retailing and service firms that have opened American operations in recent years. Japan's MITI has estimated that 840,000 Americans will be working for Japanese companies by the end of the decade.[6]

Mazda is only one company, and like all companies the world over, it has its own unique corporate culture. Generalizing about all Japanese employers from the experience of one auto plant in Michigan is, of course, problematic. The success of union dissident movements at Flat Rock and at the Toyota-run NUMMI plant can be taken as a sign of worker discontent with the Japanese JIT/team system. But those who defend the Japanese system can point to the rejection of the UAW at Nissan-Smyrna and Honda-Marysville to support their claim that the Japanese are offering Americans a more

harmonious, less contentious work environment. Without studying a representative cross-section of plants run by the Japanese in detail, it would be impossible to draw sweeping conclusions about their treatment of workers. For example, the fact that one Japanese manufacturer has failed to enforce its own established safety procedures does not mean that all Japanese employers are negligent about safety. No two Japanese plants are exactly alike, just as no two American plants are identical; to think otherwise would be to engage in the stereotyping and over-generalizing that too often have characterized American and Japanese perceptions of one another in the past.

But just as American companies share much in common, so too do Japanese firms. Like Mazda, other Japanese companies view the employer-employee relationship from a different perspective than do their American opposite numbers. This difference will surely not be lost on Americans who go to work for a Japanese company. They will be expected to give much more of themselves than they are accustomed to giving. Not only will these American workers be required to make a greater physical effort to keep up with the JIT production pace, they will be expected to commit themselves more fully to their new employer and identify more strongly with its corporate philosophy. As Mazda hirees were told repeatedly during their orientation at Flat Rock, one does not simply go to work for a Japanese company, one becomes a part of a Japanese company, embracing its goals as one's own, merging one's interests with its interests, until the traditional (American) barriers between employer and employee have all but disappeared.

Differences in style will separate one Japanese employer from another, but the substance of the emotional demands made on American workers will remain unchanged. The demands are rooted too deeply in Japanese culture to be altered significantly by corporate affiliations. That this Japanese culture differs sharply from American culture in its ideas about individuals and groups, and the obligations owed by each to the other, has, as the experience of workers at Flat Rock has shown, created difficulties for Americans trying to adjust to a Japanese management system.

A Japanese parable about an ancient traveler illustrates the difference between the two cultures: Walking alone on a remote country trail, the traveler happened upon a well pump, and being thirsty, pumped some water into the well's cup. When he finished drinking, the traveler washed the cup and rehung it over the well. To the Japanese the ancient traveler exemplified what Mazda, centuries later,

would call "team-spiritedness." By drinking from the strange cup without first washing it, he showed his unquestioning trust in his fellow Japanese. By washing the cup when he was finished, even though unobserved, he demonstrated his sense of loyalty to them.

Trust and loyalty came quite naturally to the ancient Japanese traveler. He was so much a part of his group, and it was so much a part of him, he could see no reason to separate its interests from his own. His modern descendants in the Japanese plant and office share this strong identification with the group, in both the form of their country and their company. These Japanese workers would no sooner seek to protect themselves against their company-group by erecting an elaborate defense of work rules and regulations than members of an American family would seek to lock up their valuables from one another. To the Japanese worker, the company is the family, and families do not need the reassurance of formal rules to feel secure.

But Americans, at least in the late 20th century, find it difficult to feel this way about any group, with the possible exception of their own biological families. Few American travelers would drink from the unknown cup without first washing it very thoroughly. Experience has taught them that they cannot trust the previous traveler, an unseen stranger, to have cleaned the cup before them. Better to be safe than sorry. Indeed, most Americans would count themselves lucky if the stranger had not taken the cup with him to sell in the next town.

It is not surprising, then, that American workers, products of a contentious, fragmented society, a society of car alarms and double deadbolt locks, feel suddenly vulnerable when the rules and regulations that had protected them at U.S. companies are removed by their new Japanese employers.

The Japanese have tried to overcome the fears of their American employees by encouraging workers to become part of the corporate family. If you commit yourself to us, they say, we will commit ourselves to you. Then there will be no more mistrust, no more contentiousness, no need for protective rules. Many Americans will undoubtedly welcome the invitation to join a Japanese corporate family. But if there is a lesson to be learned from Mazda–Flat Rock, it is that this familial bonding will often be difficult for both Americans and Japanese.

Becoming part of a Japanese corporate family requires that American workers give up some of the rights and privileges they have been taught to value. The sharp distinction between personal time and company time is one of the notions that Americans are expected to

relinquish. Japanese workers think nothing of remaining at their work stations after the quitting bell has sounded to clean up or work on a *kaizen* project, without pay. Nor do they hesitate to work overtime, come in on holidays, or give up vacations to help their company meet its production quotas. Like Mazda, most Japanese companies want their American employees at least to approximate this level of dedication.

Inevitably there will be conflicts between the demands made on the time of workers by their corporate family and their biological families: The overtime that is suddenly scheduled on the evening of a school play, the anticipated vacation that must be canceled, the sick child who must be left with a sitter during a busy model changeover at the car plant. Japanese workers are accustomed to balancing these competing loyalties. Americans are not. When an American places the demands of family over work, the Japanese look on him or her as weak and disloyal. When the Japanese voice their objections to the American, he or she sees them as callous.

Americans, it seems, must also be prepared to give up a measure of privacy to become part of the Japanese corporate family. Mazda's "open administration area" at Flat Rock is typical of the American offices of most Japanese companies. But it is more than a lack of their own physical space that Americans must get used to. The Japanese, with their emphasis on what they call "open communication," leave the worker with less psychological space as well. Employees of Japanese companies quickly become accustomed to working under the watchful eye of others, be they advisors from Japan or teams of their own peers. There can be few secrets among corporate family members. Secrets breed mistrust. Workers at the Japanese plant or office must accept having their work habits critiqued and their mistakes discussed openly in front of others, even when this proves to be embarrassing, as it did for the two Mazda team members who had to go through the plant and relive their fight over the public address system.

As these Mazda workers discovered, the individual is expected to sacrifice his or her own interests or comfort or pride to the good of the group at a Japanese company. This is the biggest concession that Americans must make to become part of the corporate family. Individualism is not a cherished virtue in the Japanese plant or office. Neither is thinking for oneself. Both American and Japanese managers at Mazda made no secret of that. No decision at Mazda is made by the individual acting alone, David Merchant, the former vice president of personnel, had told visitors. The individualism of Amer-

ican workers made it difficult to forge them into an efficient team, Osamu Nobuto had lamented to the *Detroit News.*[7] Of course, becoming part of the Mazda team means much more than donning the company uniform and participating in morning calisthenics. It also means conforming to a group way of thinking, of not only doing what one is told but of *wanting* to do what one is told. Everyone must agree with a consensus decision. Everyone must choose *voluntarily* to wear caps. Everyone must have the "will to participate." In making these demands, the team system, as practiced at Flat Rock, is a great leveler of individual differences. But it is not, as those who support the team system would argue, a democratizer of the workplace. If it were, it would seek to achieve equality. As it is it seeks merely conformity. Americans who do not conform to the prescribed group way of thinking, as many at Mazda do not, will not lose their jobs, but neither will they be accepted into the corporate family.

There is, of course, good reason to question whether any American can ever be fully accepted into the Japanese corporate family, regardless of how hard he (or especially she) tries to conform to its ways. The Japanese, with few exceptions, have not accepted Americans (particularly black Americans) as their equals. They have often been reluctant to entrust Americans with the responsibility of mig welding the C-pillar of an automobile, no less with that of running a $550 million automobile plant. Americans can gain admission into the corporate family as stepchildren, perhaps, or as distant cousins, but not as full-fledged sons and daughters—and certainly not as parents. Americans, it must be admitted, were guilty of the same hubris during their halcyon days, but this is of little consolation to Denny Pawley and the other American managers at Japanese firms who have had their career paths blocked simply because of their national origin. Unlike American, British, and German multinationals, which typically appoint native managers to head their overseas operations, Japanese corporations invariably select Japanese managers to run their foreign ventures.

If, as Denny Pawley has suggested, the Japanese do not want "American all-stars" at their plants and offices, one must wonder whether the country's future all-stars will have enough opportunities to shine. Now that 25 percent of the passenger cars made in this country are produced in Japanese "transplants," will one out of four future Henry Fords and Walter Chryslers have to go looking for jobs elsewhere? What happens when this pattern is repeated in electronics, computers, and other industries? A nation that fails to provide

ample opportunities for its best and brightest managers and engineers will be ill prepared to regain its competitive edge in the next century.

Most Americans at Flat Rock, managers and workers alike, seem to be aware that their opportunities to advance and acquire greater responsibilities are limited by the fact that they are not Japanese. There is often an awkwardness about these Americans, especially the managers, when they talk about the relative roles of Americans and Japanese at the plant. They will admit, at least tacitly, that major decisions will always come out of Japan, that the president of the plant will always be Japanese, that their actions will always require the approval of Japanese advisors. These Americans find themselves moving about in a shadowy work environment, where words and titles and appearances often bear no relation to reality: *I may say I'm a purchasing agent and act like a purchasing agent, but in reality my Japanese advisor does all the purchasing.* It is an environment that encourages one *not* to "walk like one talks." It is an environment in which some Americans feel an encroaching sense of inferiority.

Americans should not expect Japanese corporations to look after the long-term interests of the U.S. worker and manager. They should not be disappointed when the Japanese do not run their American plants and offices in accordance with American notions about the rights and responsibilities a group and its members owe one another. The Japanese are not hostile toward Americans or American values; they are simply taking a management system that has worked well for them at home and exporting it to another country. In doing this they are acting no differently than Americans and Europeans have acted. If by exporting their management system the Japanese threaten to undermine American cultural values in the workplace, it is up to Americans to see that those values are preserved. American workers and managers must draw on that most American of virtues, self-reliance, and approach the Japanese management system from a critical and independent perspective, accepting those things about it that fit, rejecting those that do not, and insisting that their Japanese employers listen to their ideas for improvements. Ultimately this will have to be done as it is now being done at Flat Rock, by American employees banding together on the shop floor and in the office to pressure the Japanese into making their system more reflective of American cultural values. Only when American employees are willing to take this stand will they be able to have a third-culture plant or office that serves the interests of two equal partners.

Epilogue
The Union's Choice

IN July 1989, two months after the dissident victory at Flat Rock, workers at Nissan's Smyrna, Tennessee, plant voted 1,622 to 711 against joining the UAW. It is impossible to determine exactly what role the success of the Mazda dissidents played in the election at Nissan. The UAW's defeat stemmed from a complex web of causes, most of which were unrelated to internal union political battles. Nissan management mounted an aggressive campaign in opposition to the UAW, leveling many of the same charges against the union that the USA incumbents had made against the dissidents in the Local 3000 election—unionization would bring radicals and rabble-rousers to the plant and would make Smyrna less competitive, endangering job security. These charges carried far more weight in rural central Tennessee than they did in urban southeastern Michigan. Workers in Tennessee, one of the most staunchly antiunion states in the country (only 14 percent of its work force is unionized, compared to 53 percent in Michigan)[1] were products of a culture that encouraged mistrust of organized labor. They were prepared to be receptive to an antiunion message. This was especially true of workers at Smyrna, who had been screened by Nissan for their negative attitudes toward organized labor. The relatively high wages Nissan paid its employees also discouraged unionization. In 1989 production workers at Smyrna earned $14.85 per hour in wages and bonuses. That was less

than Big Three wages, but more than Mazda wages, more than the
$13.14 average hourly manufacturing wage in the United States, and
well above the $9-per-hour average manufacturing wage in Tennes-
see. As one Nissan worker who voted against the union explained at
a company-sponsored press conference following the election: "If
you worked for minimum wage like I have, you appreciate what
you're making now. You don't bite the hand that feeds you."[2]

Like Nissan, other Japanese automakers in the United States,
including Mazda, have paid relatively high wages. (Their greater
efficiency comes from hiring fewer workers and having them do more
work, not from paying them penurious wages.) By keeping their pay
scales close to Big Three rates, the Japanese have deprived the UAW
of its most attractive organizing issue. If the UAW cannot promise
workers at Japanese plants more money, it must be able to rally them
around other issues in order to win their approval. Such issues do
exist. The intense JIT work pace and its threat to safety and health,
as well as the broad, and often abused, discretionary power of su-
pervisors at Japanese-owned plants, provide potentially good rally-
ing points for organizing campaigns. But the UAW, intent on creating
a cooperative image with Japanese automakers, has refused to chal-
lenge management over these issues. As a result the UAW has not
been able to persuade nonunion workers at Japanese plants that it
can contribute to the development of a better, more equitable team
system. It was not surprising, then, that workers at Nissan-Smyrna,
who were already earning over one dollar more per hour than their
opposite numbers at unionized Mazda–Flat Rock, did not feel com-
pelled to become part of a union that, in exchange for its two hours
of wages per month in dues, simply promised to go along with the
team system that was already in place. Seeing Mazda team members
replace their incumbent union leaders lent credence to the charge
often made by Nissan that the union had no positive contribution to
make to the well-being of workers at a team plant. If the union was
doing anything good at Flat Rock, many Nissan workers undoubt-
edly asked themselves, why did the people up there vote in the dis-
sidents?

Would the UAW have been more successful at organizing Nissan-
Smyrna, Honda-Marysville, and other Japanese-owned plants had it
abandoned its cooperative strategy and appealed to workers with a
more militant message? The answer to this question cannot be known
for certain, but the history of JIT/team plants that are unionized
indicates that workers at these facilities want an aggressive and in-

dependent union to counter management's power. Less than one week after Keeling's victory at Flat Rock, New Directions candidates won five of seven delegate seats to the UAW convention from the 3,850-employee General Motors assembly operation in Van Nuys, California, a team plant since May 1987, "People's Caucus," a dissident group opposed to close union-management cooperation at the NUMMI team plant managed by Toyota, won two of seven seats on the local bargaining committee, as well as other key positions, in 1988 elections.

In the wake of its defeat at Flat Rock, and the subsequent failure to organize Nissan's Tennessee plant, the UAW administration must do some serious soul searching. The strategy of creating a cooperative image of the union has failed. It has not won the trust of the Japanese automakers the UAW's leaders had hoped to impress, and it has alienated those team plant workers who are already represented by the union. Mazda–Flat Rock remains the only wholly Japanese-owned plant organized by the UAW. Blaming the dissidents for this is not only unfair, it runs counter to the best long-term interests of the union. Eventually Solidarity House will have to embrace many of the ideas advocated by dissidents like Keeling and Tucker if the UAW is to develop a team plant policy that makes it possible for the union to serve the interests of workers aggressively, without unduly limiting the flexibility that is essential to the success of the team concept.

As the dissidents have repeatedly insisted, the UAW cannot continue to stifle its independent voice in the name of cooperation. To fulfill its mission as a watchdog of worker interests, the union must maintain a professional distance from management. When the union becomes involved in the creation and implementation of management policies as it did at Flat Rock, where union meetings included attendance lectures, it loses both the will and the right to criticize those policies when they conflict with the interests of workers. The union-management relationship need not be combative, but it must always contain an element of adversarial tension—even at the most harmonious of team plants. To think otherwise is, as the workers at Flat Rock have discovered, unrealistic. A union representative must be "biased" in favor of workers, just as an attorney must be in favor of his or her clients—or an automaker in favor of its corporate interests. The legitimate needs of employee and employer diverge from one another at too many points to expect the union and management to view the worker-company relationship from the same

perspective. In its drive to increase profits, management will strive to obtain the maximum output from the smallest number of employees, while paying them the lowest wages possible. This is not because individual managers are necessarily unfair or greedy; they are simply following an imperative that must be followed in a competitive industry—increase profits by holding down costs. Understandably, this puts management at odds with workers, who, though they may be sincere about providing a fair day's work for a fair day's pay, will invariably seek to increase wages and reduce job stress. Neither side is "wrong" or unreasonable; each is entering the employer-employee covenant with goals and interests that put it in an inherently adversarial position in relation to the other. It is only through the interaction of these two adversarial forces that a compromise management system—one that allows the company to operate its plant efficiently while still protecting the interests of workers—can be reached. The UAW must convince workers that it can, by providing an independent, countervailing power to management, contribute to the development of such an equitable system in a team plant, if it hopes to reach the 25 percent of the American auto industry that will soon be controlled by Japanese manufacturers.

The UAW administration has often defended its policy of granting sweeping discretionary power to management at Mazda–Flat Rock and other team plants by arguing that such managerial "flexibility" is necessary for a team system to operate efficiently. But even if this were true, there are still checks that can be placed on management's power without resorting to the rigid work rules and job classifications of the past. One possibility would be for the union and management at a team plant to agree on a reserve set of alternate work rules that could be implemented in place of their contract's normal, flexible provisions, should management abuse its discretionary power. For example, a vaguely worded provision that allows management to assign unannounced overtime under unspecified "special circumstances" could be replaced by an ironclad rule that prohibits unannounced overtime assignments for any reason, if management abuses its flexible power by assigning unannounced overtime as a matter of routine, as Mazda has done at Flat Rock. The question of whether management has abused its flexible power is one that would have to be decided by the union alone during periodic reviews (perhaps twice a year) of management's performance. The union should also be given the power to determine the amount of time, within prearranged limits, that the stricter reserve work rules

would be in effect (10, 30, or 60 days), depending on the seriousness of management's offense. The availability of reserve work rules would allow management to maintain the flexibility that it claims is needed in a team plant while still providing workers with protection against managerial abuses of discretionary power. By having the power to invoke reserve rules, the union would be able to pressure management to live up to the spirit of its flexible team contract without having to resort to the threat of a disruptive strike during triennial contract negotiations. The union's actions could be limited only to those provisions that have been abused. Stricter work rules could, for example, be invoked to cover overtime assignments, while the rest of the team contract remained unchanged.

In all likelihood Mazda and other team-oriented manufacturers would complain that the implementation of such a reserve rule plan would place too much unchecked power in the hands of the union. What would prevent the union, they would probably argue, from invoking reserve rules indiscriminately, without justification? But the unchecked power of the union would only serve to balance the unchecked power already enjoyed by management under the normal, weakly-worded team plant contract, in which everything from training schedules to disciplinary standards is left to the unilateral discretion of the company. Under this plan, management would not be giving anything more than the level of trust it has asked of workers. If Japanese manufacturers are sincere about their widely-publicized promises to make American workers partners in their team plants, they must recognize that in any true partnership trust is a two-way street.

Notes

Chapter 1

1. The Japanese share of U.S. market in 1977 is from *Ward's Automotive Yearbook 1978*, p. 23. The 1982 market share is from *Ward's Automotive Yearbook 1983*, p. 11.

Chapter 2

1. Usery's quote is from Michael Brody, "Toyota Meets U.S. Auto Workers," *Fortune*, 9 July 1984, p. 54.
2. The Nissan worker's quote is from Carey W. English, "UAW vs. Japanese: An Uphill Battle," *U.S. News & World Report*, 4 July 1983, p. 76.
3. K. Yamamoto's quote is from "Face to Face: Kenichi Yamamoto of Mazda," *Japanese Motor Business Quarterly*, June 1987, p. 13.
4. Ted Barrett's quote is from "The Deliberate Style of the UAW Winner," *Business Week*, 29 November 1982, p. 34.
5. Bieber's quote is from "Bieber, Owen F(rederick)," *Current Biography Yearbook*, 1986, p. 46.
6. Big Three profits are reported in *Moody's*. Japan's total exports are from *Foreign Exchange Statistics Monthly*, Bank of Japan, December 1957.
7. In 1955, 57,115 of the 7,169,908 cars sold in the United States were imports, according to *Ward's Automotive Yearbook 1956*, pp. 155, 193.
8. The Big Three losses are from *Moody's*. The market share of imports is from *Ward's, 1984*. Union membership is from Dave Elsila, *We Make Our Own History* (Detroit: International Union, UAW, 1986), p. 144. The number of autoworkers on indefinite layoff is from *Ward's, 1983*, p. 12.
9. The $8-an-hour cost advantage of Japanese automakers was reported in "The UAW's Next Try May Yield Less at GM," *Business Week*, 22 March 1982, p. 32.

10. The personal holiday concession raising annual work hours by 4 percent is from Harry C. Katz, *Shifting Gears: Changing Labor Relations in the U.S. Automobile Industry* (Cambridge, Mass.: MIT Press, 1987), p. 56.

11. The Bieber quote is from Helen Fogel, " 'The Lone Ranger' Has Firm Control of His Union," *Detroit News,* 19 June 1989, sec. D, p. 2.

12. The Shoemaker quotes are from a personal interview conducted by the authors.

13. The UAW commitment to flexibility is taken from the *Letter of Intent* signed with Mazda. The no-layoff promise from Mazda is taken from the UAW-MMUC contract. The promise to provide meaningful joint programs is from the *Letter of Intent.*

Chapter 3

1. The $125 million incentive was calculated by the authors based on interviews with Michigan Department of Commerce officials William Luntz and Read Ross. Similar estimates ($120 to $130 million) have been reported by other researchers including Martin and Susan Tolchin, *Buying Into America* (New York: Times Books, 1988), p. 313.

2. The James Blanchard quote is from Craig Farrand, "Mazda to Break Ground in Flat Rock April 1," *Mellus Newspapers,* 5 December 1984, sec. A, p. 11.

3. Luncheon speech reported in "Flat Rock Gives OK to Mazda Tax Break," *Mellus Newspapers,* 20 February 1985, sec. A, p. 8.

Chapter 4

1. The Nobuto pledge to Anders is from a letter written by Osamu Nobuto to Mayor Ted Anders, 3 June 1985.

2. The comparison figures are from Gerry Kobe, "Capital Performance! Mazda Flat Rock Versus GM Fairfax: Does a Billion Bucks Mean Better Efficiency?" *Automotive Industries,* June 1988, p. 56.

3. The Yamamoto quote is from Dale Thomas, "The End of One Era; The Beginning of a New One," *Mellus Newspapers,* 5 June 1985, sec. A, p. 3.

4. The Nobuto quote about the need to avoid ambiguity in Japanese-American communications is from Ric Bohy, "The Third Culture," *Detroit News,* 20 December 1987, sec. A, p. 17.

5. The Pawley quote about his personal history is from a telephone interview with the authors conducted on 21 April 1988.

6. The Pawley quote about union contracts is from Ric Bohy, "The Third Culture," *Detroit News,* 20 December 1987, sec. A, p. 17.

7. The Pawley quote about Japanese plans is from ibid., p. 16.

Chapter 5

1. The Pawley quote about the characteristics sought in a Mazda employee is from Louise Kertesz, "Team Concept Makes Mazda Flat Rock a Different Plant," *Automotive News,* 29 February 1988, p. 36.

2. The Merchant quotes about using the minds of workers are from a personal interview with the authors conducted at the Mazda plant on 8 April 1988.

3. The Merchant quotes about the screening process are from a speech given at Mercy College, Detroit, as reported by Dale Thomas, "Motivation Is the Key to Mazda's Hiring Goal," *Mellus Newspapers,* 12 March 1986.

4. The material about the Michigan Casting Center was related to the authors by several supervisors and hourly employees who worked at the foundry. Still employed by Ford, they understandably wished to remain anonymous.

5. The study of minority hiring at Japanese-owned auto plants conducted by Robert E. Cole and Donald R. Deskins, Jr., of the University of Michigan, was reported by Louise Kertesz, *Automotive News,* 29 August 1988, p. 1.

6. The average age of the plant's work force is from "Inside Mazda's Flat Rock Assembly Plant," *Japanese Motor Business Quarterly,* December 1987, p. 8. The experience level of the work force is a consensus of many interviews the authors conducted with Mazda managers, workers, and union officials, as well as reports in many printed sources, including John Lippert and Nunzio Lupo, "A Not-So Happy Birthday," *Detroit Free Press,* 28 August 1988, sec. F, p. 1. The percentage of women in the work force was obtained from *Mazda Motor Manufacturing (USA) Corp. Equal Employment Opportunity Status Report,* 31 March 1988.

Chapter 6

1. The United Way Campaign example is from *Interact: Interpersonal Problem Solving,* May 1984, pp. 4, 7.

2. Merchant's comments on consensus and voting are from a personal interview with the authors conducted at the Mazda plant on 8 April 1988.

3. Pawley's comments on consensus are from a telephone interview with the authors conducted on 21 April 1988.

4. The quote about *kaizen* is from *MMUC Production System Concept and Outline,* Mazda Motor Manufacturing (USA) Corp., 1986, p. 3.

5. The warning about waste is from ibid., p. 5.

6. The warning against idle time is from ibid.

7. The quote about trying *kaizen* around the house is from Joe Hoshaw, Jr., "Moving to Mazda," *Mellus Newspapers,* 14 January 1987.

8. The Nobuto quote about Americans training in Japan is from Joe Hoshaw, Jr., "Kaizen: Mazda Trainees Off to Japan," *Mellus Newspapers,* 16 July 1986.

Chapter 7

1. The Pawley quote about new Mazda workers is from James V. Higgins, "Nothing's Goofy About Mazda's VP," *Detroit News,* 31 August 1987, sec. D, p. 1.

2. Compared to Mazda, with its fewer than 200 skilled trades workers, Chrysler-Newark has 411, Ford–St. Louis 422, and GM-Framingham 431, according to Mike Parker and Jane Slaughter, *Choosing Sides: Unions and the Team Concept* (Boston: South End Press, 1988), p. 80.

3. Yamamoto's comments about combining Japanese and American culture are from Ric Bohy, "Kansei in the USA," *Detroit News,* 30 August 1987, sec. A, p. 12.

4. Nobuto's comments are from the text of his speech to the University of Michigan Eighth International Automotive Industry Conference, Ann Arbor, Mich., 22 March 1988.

5. A study conducted by Michigan State University sociologists Richard Child Hill, Michael Indergaard, and Kuniko Fujita concluded that spin-off jobs created by the Mazda plant "haven't come close to matching original Downriver expectations," James V. Higgins, "Area Changes Tune on Mazda Plant," *Detroit News,* 30 March 1988, sec. C, p. 1. Even the most optimistic projections by the State Department of Commerce were, by 1986, scaled down to 8,500 spin-off jobs, about half the number forecast by the governor and other state officials when they were promoting the 100 percent abatement plan. See "Attracting New Investment," *Meeting the Challenge: Annual Report Cabinet Council on Jobs and Economic Development,* Michigan State Government, Lansing, December 1986, p. 18.

6. The Dingell quote is from Robert C. Christopher, *The Japanese Mind* (New York: Simon & Schuster, 1983), p. 175.

7. The "Japs" quote was made by Detroit city councilman Jack Kelly as reported by Linda Jones, "Kelly: Forget Japanese," *Detroit News,* 31 May 1989, sec. B, p. 1.

8. The worker's quote about working without pay on personal time is from Louise Kertesz, "Team Concept Makes Mazda Flat Rock a Different Plant," *Automotive News,* 29 February 1988, p. 36.

9. Mr. Ueno made his comments to the authors in a taped interview conducted with the authors at the Mazda plant on 11 May 1988.

10. Mr. Ramp's comments are taken from a taped interview conducted with the authors at the Mazda plant on 31 August 1988.

11. The number of female employees at Mazda was arrived at by taking 27 percent (the percentage of females in the MMUC work force, according to *Mazda Motor Manufacturing [USA] Corp. Equal Employment Opportunity Status Report,* 31 March 1988) of 3,078 (the total number of employees at MMUC, according to the *Mazda Motor Manufacturing [USA] Corp. Newsletter,* vol. 3, no. 18, 26 August 1988, p. 2.).

12. Takashi Itakura's quote about American men and women is from Ric Bohy, "Third Culture a Product of Adjustments," *Detroit News,* 30 August 1987, sec. A, p. 12.

13. The Honda hiring radius and its impact on Columbus, Ohio, blacks, as well as the Equal Employment Opportunity settlements paid by Honda, are discussed by Michel McQueen and Joseph B. White, "Blacks, Women at Honda Unit Win Back Pay," *Wall Street Journal,* 24 March 1988, p. 1. The minority hiring figures are from Louise Kertesz, "Japanese Rapped on Black Jobs," *Automotive News,* 29 August 1988, p. 1.

14. The Chrysler contribution to the income of black Americans is from Jacob M. Schlesinger, "Shift of Auto Plants to Rural Areas Cuts Hiring of Minorities," *Wall Street Journal,* 12 April 1988, p. 1.

15. The Judson quote about avoiding confrontation is from John Lippert and Nunzio Lupo, "Mazda Union Head Is Hit From All Sides," *Detroit Free Press,* 28 August 1988, sec. F, p. 2.

Chapter 8

1. The Pawley quote about the upcoming years at Mazda is from Louise Kertesz, "Team Concept Makes Mazda Flat Rock a Different Plant," *Automotive News,* 29 February 1988, p. 36.

2. Pawley expressed this view during a telephone interview with the authors on 21 April 1988. (Unless otherwise noted, all quotes by Pawley in this chapter are taken from that interview.)

3. James V. Higgins, "U.S. Bosses Face Tough Sailing in Japanese Plants," *Detroit News,* 28 March 1988, sec. D, p. 1.

4. Leah Nathans, "A Matter of Control," *Business Month,* September 1988, p. 46.

5. Ibid., p. 52.

6. Yoshinori Taura's quote about laid-off American Mazda workers is from James V. Higgins, "Mazda Expects Rise in U.S. Sales," *Detroit News,* 15 June 1988, sec. C, p. 2.

7. Mazda originally projected a 5 percent turnover rate for the plant, as reported by John Lippert and Nunzio Lupo, "A Not-So Happy Birthday," *Detroit Free Press,* 28 August 1988, sec. F, p. 2.

8. UAW Local 3000 estimated the number of maintenance unit leaders in the plant at 20 for the authors in the summer of 1989.

9. Mazda's target defect rate was 15 percent, according to John Lippert and Nunzio Lupo, "A Not-So Happy Birthday," *Detroit Free Press,* 28 August 1988, sec. F, p. 1. Lippert and Lupo reported that at times in the summer of 1988 the defect rate at the plant reached as high as 70 percent. A 25 percent defect rate at the plant was reported by Greg Gardner, "Mazda President Sees Gears Meshing," *Detroit Free Press,* 24 April 1989, sec. C, p. 3. These figures were corroborated in numerous interviews the authors conducted with Mazda workers, including employees assigned to the reprocessing shop.

10. The worker's quote about management needing a refresher course in the team system is from John Lippert and Nunzio Lupo, "A Not-So Happy Birthday," *Detroit Free Press,* 28 August 1988, sec. F, p. 2.

Chapter 9

1. The number of American employees, a little over 2,990, is from the *Mazda Motor Manufacturing (USA) Newsletter,* 6 May 1988, p. 3, which lists 3,242 employees, including 251 Japanese dispatches at the plant as of 2 May 1988. The employment figure for late August, 3,078 Americans, is taken from the *Mazda Motor Manufacturing (USA) Newsletter,* 26 August 1988, p. 2, which lists 3,322 employees, including 244 Japanese dispatches at the plant as of 22 August 1988.

2. The worker's comments comparing Mazda to GM are from John Lippert and Nunzio Lupo, "A Not-So Happy Birthday," *Detroit Free Press,* 28 August 1988, sec. F, p. 2.

3. Ray Marshall's comments are from Mike Parker and Jane Slaughter, "Behind the Scenes at NUMMI Motors," *New York Times,* 4 December 1988, sec. F, p. 2.

4. The story of the female employee who broke her ankle is from Mike Parker and Jane Slaughter, *Choosing Sides,* pp. 23, 24. During a taped interview with the authors at the Mazda plant on 5 May 1988, Don Kricho, the MMUC director of safety and health, said that the "worst [injury] incident" he could recall occurred when a female employee "rushing to complete a job" fell off a platform, fracturing her ankle and incurring "pretty serious damage" to her heel.

5. *Collective Bargaining Agreement Between Mazda Motor Manufacturing (USA) Corporation and International Union, United Automobile, Aerospace and Agricultural Implement Workers of America, UAW,* 7 March 1988, p. 40.

6. The vacation comparisons between the United States and Japan are based on figures provided by U.S. Department of Labor and Japanese Ministry of Labor as reported by Brendan Boyd, "Moneylist: Time Off," *Detroit News,* 16 November 1988, sec. C, p. 1.

7. Mazda-UAW *Collective Bargaining Agreement,* p. 49.

8. James Korowin's comments are from Louis Kertesz, "Injury, Training Woes Hit New Mazda Plant," *Automotive News,* 13 February 1989, p. 52.

9. Bill Judson's comments about line speed and SMPs are from ibid.

10. Judson's comments about Japanese philosophy and American managers are from Louise Kertesz, "Mazda Faction Battles UAW Establishment," *Automotive News,* 13 March 1989, p. 20.

11. Nobuto's comments about American suppliers are from the text of his speech to the University of Michigan Eighth International Automotive Industry Conference, Ann Arbor, Mich., 22 March 1988.

12. Nobuto's comments about American individualism are from Ric Bohy, "The Third Culture," *Detroit News,* 20 December 1987, sec. A, p. 17.

13. The Michigan State University study was reported by James V. Higgins, "Area Changes Tune on Mazda Plant," *Detroit News,* 30 March 1988, sec. C, p. 1; and Charles Slat, "Reality of Mazda's Impact Not as Strong as Hopes," *Monroe (Michigan) Evening News,* 24 March 1988, pp. 1, 14.

14. Job and incentive figures were provided to the authors by State of Michigan Department of Commerce officials William Lontz and Read Ross, and Robert Fraser of the State of Michigan Jobs Training Program.

15. The GAO study and Lloyd Bentsen's comments are from John E. Peterson, "Bentsen: Foreign Cars Cost U.S. Jobs," *Detroit News*, 11 July 1989, sec. E, p. 1.

Chapter 10

1. Don Kricho's quote about healthy employees fitting into the team environment is from Joe Hoshaw, Jr., "Health Kick: Mazda Fitness Center a 'Pro Active' Activity," *Mellus Newspapers*, 2 December 1987, sec. C, p. 1.

2. The American manager's comments about employee health and Mazda are from ibid., p. 3.

3. Don Kricho made these comments to the authors during a taped interview at the Mazda plant on 5 May 1988.

4. The Michigan OSHA (MIOSHA) recordable injury rate at the Flat Rock plant was 35.4 in June 1988 and 53.4 in September 1988, according to a copy of the May 1989 *Mazda Safety Report* obtained by the authors. The recordable injury rate is arrived at by multiplying the number of recordable injury incidents by 200,000 and dividing this by the total number of hours worked at the plant.

5. The number of workdays lost (1,763) in the Flat Rock plant's first year of two-shift production (June 1988 to May 1989) and the lost workday rate of 42.56 per 100 workers is taken from the May 1989 *Mazda Safety Report*. The number of recordable incidents at Flat Rock between June 1988 and May 1989 (152) is listed in the May 1989 *Mazda Safety Report*, as is the 3.67 per 100 worker incident rate. The lost workday rates and recordable incident rates for other Michigan automobile plants are from *Occupational Injury and Illnesses Michigan Survey 1987*, Michigan Department of Labor MIOSHA Information Division, Lansing, April 1989, p. 63. MIOSHA defines automobile and car body assembly plants as "establishments primarily engaged in manufacturing or assembling complete passenger automobiles, trucks, commercial cars and buses." This is not to be confused with the category for motor vehicle parts and accessories, which has a higher injury rate and is defined as facilities engaged in the manufacture of vehicle components "but not engaged in manufacturing complete vehicles."

6. The local news headline is from the *Detroit Free Press*, 14 February 1989, sec. C, p. 6.

7. The Mazda memo quoted is headed "Health and Fitness," dated 20 June 1989.

8. The figures cited are from the May 1989 *Mazda Safety Report*.

9. The quote about MMUC's sensitive position is from the *MMUC Employee Handbook (For Team Leaders and Team Members)*, p. N3.

10. The warning about not talking to the media is from ibid., p. N4.

11. Story of "Brother Jim" is in the *New Directions Coalition Newsletter*, 10 March 1989.

12. The 5.1 percent incidence of carpal tunnel syndrome is cited by T. J. Armstrong et al., "Ergonomics and the Effects of Vibration in Hand-Intensive Work," *Scandinavian Journal of Work Environment and Health*, vol. 13, 1987, p. 288.

13. The quote about the "mini-epidemic" of carpal tunnel syndrome at Flat Rock is from Louise Kertesz, *Automotive News*, 13 February 1989, p. 53.

14. The comparison between Chrysler–Sterling Heights and Mazda–Flat Rock is from ibid., p. 1.

15. Osamu Nobuto's letter appeared in *Automotive News*, 27 February 1989, p. 12.

16. The study cited was conducted by Barbara A. Silverstein, Lawrence J. Fine, and Thomas J. Armstrong, "Occupational Factors and Carpal Tunnel Syndrome," *American Journal of Industrial Medicine*, vol. 11, 1987, pp. 343–58.

17. The story of the injured worker who was ordered to use a hand-held power tool despite being on a medical restriction is taken from Marney Rich Keenan, "Wrist Action: Carpal Tunnel Syndrome Hits a Nerve With America's Workers, and Many Are Fighting Back," *Detroit News*, 6 June 1989, sec. G, p. 5.

18. The quote about protecting employees and the company is from a memo circulated at the plant in early March 1989.

19. The letter from skilled trades workers appeared in *MMUC New Horizons* newsletter, vol. 3, December/January 1989, p. 4.

20. The Survey of Japanese workers is from *Japan Labor Bulletin*, 1 February 1989, p. 3.

21. The UAW official's quote about injuries is from Louise Kertesz, "Injury, Training Woes Hit New Mazda Plant," *Automotive News*, 13 February 1989, p. 52.

22. Judson and Lofton expressed this sentiment to the authors in a taped interview conducted at UAW Region 1A headquarters on 16 August 1988.

23. The Lofton quote is from ibid.

Chapter 11

1. The UAW statistics about the decline in the earnings of displaced workers are from Marjorie Sorge, "A Crack in the Middle Risks UAW's Solid Ground," *Detroit News*, 19 April 1987, sec. D, p. 3.

2. A report on the NLRB ruling, as well as the Mazda quote about the "rights" of employees, are from Louise Kertesz, "Mazda Faction Battles UAW Establishment," *Automotive News*, 13 March 1989, p. 3. The NLRB ruling was also reported by John Lippert, "Mazda Plant Dissidents Want NLRB To Back Their Buttons," *Detroit Free Press*, 10 March 1989, p. 4.

3. The Bill Judson quote about the self-serving motives of the dissidents is from Louise Kertesz, "Mazda Faction Battles UAW Establishment," *Automotive News*, 13 March 1989, p. 20

4. The accounts of Tucker's campaign and Judge Suhrheinrich's ruling are from Jacob M. Schlesinger, "UAW's Leadership Faces Crack in Unity," *Wall Street*

Journal, 6 September 1988, p. 6; and Helen Fogel, "UAW Critic Wins Disputed Election," *Detroit News,* 3 September 1988, sec. C, pp. 1, 2.

5. The status of the Douglas campaign is from Helen Fogel, "Dissident Wins Four More Delegates in Bid For UAW Executive Board," *Detroit News,* 1 April 1989, sec. D, p. 1.

6. The UAW "flower fund" was described by Jacob M. Schlesinger and Gregory A. Patterson, "UAW Plays Hardball With Dissidents Who Say Union Is Too Close To Firms," *Wall Street Journal,* 27 February 1989, sec. A, p. 12; and by Helen Fogel, "Heated Union Battles Put High Price Tag On Campaigns," *Detroit News,* 13 March 1988, sec. D, p. 1.

7. Victor Reuther's comments are from Jacob M. Schlesinger and Gregory A. Patterson, "UAW Plays Hardball With Dissidents Who Say Union Is Too Close To Firms," *Wall Street Journal,* 27 February 1989, sec. A, p. 12.

8. The headlines and quotes are from Greg Gardner, "UAW Vote at Mazda Plant Is Seen As a Test of Japanese Concept," *Detroit Free Press,* 9 May 1989, sec. C, p. 5; and the *Detroit News,* 18 April 1989, sec. D, p. 3; and "UAW Leadership Faces Tests," ibid., 10 May 1989, sec. C, p. 1. (The industry expert quoted in the Gardner article is Harley Shaiken of the University of California at San Diego.)

9. The quote from the UAW staff member is from "Dissident at UAW Is Elected As Leader of Mazda Plant Local," *Wall Street Journal,* 12 May 1989, sec. C, p. 15.

10. The quotes about the dissidents made by a UAW officer are from Greg Gardner, "Dissident Wins Vote at Mazda," *Detroit Free Press,* 11 May 1989, sec. C, pp. 5, 7.

11. Leadbetter's quote about the naïveté of the dissidents is from ibid., p. 7.

Chapter 12

1. The details of the new attendance policy were provided to the authors by Phil Keeling and Mazda workers, also by John Lippert, "At Mazda, Work Attendance Wins Bonus—or Pink Slip," *Detroit Free Press,* 11 October 1989, sec. A, p. 1.

2. On the eve of the Local 3000 election, Osamu Nobuto insisted that *kaizen* would always be practiced at the plant, according to Greg Gardner, "Mazda President Sees Gears Meshing," *Detroit Free Press,* 24 April 1989, sec. C, p. 3.

3. Norimasa Furuta's comments were taken from William J. Mitchell, "Mazda Learns From Flat Rock Experience," *Detroit Free Press,* 21 May 1989, sec. C, pp. 1, 3.

4. Greg Drudy's comments from Pat McCaughan and David Sedgwick, "2 Top Mazda Negotiators Quit," *Detroit News,* 12 October 1989, sec. A, p. 1.

5. The unnamed Mazda spokesperson was quoted by Gregory A. Patterson, "Mazda's 2 Top American Aides at Plant in U.S. Quit, Are Succeeded by Japanese," *Wall Street Journal,* 13 October 1989, sec. A, p. 4. Jim Gill's comments are from Pat McCaughan, and David Sedgwick, "2 Top Mazda Negotiators Quit," *Detroit News,* 12 October 1989, sec. A, p. 1.

6. Japanese plant and employment figures are from Takashi Hoshino, "Japanese Manufacturers Taking Root in Local Communities of the USA," Long Term Credit Bank of Japan, *Economic Review*, no. 96, February 1989. MITI projection from William J. Holstein, Pete Engardio, and Dan Cook, "Japan, U.S.A.," *Business Week*, 14 July 1986, p. 46.

7. Nobuto's comments are from Ric Bohy, "The Third Culture Plant," *Detroit News*, 20 December 1987, sec. A, p. 17.

Epilogue

1. The percentages of the work force unionized in Tennessee and Michigan reported by David Sedgwick, "Nissan Vote Stalls UAW Drive," *Detroit News*, 28 July 1989, sec. E, p. 2.

2. The relative wages and the Nissan worker's quote are from ibid.

Bibliography

Books

Abegglen, James C., and Stalk, George, Jr. *Kaisha: The Japanese Corporation*. New York: Basic Books, 1985.

Baldwin, Nick, Georgano, G. N., Sedgwick, Michael, and Laban, Brian. *The World Guide To Automobile Manufacturers*. New York: Facts on File, 1987.

Balzer, Richard. *Clockwork: Life In and Outside an American Factory*. New York: Doubleday, 1976.

Christopher, Robert C. *The Japanese Mind*. New York: Simon & Schuster, 1983.

Clark, Rodney C. *The Japanese Company*. New Haven: Yale University Press, 1979.

Cole, Robert E. *Japanese Blue Collar*. Los Angeles, University of California Press, 1971.

Cole, Robert E., and Yakushiji, Taizo, eds. *The American and Japanese Auto Industries in Transition*. Ann Arbor: Center For Japanese Studies, University of Michigan, 1984.

Cray, Ed. *Chrome Colossus*. New York: McGraw-Hill, 1980.

Dower, John W. *War Without Mercy: Race and Power in the Pacific War*. New York: Pantheon Books, 1986.

Elsila, Dave, ed. *We Make Our Own History: A Portrait of the UAW*. Detroit: International Union, UAW, 1986.

Fallows, James. *More Like Us: Making America Great Again*. Boston: Houghton Mifflin, 1989.

Gartman, David. *Auto Slavery: The Labor Process in the American Automobile Industry 1897–1950*. New Brunswick, N.J.: Rutgers University Press, 1986.

Gibney, Frank, *Miracle By Design*. New York: Times Books, 1982.

———. *Japan: The Fragile Superpower*, rev. ed. New York: New American Library/ Meridian, 1985.

Halberstam, David. *The Reckoning.* New York: William Morrow, 1986.

Imai, Masaaki. *Kaizen: The Key To Japan's Competitive Success.* New York: Random House, 1986.

Juravich, Tom. *Chaos on the Shop Floor: A Worker's View of Quality Productivity and Management.* Philadelphia: Temple University Press, 1985.

Kamata, Satoshi. *Japan in the Passing Lane.* New York: Pantheon, 1982.

Kannan, N. P., Rebibo, Kathy L., and Ellis, Donna L. *Downsizing Detroit: The Future of the U.S. Automobile Industry.* New York: Praeger, 1982.

Katz, Harry C. *Shifting Gears: Changing Labor Relations in the U.S. Automobile Industry.* Cambridge, Mass.: MIT Press, 1987.

Kline, John M. *State Government Influence in U.S. International Economic Policy.* Lexington, Mass.: D. C. Heath, 1983.

Kochan, Thomas, Katz, Harry, and Mower, Nancy. *Worker Participation and American Unions.* Cambridge, Mass.: MIT Press, 1984.

Lacey, Robert. *Ford: The Men and the Machine.* Boston: Little, Brown, 1986.

Norbye, Jan P. *The Wankel Engine.* Radnor, Pa.: Chilton Books, 1971.

Ouchi, William G. *Theory Z: How American Business Can Meet the Japanese Challenge.* Reading, Mass.: Addison-Wesley, 1981.

Parker, Mike. *Inside the Circle: A Union Guide to QWL.* Boston: South End Press, 1985.

Parker, Mike, and Slaughter, Jane. *Choosing Sides: Unions and the Team Concept.* Boston: South End Press, 1988.

Pascale, Richard Tanner, and Athos, Anthony G. *The Art of Japanese Management.* New York: Simon & Schuster, 1981.

Plath, David W., ed. *Work and Lifecourse in Japan.* Albany: State University of New York Press, 1983.

Prestowitz, Clyde V., Jr. *Trading Places: How We Allowed Japan To Take the Lead.* New York: Basic Books, 1988.

Rae, John B. *The American Automobile Industry.* Boston: Twayne Publishers, 1984.

Reischauer, Edwin O. *The Japanese.* Cambridge, Mass.: The Belknap Press of Harvard University, 1981.

———. *The Japanese Today.* Cambridge, Mass.: The Belknap Press of Harvard University, 1988.

Rothschild, Emma. *Paradise Lost: The Decline of the Auto-Industrial Age.* New York: Random House, 1973.

Schonberger, Richard J. *Japanese Manufacturing Techniques: Nine Hidden Lessons in Simplicity.* New York: Free Press, 1982.

———. *World Class Manufacturing: The Lessons of Simplicity Applied.* New York: Free Press, 1986.

Sethi, S. Prakash, Namiki, Nobuaki, and Swanson, Carl. *The False Promise of the Japanese Miracle.* Marshfield, Mass.: Pitman Publishing, 1984.

Sobel, Robert. *Car Wars.* New York: E. P. Dutton, 1984.

Taylor, Jared. *Shadows of the Rising Sun.* New York: William Morrow, 1983.

Toland, John. *The Rising Sun.* New York: Random House, 1970.

Tolchin, Martin, and Tolchin, Susan. *Buying Into America.* New York: Times Books, 1988.

Vogel, Ezra. *Japan As Number One: Lessons For America.* Cambridge, Mass.: Harvard University Press, 1979.

Wells, Donald M. *Empty Promises.* New York: Monthly Review Press, 1987.

White, Merry. *The Japanese Overseas: Can They Go Home Again?* New York: Free Press, 1988.

Widick, B. J., ed. *Auto Work and Its Discontents.* Baltimore: Johns Hopkins University Press, 1976.

Yates, Brock. *The Decline & Fall of the American Automobile Industry.* New York: Random House, 1983.

Yoshiaki, Shimabukuro. *Consensus Management in Japanese Industry.* Tokyo: I.S.S. Inc., 1982.

Correspondence, Speeches, Reports, and Government Publications

Adler, Kim, Ford Motor Company Corporate News/Public Affairs spokesperson. Letter responding to authors' questions concerning Michigan Casting Center and Ford-Mazda relationship, 12 July 1988.

Anders, Ted, mayor of Flat Rock. Letter to Yoshiki Yamasaki, president of Toyo Kogyo Company, Inc. (forerunner of Mazda), proposing meeting to discuss tax abatement, 27 March 1984.

———. Text of speech delivered at Mazda groundbreaking ceremony, 29 May 1985.

The Auto in Michigan Project Newsletter. Michigan Modernization Service (MMS), a state government agency, winter 1987–88 (special edition; 24 pages).

———. January 1988 (8 pages).

———. May 1988 (8 pages).

Blanchard, James J., governor, State of Michigan. Four-page letter responding to authors' questions about Mazda incentive package, 9 February 1988.

Cabinet Council on Jobs and Economic Development, Michigan State Government. *Meeting the Challenge: Annual Report, 1986,* pp. 16–18.

Congressional Record. 7 August 1987, vol. 133, no. 133. Report by Rep. John J. LaFalce (D., N.Y.), "Crisis In The American Auto Industry."

Flaherty, Darleen, archivist, Ford Industrial Archives. Letter answering authors' questions concerning Michigan Casting Center, 25 February 1988.

Ford Motor Company. Industrial Archives, Accession No. AR-85-57043. Press release about environmental features of Michigan Casting Center, 6 January 1972.

———. Press release announcing opening of Michigan Casting Center, 6 January 1972.

———. Script of public relations film about the Michigan Casting Center.

———. Suggested "stock speech" introducing and concluding 12-minute public relations film on Ford plants in the Downriver area, about 1980.

Hagman, Sandra. *Education in Michigan: Background For Japanese Families.* Internal report, Mazda Motor Manufacturing (USA) Corp, about 1985.

Hamilton, Winthrop W., vice president, marketing & business planning Tenneco Automotive. Letter answering authors' questions concerning the relationship between U.S. suppliers and Japanese "transplants" (three pages), 27 June 1988.

Hartwig, M. A., Mazda Information Bureau. Letter to Flat Rock mayor Ted Anders outlining details of groundbreaking ceremony for Flat Rock plant (two pages), 20 May 1985 (from Ted Anders' files).

Interact Performance Systems, Inc. *Interpersonal Problem Solving.* Lesson program used in Mazda's original training program at Flat Rock, 1987.

International Union, United Automobile, Aerospace and Agricultural Implement Workers of America (UAW). *UAW-Ford Report* (a 24-page report on 1987 contract agreement), September 1987.

———. *Letter of Intent.* Draft of original letter and additional amendments from UAW files. August 1984 and September 1984.

———. *UAW-Mazda Special Report* (a 20-page report on the UAW-Mazda contract), March 1988.

International Union, United Automobile, Aerospace, and Agricultural Implement Workers of America (UAW), and Ford Motor Company. *Agreements Between UAW and The Ford Motor Company,* vol. 1, 17 September 1987.

International Union, United Automobile, Aerospace and Agricultural Implement Workers of America (UAW), and Mazda Motor Manufacturing (USA) Corporation. *Collective Bargaining Agreement, March 7 1988 Through March 3 1991,* 7 March 1988.

Japan National Tourist Organization. *Japan: Images and Reflections.* Tokyo: 1986.

———. *Your Guide To Japan.* Tokyo: 1987.

Japanese School of Detroit. *School Handbook* (20 pages). Bloomfield Hills, Mich.: 1987.

Kelley, Frank J., attorney general, State of Michigan. Letter to authors explaining legal opinion on Mazda's eligibility for 100 percent property tax abatement (2 pages). 9 May, 1988.

———. *Report of the Attorney General.* Opinion No. 5678. 27 March 1980, pp. 674–81 (ruling on 100 percent abatement eligibility for rehabilitation projects.)

Kullberg, Duane R., managing partner, chief executive office, Arthur Andersen & Company. "U.S.–Japan Relations." From *Vital Speeches of the Day,* 15 March 1988, pp. 335–38.

LaFalce, John J., U.S. Representative (D., N.Y.), chairman, House Committee on Small Business. Letter to authors concerning "Fair Practices in Auto Trade Act," 8 March 1988.

Lontz, William D., deputy director, manufacturing development group, Michigan Department of Commerce. Letter to authors (two pages), 27 April 1988.

Luria, Daniel. *Technology, Work Organization and Competitiveness: Automotive Subsystem Cost Reduction, 1986–1992*. Center for Social and Economic Issues, Industrial Technology Institute. Ann Arbor, Mich., December 1987.

Mazda Motor Corporation (Hiroshima). *Annual Report,* 1986.

Mazda Motor Manufacturing (USA) Corporation. *MMUC Employee Handbook (For Team Leaders and Team Members)*, May 1987 (updated February 1989).

———. *Equal Employment Opportunity Status Report,* 31 March 1988.

———. *Health and Fitness* (internal company report), 20 June 1989.

———. *MMUC Production System Concept and Outline* (37-page training manual), 1986.

———. *New Horizons* (six-page employee newsletter), December/January 1989.

———. *Newsletter and Cafeteria Menu,* 6 May 1988, 26 August 1988.

———, Production Engineering Department, 1E Sec. *Kaizen Simulation* (86-page training manual), 1986(?).

———. *Safety Report,* May 1989.

———. *Useful School Expressions For Children.* Instructional material for children of Mazda managers.

Michigan Department of Labor, MIOSHA Information Division. *Occupational Injuries and Illnesses Michigan Survey 1987,* April 1989. Ref. #184075.

National Safety Council. *Worker Injury and Illness Rates,* 1987, p. 27.

Nobuto, Osamu, president Mazda Motor Manufacturing (USA) Corporation. Letter to Flat Rock mayor Ted Anders (two pages), 3 June 1985 (from Ted Anders' files).

———. Speech to the University of Michigan Eighth International Automotive Industry Conference, 22 March 1988 (seven pages).

"The Power Report on Automotive Marketing." *Forecaster's Perspective,* March 1988, p. 3.

Rinaldi, Mike, president of UAW Local 3000. Letter to Flat Rock mayor Ted Anders about Ford's plans to close the Michigan Casting Center, 16 April 1981 (from Ted Anders' files).

Wada, Yoshihiro, senior managing director and general manager corporate planning, Toyo Kogyo Co. Inc. (Mazda). Letter to Flat Rock mayor Ted Anders, 29 March 1984 (from Ted Anders' files).

Walters, Peter, deputy director Michigan State Department of Commerce. Letter to Flat Rock mayor Ted Anders concerning details of Mazda tax abatement. 18 September 1985 (2 pages, from Ted Anders' files).

Interviews

Alessandro, Kathy, former official with Downriver Community Conference, government agency that assisted Mazda in employee screening process.

Anders, Ted, former mayor of Flat Rock.

Bagnell, David, president, Monroe (Michigan) Chamber of Commerce, organizer of Host Family Program for transplanted Japanese executives.

Bolton, Robert, director, Monroe (Michigan) County Employment and Training Department, assisted in job-screening process for Mazda supplier firms.

Bonello, Jeffrey, manager international business development, Greater Detroit Chamber of Commerce.

Crowley, Walter, president, Michigan Injured Workers.

DeSana, James, former Michigan state senator, leading advocate of Mazda incentive package.

Farrand, Craig, editor, *Mellus Newspapers*.

Fraser, Robert, director, State of Michigan Jobs Training Program.

Gillespie, Aaron, former lieutenant, Flat Rock Police Department.

Greathouse, Pat, former executive vice president (international relations), UAW.

Hagman, Sandra, professional dispatch services personnel, Mazda Motor Manufacturing (USA) Corporation.

Hemingway, Ben, UAW representative at Mazda plant.

Hennigar, Nancy, Mazda Motor Manufacturing (USA) Corporation public relations officer.

Higgins, Jamie, former Flat Rock City Council member.

Hosler, Jim, Monroe (Michigan) host family member.

Jones, Richard C., mayor of Flat Rock, 1985 to present.

Joyce, Frank, assistant director, public relations, UAW.

Judson, Bill, president, UAW Local 3000.

Korneski, Alfred, former Flat Rock Chief of Police.

Kricho, Don, director of safety and health, Mazda Motor Manufacturing (USA) Corporation.

Lofton, Ernest, director, Region 1A, UAW.

Lontz, William, deputy director, manufacturing development group, Michigan Department of Commerce, part of the state team that negotiated the Mazda incentive package.

Luria, Daniel, manager industry affairs and policy, Industrial Technology Institute, University of Michigan.

Miyamoto, Masanobu, purchasing manager, Mazda Motor Manufacturing (USA) Corporation.

Maruyama, Masatoshi, quality engineering specialist, Mazda Motor Manufacturing (USA) Corporation.

Matsui, Yuji, production planning/production control manager, Mazda Motor Manufacturing (USA) Corporation.

Mazour, Glen, Japanese Business Consultants, who worked with Mazda and supplier firms.

McNally, Jay, editor, *Flat Rock Guardian* newspaper.

Meade, Pam, Monroe (Michigan) host family member.

Merchant, David, vice president, personnel, Mazda Motor Manufacturing (USA) Corporation.

Metty, Harold F., Flat Rock City Council member.

Nagle, Nancy, former official with Downriver Community Conference.

Palmer, Charles, attorney representing injured Mazda workers.

Parker, Mike, labor activist, opponent of team plant concept.

Pawley, Denny, former vice president of manufacturing, Mazda Motor Manufacturing (USA) Corporation.

Ramp, Bob, UAW representative at Mazda plant.

Reid, James, chairman, Standard Products, an automotive supplier.

Ross, Read, intake services, manufacturing development group, Michigan Department of Commerce, who participated in the negotiation of the Mazda incentive package.

Sano, Makoto, Japanese executive with Delta Kogyo, Mazda's seat supplier, transferred to Michigan.

Shichi, Asae, professor, Japanese studies, Oakland (Michigan) University, conducts cultural assimilation classes for Japanese executives in Detroit area.

Shimada, Tadashi, senior advisor, production, Delta USA Corp., American subsidiary of Mazda's seat supplier, Delta Kogyo.

Shoemaker, Richard, administrative assistant to Owen Bieber, president of the UAW.

Turner, Barb, Monroe (Michigan) host family member.

Ueno, Hiroshi, production engineering manager, Mazda Motor Manufacturing (USA) Corporation.

Wilkins, Thomas, former mayor pro tem of Flat Rock.

Williams, Mary, materials handling, Mazda Motor Manufacturing (USA) Corporation.

Woodcock, Leonard, former president, UAW.

Articles

Alpert, Bruce. "Racism Prevalent in Japan, Black Americans Say." *Detroit News,* 28 February 1989, sec. A, pp. 3, 6.

Armstrong, Thomas J., Fine, Lawrence J., Radwin, Robert G., and Silverstein, Barbara S. "Ergonomics and the Effects of Vibration in Hand Intensive Work." *Scandinavian Journal of Work Environment and Health,* vol. 13, 1987, pp. 286–89.

Armstrong, Thomas J., Radwin, Robert G., Hansen, Doan J., and Kennedy, Kenneth W. "Repetitive Trauma Disorders: Job Evaluation and Design." *Human Factors,* 1986, pp. 325–36.

Bernstein, Aaron, et al. "Japan, U.S.A." *Business Week,* 14 July 1986, pp. 45–50.

Bohy, Ric. "Kansei in the U.S.A." *Detroit News,* 30 August 1987, sec. A, pp. 1, 12–13.

———. "The Third Culture." *Detroit News,* 20 December 1987, sec. A, pp. 1, 16–17.

———. "When Cultures Meet: A Restrained Welcome As Japan Moves In Downriver." *Detroit News,* 11 January 1987, sec. A, pp. 1, 8–9.

Boyer, Edward. "Are Japanese Managers Biased Against Americans?" *Fortune,* 1 September 1986, pp. 72–74

Cannon, Lawrence J., Bernacki, Edward J., and Walter, Stephen D. "Personal and Occupational Factors Associated with Carpal Tunnel Syndrome." *Journal of Occupational Medicine,* April 1981, pp. 255–58.

Crittendon, Denise, "Japanese Criticized For 'Slurs.' " *Detroit News,* 3 August 1988, sec. A, pp. 1, 4.

Drucker, Peter F. "Workers' Hands Bound By Tradition." *Wall Street Journal,* 2 August 1988.

Edid, Marilyn. "Why Mazda Is Settling In The Heart Of Union Territory." *Business Week,* 9 September 1985, pp. 94–95.

English, Carey W. "UAW vs. Japanese: An Uphill Battle." *U.S. News & World Report,* 4 July 1983, pp. 75–76.

"Face to Face: Kenichi Yamamoto of Mazda." *Japanese Motor Business Quarterly,* June 1987, pp. 3–17.

Fallows, James. "The Japanese Are Different From You and Me." *Atlantic Monthly,* September 1986, pp. 35–41

Farrand, Craig. "Putting Together the Pieces: Mazda's Move Downriver a Mix of Cultures and Attitudes." *Mellus Newspapers,* 23 October 1985, sec. A, pp. 1, 16.

———. "Who Will Work in Flat Rock?" *Mellus Newspapers,* 23 October 1985, sec. A, p. 3.

———. "Will Japanese Take Over Ford Plant? Signs Hopeful." *Mellus Newspapers,* 12 September 1984; sec. A, pp. 1, 8–9.

Feldman, Robert G., Goldman, Rose, and Keyserling, W. Monroe. "Peripheral Nerve Entrapment Syndromes and Ergonomic Factors." *American Journal of Industrial Medicine,* 1983, pp. 661–81.

Finegan, Jay. "Beware of the Trojan Horse." *Inc,* December 1987, pp. 27–29.

Fogel, Helen. "Bieber Returns Fire in Political Skirmishing With UAW Dissidents." *Detroit News,* 16 April 1989, sec. N, pp. 1, 3.

———. "Companies Run by Japanese Rate Staff." *Detroit News,* 5 June 1988, sec. F, pp. 1, 2.

———. "Dissident Wins Vote at Mazda." *Detroit News,* 11 May 1989, sec. E, pp. 1, 2.

———. " 'The Lone Ranger' Has Firm Control of His Union." *Detroit News,* 19 June 1989, sec. D, pp. 1, 2.

Gardner, Greg. "Mazda President Sees Gears Meshing." *Detroit Free Press,* 24 April 1989, sec. C, p. 3.

———. "UAW Vote at Mazda Plant Is Seen As a Test of Japanese Concept." *Detroit Free Press,* 9 May 1989, sec. C, p. 5.

Hampton, William J. "How Does Japan Inc. Pick Its American Workers?" *Business Week,* 3 October 1988, pp. 84, 88.

———. "Mazda's Bold Embrace of the United Auto Workers." *Business Week,* 17 December 1984, p. 40.

Hayashi, Kichiro. "The Internationalization of Japanese-Style Management." *Japan Update,* autumn 1987, pp. 20–23.

Higgins, James V. "High Hopes and History on the Line at Flat Rock." *Detroit News,* 30 August 1987, sec. F, pp. 1, 4–5.

———. "Mazda Says It Will Try to Avoid Layoffs." *Detroit News,* 31 May 1985, sec. A, p. 13.

———. "U.S. Bosses Face Tough Sailing in Japanese Plants." *Detroit News,* 28 March 1988, sec. D, p. 1.

Holstein, William J. "Will Sake and Sour Mash Go Together?" *Business Week,* 14 July 1986, pp. 53–55.

Holusha, John. "Japanese Faulted Over Black Hiring." *New York Times,* 27 November 1988, p. 16.

———. "Mixing Cultures on the Assembly Line." *New York Times,* 5 June 1988, sec. A, pp. 1, 8.

———. "No Utopia, But To Workers It's a Job." *New York Times,* 29 January 1989, sec. 3, pp. 1, 10.

Hoshaw, Joe, Jr. "Health Kick: Mazda Fitness Center A 'Pro-Active' Activity." *Mellus Newspapers,* 2 December 1987, sec. C, pp. 1, 3.

———. "Mazda Plant Gets Regal Opening." *Mellus Newspapers,* 14 October 1987, sec. D, pp. 1, 3.

———. "Moving To Mazda." *Mellus Newspapers,* 14 January 1987.

"Inside Mazda's Flat Rock Assembly Plant." *Japanese Motor Business Quarterly,* December 1987, pp. 4–14.

"Japan's Ambitions in the U.S. Car Sector." *Japanese Motor Business Quarterly,* September 1987, pp. 36–43.

"Japan's Turnaround Artists." *Forbes,* 16 July 1984, p. 153.

Junkerman, John. "Nissan Tennessee: It Ain't What It's Cracked Up To Be." *The Progressive,* June 1987, pp. 16–20.

Kertesz, Louise. "Infighting Heats Up As UAW Vote Nears." *Automotive News,* 17 April 1986, p. 6.

———. "Injury, Training Woes Hit New Mazda Plant." *Automotive News,* 13 February 1989, pp. 1, 52–53.

———. "Japanese Rapped On Black Jobs." *Automotive News,* 29 August 1988, pp. 1, 53.

———. "Mazda Faction Battles UAW Establishment." *Automotive News,* 13 March 1989, pp. 3, 20.

———. "Team Concept Makes Mazda Flat Rock a Different Plant." *Automotive News,* 29 February 1988, p. 36.

Kobe, Gerry. "Capital Performance! Mazda Flat Rock Versus GM Fairfax: Does a Billion Bucks Mean Better Efficiency?" *Automotive Industries,* June 1988, pp. 55–57.

Kolata, Gina. "As Complaints Grow, Doctors Seek Data On Repetitive Motion Injuries." *New York Times,* 8 December 1988, sec. B, p. 27.

Kraar, Louis. "Japan's Automakers Shift Strategies." *Fortune,* 11 August 1980, pp. 106, 108–11.

Kurtenbach, Elaine. "Japanese Fear Being Worked To Death." *Detroit News,* 2 July 1989, sec. H, p. 4.

Lehner, Urban C. "Mazda Ponders If U.S. Workers Can Hustle." *Wall Street Journal,* 1 May 1984, p. 38.

Lippert, John. "At Mazda, Work Attendance Wins Bonus—Or Pink Slip." *Detroit Free Press,* 11 October 1989, sec. A, p. 1.

———. "Racing To Cut Time on the Assembly Line." *Detroit Free Press,* 7 February 1988, sec. G, pp. 1, 2.

Lippert, John, and Lupo, Nunzio. "A Not-So Happy Birthday." *Detroit Free Press,* 28 August 1988, sec. F, pp. 1, 2.

Massing, Michael, "Detroit's Strange Bedfellows." *New York Times Magazine,* 7 February 1988, pp. 20+.

McCaughan, Pat, and Sedgwick, David. "2 Top Mazda Negotiators Quit." *Detroit News,* 12 October 1989, sec. A, pp. 1, 10.

McIlnay, Annabelle. "Mazda in Michigan: U.S.–Japanese Success." *Managing Automation,* December 1987, p. 20.

McKinney, Mavis. "International School Could Come Downriver." *Mellus Newspapers,* 29 May 1985, sec. A, pp. 1, 15.

McQueen, Michel, and White, Joseph. "Blacks, Women at Honda Unit Win Back Pay." *Wall Street Journal,* 24 March 1988, p. 2.

"Meeting Mr. Big Face." *Wall Street Journal,* 14 November 1988, sec. R, p. 10.

Mitchell, William J. "Mazda Learns From Flat Rock Experience." *Detroit Free Press,* 21 May 1989, sec. C, pp. 1, 3.

Nag, Amal. "Mazda Will Begin Making Cars in U.S. in Fall '87, Employing UAW Workers." *Wall Street Journal,* 3 December 1984, p. 8.

Nathans, Leah. "A Matter Of Control." *Business Month,* September 1988, pp. 46, 50–52.

Naughton, Keith. "Brother Victor: Surviving Reuther Brother Speaks Out Against Union He Helped Form."*Detroit News,* 11 June 1989, sec. P, pp. 1, 3.

Nolan, Harriet. "Detroit Companies Study Japanese." *Crain's Detroit Business,* 14 October 1985, pp. 1, 29.

Nussbaum, Bruce, et al. "Help Wanted From The Multinationals." *Business Week,* 29 February 1988, p. 68.

"Owen Bieber: United Auto Workers' Man in the Middle." *U.S. News & World Report,* 24 September 1984, p. 7.

Parker, Mike, and Slaughter, Jane. "Behind The Scenes At NUMMI Motors." *New York Times,* 4 December 1988, sec. III, p. 2.

———. "The Factory That Runs on Anxiety." *Washington Post,* 9 October 1988, sec. D, p. 3.

Patterson, Gregory A. "Auto Assembly Lines Enter A New Era." *Wall Street Journal,* 28 December 1988, sec. A, p. 2.

———. "Mazda's 2 Top American Aides At Plant In U.S. Quit, Are Succeeded By Japanese." *Wall Street Journal,* 13 October 1989, sec. A, p. 4.

Pauly, David, and Coppola, Vincent. "Nissan Takes On The UAW." *Newsweek,* 21 February 1983, p. 64.

Reich, Robert B., and Mankin, Eric D. "Joint Ventures With Japan Give Away Our Future." *Harvard Business Review,* March–April 1986, pp. 78–83.

Schlesinger, Jacob M. "Shift of Auto Plants To Rural Areas Cuts Hiring Of Minorities." *Wall Street Journal,* 12 April 1988, pp. 1, 28.

———. "UAW's Leadership Faces Crack In Unity." *Wall Street Journal,* 6 September 1988, p. 6.

———. "UAW Starts Nissan Organizing Drive In Test Of Japanese-Owned U.S. Plants." *Wall Street Journal,* 20 January 1988, p. 13.

Sedgwick, David. "Nissan Vote Stalls UAW Drive." *Detroit News,* 28 July 1989, sec. E, pp. 1, 2.

———. "UAW Policy Faces Test At Mazda." *Detroit News,* 18 April 1989, sec. D, pp. 1, 3.

Silverstein, Barbara A., Fine, Lawrence J., and Armstrong, Thomas J. "Occupational Factors and Carpal Tunnel Syndrome." *American Journal of Industrial Medicine,* vol. 11, 1987, pp. 343–58.

Slat, Charles. "Proud Day For Mazda Plant." *Monroe* (Michigan) *Evening News,* 10 October 1987, sec. A, p. 3.

———. "Reality of Mazda's Impact Not As Strong As Hopes." *Monroe Evening News,* 24 March 1988, sec. A, pp. 1, 14.

Sorge, Marjorie. "A Crack In The Middle Risks UAW's Solid Ground." *Detroit News,* 19 April 1987, sec. D, pp. 1, 3.

Stavro, Barry, "Made In The U.S.A." *Forbes.* 22 April 1985, pp. 50–51, 54.

Sundstrom, Geoff. "U.S. Slaps Japan On Parts Buys." *Automotive News,* 4 April 1988, pp. 1, 62.

Thomas, Dale. "Motivation Is The Key To Mazda's Hiring Goal." *Mellus Newspapers,* 12 March 1986.

———. "The End Of One Era; The Beginning Of A New One." *Mellus Newspapers,* 5 June 1985, sec. A, pp. 3, 8.

Toy, Stewart, et al. "The Americanization Of Honda." *Business Week,* 25 April 1988, pp. 90–95.

"Toyo Kogyo: A 'Sure Loser' Stages A Spectacular Turnaround." *Business Week*, 25 January 1982, pp. 104–7.

"Update On Mazda." *Japanese Motor Business Quarterly*, March 1988, pp. 20–39.

Wilkerson, Isabel. "Influx Of Japanese Changing Style Of Midwest." *New York Times*, 15 February 1987, sec. A, pp. 1, 26.

Index